Representing the Disadvantaged

The limited attention Congress gives to disadvantaged or marginalized groups, including Black Americans, LGBTQ, Latinx, women, and the poor, is well known and often remarked upon. This is the first full-length study to focus instead on those members who do advocate for these groups and when and why they do so. Katrina F. McNally develops the concept of an "advocacy window" that develops as members of Congress consider incorporating disadvantaged-group advocacy into their legislative portfolios. Using new data, she analyzes the impact of constituency factors, personal demographics, and institutional characteristics on the likelihood that members of the Senate or House of Representatives will decide to cultivate a reputation as a disadvantaged-group advocate. By comparing legislative activism across different disadvantaged groups rather than focusing on one group in isolation, this study provides fresh insight into the trade-offs that members face as they consider taking up issues important to different groups. This title is also available as Open Access on Cambridge Core.

Katrina F. McNally is an Assistant Professor at Eckerd College in St. Petersburg. She received her PhD from the University of Maryland, College Park.

T0382342

Representing the Disadvantaged

Group Interests and Legislator Reputation in US Congress

KATRINA F. MCNALLY
Eckerd College, Florida

CAMBRIDGE
UNIVERSITY PRESS

CAMBRIDGE
UNIVERSITY PRESS

Shaftesbury Road, Cambridge CB2 8EA, United Kingdom

One Liberty Plaza, 20th Floor, New York, NY 10006, USA

477 Williamstown Road, Port Melbourne, VIC 3207, Australia

314–321, 3rd Floor, Plot 3, Splendor Forum, Jasola District Centre, New Delhi – 110025, India

103 Penang Road, #05–06/07, Visioncrest Commercial, Singapore 238467

Cambridge University Press is part of Cambridge University Press & Assessment, a department of the University of Cambridge.

We share the University's mission to contribute to society through the pursuit of education, learning and research at the highest international levels of excellence.

www.cambridge.org
Information on this title: www.cambridge.org/9781009514514

DOI: 10.1017/9781108974172

First published 2021
First paperback edition 2024

A catalogue record for this publication is available from the British Library

ISBN   978-1-108-83822-1   Hardback
ISBN   978-1-009-51451-4   Paperback

For G&G

Contents

Figures

Tables

This title is part of the Cambridge University Press *Flip it Open* Open Access Books program and has been "flipped" from a traditional book to an Open Access book through the program.

Flip it Open sells books through regular channels, treating them at the outset in the same way as any other book; they are part of our library collections for Cambridge Core, and sell as hardbacks and ebooks. The one crucial difference is that we make an upfront commitment that when each of these books meets a set revenue threshold we make them available to everyone Open Access via Cambridge Core.

This paperback edition has been released as part of our Open Access commitment and we would like to use this as an opportunity to thank the libraries and other buyers who have helped us flip this and the other titles in the program to Open Access.

To see the full list of libraries that we know have contributed to *Flip it Open*, as well as the other titles in the program please visit www.cambridge .org/fio-acknowledgements

Acknowledgments

Writing this book has been an adventure stretching over many years and many locations and, like all good adventures, it has only reached its successful conclusion with an awful lot of help along the way.

This project began as my dissertation, and I am indebted to the faculty and staff of the Government and Politics Department at the University of Maryland, College Park for their time, attention, and advice. In particular, my dissertation committee provided invaluable feedback and perspective, and this project is many times better because of it. I am grateful to Kris Miler for pushing me to develop a clearer and more robust theoretical framework, to Mike Hanmer for holding me accountable for my methodological decisions, to David Karol for providing limitless historical insight, and to Christopher Foreman for challenging me to expand my thinking beyond the world of political science alone. I also wish to thank the multiple conference participants and two anonymous reviewers for their thoughtful suggestions and improvements.

I am not the first to recognize this, and surely will not be the last, but it simply cannot be possible to have had a better mentor than the indomitable Frances Lee. Every step along the way, Frances offered encouragement, insightful suggestions, and the kindest form of constructive criticism. I walked away from every conversation with a stronger, smarter, and considerably more grammatically sound project, and I am eternally grateful.

I have been very fortunate to have extremely supportive family and friends. Much gratitude is owed to Jaime, my siblings, and my parents for their patience with my near single-minded focus on this project over the past few years. Special thanks go to my mother, who offered enthusiastic support over the course of this journey, and never doubted that this book would happen.

Finally, it is one of my greatest aspirations to at some point find the appropriate words to express my appreciation for the ceaseless support and encouragement that my wife Kari provided from beginning to end. With her, this process has been immeasurably more joyful and more grounded. For the untold hours of conversation, the many rounds of edits, the delight in the ups, the reassurance in the downs, and the laughter throughout, I thank you.

I

Introduction

Our representative democracy is not working because the Congress that is supposed to represent the voters does not respond to their needs. I believe the chief reason for this is that it is ruled by a small group of old men. – Rep. Shirley Chishom (D-NY12) in *Unbought and Unbossed*, 1970

These words were spoken by a former member of Congress who was not afraid to rock the boat, and who made a name for herself by serving as an advocate for many of those voters whose needs she felt were not being met. Rep. Shirley Chisholm was the first Black woman elected to the United States Congress, and she served as a voice for the minority and impoverished constituents of her Brooklyn congressional district. She even launched a consciously symbolic bid for the presidency to highlight the discrimination faced by women and Black Americans.

There are some signs over the course of the past decade – from Occupy Wall Street, to Black Lives Matter, to DREAMers, to the #MeToo movement – that a growing portion of American society has begun engaging in a deeper scrutiny of the inequalities within its social and political structures that Rep. Chisholm emphasized back in the 1960s and 1970s. But while popular attention has just begun to shine a brighter light on these issues, for the actual members of marginalized or disadvantaged groups, the struggle to be recognized by governing institutions – and Congress in particular – has gone on for decades. Congress is an institution that tends toward the status quo. And since its founding, that status quo has indeed tended to be in the interest of wealthy, able-bodied, white men.

Congresswoman Chisholm's observations about the deficits that exist when it comes to representing constituent needs have been supported by a considerable amount of scholarship in the intervening years, particularly

1

when it comes to the needs of some of the most disadvantaged groups in American society. For instance, prior research has shown that members of Congress are more likely to cast votes in line with the views of wealthier individuals (Carnes, 2013), and that the preferences of white Americans tend to have a greater influence over member behavior than those of non-white Americans when preferences conflict (Griffin and Newman, 2008). These examples provide clear evidence that disadvantaged groups may be less likely to see their needs addressed in Congress, but the important question is, why does it matter?

1.1 THE CASE FOR STUDYING THE REPRESENTATION OF DISADVANTAGED GROUPS

Disadvantaged groups, from racial/ethnic minorities and the poor to women and senior citizens, hold a unique place in American society. What sets them apart are the additional challenges they face relative to non-group members. These barriers can be cultural, as with groups who must navigate racism, sexism, or ageism, or material, as is the case for groups with limited access to resources. In this section, I lay out four main reasons for why it is important to study disadvantaged groups, and to care about the representation they receive.

First and foremost, the representation of disadvantaged groups matters because they are among the most vulnerable groups in American society. In *Federalist 51*, James Madison wrote of the critical importance of having a system of government that can protect the rights of the minority from the tyranny of the majority. Now, Madison may well have been talking about protecting the smaller number of wealthy, landed interests from a lower-class "mob mentality," but the importance of this idea extends beyond this initial conception. If our democratic system was designed and intended to protect the rights and needs of the minority, it is important to determine how well these less-powerful and disadvantaged minority groups actually fare within Congress. The existence of clear differences in how well disadvantaged groups are represented implies that some element of the representational system is not functioning as it should. This creates a crucial need to diagnose and understand the flaws in our system that keep disadvantaged groups from receiving more equitable representation.

Second, the representation of disadvantaged groups as a whole is not well understood. There are some disadvantaged groups, such as racial/ethnic minorities and women, that have received a considerable amount of focus from scholars, while others, such as veterans or Native

Americans, have received very little attention. This creates a situation in which there is a considerable amount of excellent and worthwhile scholarship into the representation of some specific groups, but not a good sense of what drives the representation of disadvantaged groups more broadly. Gaining a clearer, big-picture view of the representation of disadvantaged groups as a whole is an important next step in creating a more cohesive picture of how congressional representation really works. Disadvantaged groups, by their very nature, are systematically different from other groups in American society. By developing a broader theory of how disadvantaged groups generally are represented in Congress, this project offers a clearer understanding of how well our political system actually represents some of the most vulnerable people in society.

Third, relative to other Americans, members of disadvantaged groups have very real economic, educational, and health-related needs that are not fully addressed under current government policies. Economically, racial and ethnic minorities, unmarried women, and single and bisexual women are less likely to say that they are doing okay financially relative to other Americans (Federal Reserve Board, 2020). LGBTQ Americans are more likely to live in poverty and experience homelessness, and are less likely to own their own home (Freddie Mac, 2018; Movement Advancement Project et al., 2019). Americans experiencing poverty are more likely to face financial burden from medical care (Cohen and Kirzinger, 2014). When it comes to education, Black and Hispanic Americans are less likely to complete a bachelor's degree, and are more likely to be behind on student loan payments (Federal Reserve Board, 2020). Inequities also exist when it comes to healthcare. Veterans, women, and the poor are at greater risk of severe psychological distress compared to other demographic groups (Kramarow and Pastor, 2012; Weissman et al., 2015). Native Americans, Black Americans, and Puerto Ricans have increased incidence of infant mortality (MacDorman and Mathews, 2011). American Indian and Alaska Natives are more likely to report being in poor or fair health than other Americans (Villarroel, 2020). Seniors and immigrants who face discrimination suffer from a decline in their mental and physical well-being (Burnes et al., 2019; Szaflarski and Bauldry, 2019). LGBTQ Americans are more likely to have experienced discrimination from a healthcare provider (Movement Advancement Project et al., 2019). These examples are just a small sampling of the hardships that members of disadvantaged groups must navigate over the course of their lives. Given the very real challenges these groups face, it is worthwhile to gain a better understanding of the circumstances under which addressing their needs is prioritized by a member of Congress.

Finally, this study of the representation of disadvantaged groups stands apart from previous work that investigated members' representational decision-making through the lens of party pressures or committee membership. Unlike situations in which a member makes the choice to represent, for example, manufacturers, teachers, or environmentalists, there is not a single committee (with the possible exception of the Veterans Affairs committee) with its jurisdiction exclusively linked to serving disadvantaged groups. Every single committee in Congress offers opportunities to serve as an advocate for disadvantaged groups, if a member wishes to take them. Appropriators can make sure that poor communities are receiving funds to promote economic development, or push for increases in the resources devoted to studying women's health. Members of the Agriculture committee can propose amendments ensuring that food stamp requirements do not negatively impact seniors. Individuals serving on the Armed Services committee can investigate the rate of promotions for non-white service members relative to white service members. Similarly, both Democrats and Republicans can make the choice to serve as advocates for disadvantaged groups, even if their proposed solutions take on very different forms. Regardless of whether a Republican member chooses to push for tax breaks for businesses that hire veterans or a Democratic member works to fund additional job placement programs for veterans, they both can gain a reputation for veterans' advocacy. The distinct phenomenon that I explore in this study – disadvantaged-group advocacy – is clearly one that cannot be readily explained by committee or party factors alone.

1.2 INSTANCES OF DISADVANTAGED-GROUP ADVOCACY

Despite the strong tendency for legislation coming out of Congress to favor those who already wield a considerable degree of power in American society, disadvantaged groups have not been wholly without allies in the US Congress, nor have they gone entirely without legislative successes. From Social Security to the Voting Rights Act to the repeal of Don't Ask, Don't Tell, Congress has at times taken actions that are specifically intended to benefit disadvantaged groups. While disadvantaged groups clearly still face a variety of important challenges and barriers, as highlighted in the previous section, Congress has passed some substantively impactful legislation. In every fiscal year since 2008, the federal government has spent over 400 billion dollars on Medicare, and over 600 billion dollars on Social Security. Since 2010, Congress has authorized over 100 billion dollars a year on veterans' services, almost 40 billion dollars a year on housing assistance, and nearly 100 billion dollars a year on food and nutrition assistance. Yearly appropriations since 2004 have also provided over 10 billion dollars for federal litigation and judicial activities, including the work of the Civil Rights Division of the Justice Department, which works to enforce federal discrimination statutes.[1]

In each case, for any of the aforementioned high-profile pieces of legislation to have made it through the legislative process, the successful alignment of political will, popular support, and competent coalition building was essential. But while the passage of any bill is marked by a moment of clear cooperation from a number of different actors at the time the final vote occurs, none of these legislative coalitions are constructed instantaneously. Instead, they can only come into being after building on the steady, determined actions of members of Congress who make the decision to invest their time and energy in advocating on behalf of the disadvantaged groups who would benefit, often long before a successful piece of legislation ever comes to fruition.

In this book, I focus not on the specific discrepancies that exist between the representation of advantaged and disadvantaged groups in society, but instead make use of the knowledge that *some* members of Congress do choose to represent *some* disadvantaged groups, at least *some* of the time. In particular, I investigate what drives these members to make the choice to serve as an advocate for disadvantaged groups. Much is to be gained by taking a systematic look at what drives these decisions, both to fill some of the gaps in the scholarly understanding of how congressional representation works, and also for its normative implications. Building a better understanding of the reasons why members of Congress choose to advocate on behalf of disadvantaged groups can open the door to identifying how it could be possible to boost the representation that disadvantaged groups receive.

Who, then, are these members who make the choice to fight on behalf of the disadvantaged? A few short examples, pulled from the member profiles of the 110th Congress edition of Congressional Quarterly's

---

[1] All data on federal spending were taken from the Historical Table on Federal Budget Authority by Function and Subfunction: 1976–2025, as published by the Congressional Budget Office (www.whitehouse.gov/omb/historical-tables/).

Politics in America, can quickly provide a glimpse into the variety of individuals who make the decision to consciously serve as an advocate for disadvantaged groups, and provide some clues into the reasons behind their decision-making:

[Rep. Jose Serrano (D-NY16)] is always mindful that he represents one of the poorest districts in the country. As a new member of the college of cardinals, as the 12 Appropriations subcommittee chairmen are known, he will be attentive to social welfare spending for the inhabitants of the Bronx.

[Sen. Olympia Snowe (R-ME)], one of 16 women in the Senate, likes being a role model for younger generations entering politics. A 2002 Miss America pageant contestant cited her as inspiration. As the top-ranking Republican on the Small Business Committee, she encourages female entrepreneurs.

[Rep. Ciro Rodriguez (D-TX23)] was born on the Mexican side of the Rio Grande. ... He began his college studies intending to be a pharmacist but soon turned to social work. He has held jobs helping heroin addicts and patients in mental health clinics. 'My experience as a social worker had a profound influence on my decision to enter public life,' Rodriguez said in March 2007. 'I could see that many of the challenges facing my clients and those that I worked with had stemmed from the decisions being made at the public policy level. Serving in Congress allows me to be able to continue to help my clients in a broader capacity.'

[Rep. Dale Kildee (D-MI5)]'s grandparents, immigrants from Ireland, had frequent contact with Indians on the reservation near Traverse City. As a child, Kildee often heard his father say that Indians were treated unfairly. ... When lawmakers in 1997 started talking about taxing Indian-run gambling operations, Kildee founded the Native American Caucus.

Each of these members varies at least to some degree in their backgrounds and formative experiences, in the groups they choose to advocate for, and in the specific actions they have taken in Congress. But the common element that links them all is that they have made an explicit decision to build a reputation within the legislature as an advocate for a disadvantaged group. This project recognizes the centrality of these legislative reputations to the way in which members of Congress demonstrate the work that they are doing to represent their constituents. By focusing on the reputations that members of Congress build as disadvantaged-group advocates, this book offers a new way of thinking about the representational relationship. This fresh conceptualization makes an important contribution to the study of congressional representational by offering a realistic portrayal that takes into account both the way that constituents understand their representative's work within the legislature as well as the diversity of actions that a member can choose to engage in.

1.3 BIG QUESTIONS ADDRESSED BY THIS BOOK

This book strives to untangle a key thread in the representational knot by answering this question: Why build a reputation as an advocate for disadvantaged groups? To address this, I focus on three components in turn. First, what is a legislative reputation, and how common are reputations for disadvantaged-group advocacy? Second, what drives members to make the choice to form a reputation as a group advocate? Third, does this decision-making dynamic work differently in the House of Representatives and the Senate?

Before it can be known why members choose to build a reputation as a disadvantaged-group advocate, there must first be a thorough understanding of what makes legislative reputations a valuable component of representation. In this book, I present a clear definition of legislative reputations and describe what makes them different from other means of conceptualizing representation. I also develop an original measure of which members have a reputation for disadvantaged-group advocacy, differentiating across intensity of advocacy behavior. By utilizing this measure, this project presents a clear overview of how common these reputations for disadvantaged-group advocacy are among members of Congress, while also breaking them down along the important dimensions of group, party, and chamber. Gaining a better grasp of the frequency with which certain members of Congress choose to visibly integrate disadvantaged-group advocacy into their work within the institution provides important information in its own right, and also lays the foundation for a deeper analysis of why members are driven to form these reputations.

The heart of this project comes in addressing this second question – why do members of Congress choose to form reputations as disadvantaged-group advocates? I offer a new theory to explain the representational choices that members of Congress make, through the introduction of the concept of the *advocacy window*. As articulated in Mayhew's first seminal work in 1974, much of the behavior of members of Congress is driven by the urge to vigilantly guard their electoral prospects. Thus, their representational choices are constrained by their desire to secure the vote of as many of their constituents as possible. The advocacy window represents the level of discretion that individual members have in which groups they choose to incorporate into their legislative reputation without compromising their electoral margins, once relevant district characteristics, such as the size of a group within a district and the average feelings toward that group, are taken into account.

However, not all disadvantaged groups are exactly the same. Therefore, decisions to form a reputation as an advocate of a particular disadvantaged group are not made in exactly the same way, either. By leveraging differences in how worthy of government assistance different disadvantaged groups are generally perceived to be, this project is able to shed light on what drives a member's decision to form a reputation as an advocate for particular categories of disadvantaged groups. Examining the motivations of those who choose to stake their reputation on working for disadvantaged groups provides deeper insight into the character of representation provided by Congress.

The final component of this project addresses how the institutional differences between the Senate and the House create distinct incentive structures for legislators. I investigate the diverging characteristics of the decision-making environments of the Senate relative to the House – such as electoral instability and the need to share representational responsibilities with another senator – and explore how those distinctions can impact the representation that disadvantaged groups receive. Examining what drives a member to form a reputation for serving a disadvantaged group within each of the chambers of Congress provides a more complete determination of why members cultivate this reputation, as well as how distinct circumstances can alter a member's calculus. In a bicameral legislature, it is not enough for a group to only be represented in one chamber. By analyzing the differences that exist in the advocacy offered on behalf of disadvantaged groups within the House and the Senate, it becomes possible to see where representational bottlenecks exist, and thus to begin to determine the ways in which these discrepancies can be mitigated.

1.4 OVERVIEW OF THE BOOK

The central argument of this book rests on four key assumptions:

1. *Some* members do provide *some* representation to *some* disadvantaged groups at least *some* of the time, and this representation is both substantively and symbolically meaningful.
2. The means by which members of Congress provide this representation and communicate it to their constituents is by building a legislative reputation as a disadvantaged-group advocate.

3. The formation of reputations as disadvantaged-group advocates is not randomly distributed among members, and there are consistent sets of conditions that increase the likelihood that a member will build a reputation as a disadvantaged-group advocate.
4. Knowing which members of Congress choose to build reputations as disadvantaged-group advocates and why provides valuable information on how to increase the representation disadvantaged groups receive.

In the chapters to follow, I offer an original theory to explain what drives members to form a reputation as a disadvantaged-group advocate, and introduce the concept of the advocacy window as a means of understanding those choices. This project places legislative reputations at the center of understanding how congressional representation works, by focusing on the commonalities in how both members of Congress and their constituents view the political world. Through the use of empirical analysis, I investigate the impact of constituency factors, personal demographics, and institutional characteristics on the likelihood that a member will make the choice to cultivate a reputation as a disadvantaged-group advocate, and compare those results for the House and the Senate. I also take a closer look at the means by which members of Congress build and maintain their reputations, and analyze how well they line up with the expectations found in earlier research. The remainder of this section provides a brief overview of what is to come in the subsequent chapters.

Chapter 2 reviews the previous literature surrounding congressional representation and highlights the important contributions that this project offers relative to this body of scholarship, both theoretically and methodologically. It then proceeds to offer a definition of what it means to be a disadvantaged group and presents a means of categorizing disadvantaged groups based upon the extent to which the group is generally perceived to be deserving of government assistance. In this chapter, I introduce the concept of the advocacy window as a new way of conceptualizing the key factors shaping a member's decisions in cultivating legislative reputations for advocacy on behalf of disadvantaged groups. The advocacy window concept illuminates the amount of leeway members have in deciding what level of representation to offer a given disadvantaged group, once constituency characteristics are taken into account. I argue that the size of a group within a district should determine the minimum level of representation that should be expected, while the feelings toward that group by the district at large act as a cap on the potential range of representation that a member could offer without negative political repercussions.

Chapter 3 establishes what a legislative reputation is and explains why members of Congress aim to cultivate them. I present a novel measurement for legislative reputation by utilizing the member profiles found in the well-regarded *Politics in America* collection and explore the frequency with which members choose to develop reputations as disadvantaged-group advocates. This chapter demonstrates the variation in the intensity of the level of advocacy offered, and displays the differences in the reputations that tend to be formed by members of the House of Representatives compared to the Senate. It also shows the breakdown of the members who choose to form these reputations across a number of dimensions, including the disadvantaged group being represented and the party affiliation of the member.

An empirical analysis of what drives members of the House of Representatives to cultivate a reputation as a disadvantaged-group advocate is found in Chapter 4. I perform these analyses using an original dataset of the members of five Congresses sampled from within the 103rd–113th Congress time frame (ranging from 1993 to 2014). I find that the greater the size of a disadvantaged group within their district, the more likely a member of Congress is to form a reputation as a group advocate. Higher levels of district hostility toward a group reduces the odds that a member will be a group advocate, particularly for groups that are generally considered to be less deserving of government assistance. The results of this chapter also demonstrate that descriptive representatives tend to be more likely to capitalize on a wider advocacy window to increase the level of representation that they offer than nondescriptive representatives.

In Chapter 5, I perform a similar set of analyses on members of the Senate from the corresponding Congresses. I find a number of important differences in the factors most strongly influencing a senator's decision to form a reputation as a disadvantaged-group advocate relative to a member of the House. Chief among these distinctions is the diminished impact of the size of a disadvantaged group within the state. Senators are not likely to choose to build a reputation as a group advocate for any but the groups considered to be the most highly deserving of government assistance. This chapter also introduces and tests three additional hypotheses reflecting the unique institutional characteristics of the Senate, finding that the larger the number of group advocates present within a given Congress, the more likely it is that another senator will also be willing to incorporate advocacy on behalf of that group into their own reputation.

In Chapter 6, I use the measure of member reputation to reevaluate the assumptions inherent in prior research about the use of bill sponsorship and cosponsorship as a reliable indicator of representation. Specifically, I test the assumption that members who represent the disadvantaged will consistently devote a considerable portion of their bill sponsorship and cosponsorship activity to serving that disadvantaged group. Members have a myriad of representational tools at their disposal, and in this chapter I provide evidence that while bill sponsorship and cosponsorship are important, they are not the most appealing representational options in all circumstances. I find that members of Congress with reputations as disadvantaged-group advocates do frequently devote a greater portion of their sponsorship and cosponsorship activities to actions impacting their groups than non-advocates, but that this is conditioned by how deserving of government assistance the group is generally perceived to be, and how well that group's interests map onto the committee structure.

The final chapter offers concluding thoughts and reflections on the findings of the preceding chapters. In Chapter 7, I summarize the earlier findings and explore the normative implications of some of the big take-aways. This chapter focuses on the important insights that are gained by conceptualizing intentionally cultivated legislative reputations as a primary conduit through which representation takes place. Additionally, I consider the benefits of using the advocacy window as an analytical tool to reveal important information about the quality of representation that different categories of disadvantaged groups tend to receive from their representatives. The chapter closes by discussing future extensions of the research agenda.

Member Reputation and the Advocacy Window

An Integrated Theory of Representation

Understanding if and when constituent groups are represented in their legislatures are fundamental questions in understanding democracy and representation in the United States and around the world, and have long been a fixture in legislative scholarship. Though there are a number of studies that demonstrate the representational inequality that exists for members of disadvantaged groups such as racial minorities or the poor (e.g., Griffin and Newman, 2008; Carnes, 2013), gaps remain in the literature surrounding the situations in which members of Congress actually do engage in representational actions benefiting these groups. The passage of the Americans with Disabilities Act, the Civil Rights Act, the Voting Rights Act, the GI Bill, Medicare and Medicaid, the Equal Rights Amendment (which did pass through Congress, even if it was not ratified), the Violence Against Women Act, and others are a testament to the fact that Congress at times attends to the needs of disadvantaged groups. Yet, there is not a clear picture of when and why this happens. Who, then, are these members of Congress that make the choice to fight on behalf of the disadvantaged?

In this chapter, I review the current state of the literature around congressional representation and develop a theory for when and why members of Congress choose to form a reputation as a disadvantaged-group advocate. In doing so, I reexamine how scholars have conceptualized the representational relationship between members of Congress and their constituents, and offer a more realistic portrayal that takes into account the knowledge and goals of both members and citizens. This chapter also offers a specific and bounded definition for what counts as a disadvantaged group, and presents a nuanced categorization scheme within this classification based on how deserving of government assistance a group is perceived to be. After laying this definitional foundation, I then offer a broader theory explaining when and why members of Congress make the choice to foster a reputation as a disadvantaged-group advocate. This theory introduces the concept of the advocacy window as a means of understanding the constraints a member of Congress faces when making these representational decisions, as well as how different types of members respond to these constrictions. The chapter concludes by discussing the important differences between the House and the Senate, and their implications for when and why legislators working within these institutions choose to build reputations as advocates for the disadvantaged.

2.1 PRIOR LITERATURE

A fundamental, perennial pursuit for political scientists has been determining the extent to which our political institutions are representative of the people. Particularly for an institution like the US Congress, designed to be a representative body that is responsive to the needs and desires of constituents, it is of great interest to know whether it lives up to that intended purpose. For many decades, political scientists and theorists have been focused on unlocking the true nature of the relationship between representative and represented, and attempting to elucidate the most important connecting threads. This exploration has focused principally on the answers to three questions. First, who is it that is being represented? Second, what are the means by which representation happens? Third and finally, what is the quality of the representation provided?

2.1.1 Defining Constituency

There is a long history of work evaluating the dyadic relationship that exists between members of Congress and their constituents (Miller and Stokes, 1963; Cnudde and McCrone, 1966; Fiorina, 1974; Kuklinski and Elling, 1977; Erikson, 1978; McCrone and Kuklinski, 1979; Weissberg, 1979; Erikson and Wright, 1980; Canes-Wrone et al., 2002). The object behind all of these projects is to determine the extent to which a member's ideology or legislative actions align with the interests and opinions of the entire geographic constituency. But, more often than not, members tend to envision their constituency not as one cohesive entity, but rather parcel it out into smaller constituencies of interest. Richard Fenno, in *Home Style*, finds that the majority of the members of Congress he follows tend to describe their constituencies in terms of the smaller groups that make them up. He states that "House members describe their district's internal makeup using political science's most familiar demographic and political variables: socioeconomic structure, ideology, ethnicity, residential patterns, religion, partisanship, stability, diversity, etc. Every congressman, in his mind's eye, sees his geographic constituency in terms of some of these variables" (p. 2). More recent research confirms that members of Congress see their districts in terms of subconstituencies, and emphasizes that the critical factor in understanding congressional representation is which of these smaller components of a constituency are being recognized and attended to (Bishin, 2009; Miler, 2010).

Given the crucial role that groups and group membership play in politics and political understanding, this subconstituency focus is not surprising. A plurality of the electorate root both their party identification (Green et al., 2002) and their broader political understandings in terms of group identities (Campbell et al., 1960; Converse, 1964; Conover, 1984; Popkin, 1991; Lewis-Beck et al., 2008). Recognizing this, it would make sense that members of Congress also base their representational strategies around the groups in their district to whom they must appeal for their own reelection. Previous scholars seeking to evaluate the impact of constituent groups upon member behavior have acknowledged this, but they have tended to evaluate groups in isolation, be it nonvoters (Griffin and Newman, 2005), primary voters (Brady, Han, and Pope, 2007), African Americans and Latinos (Griffin and Newman, 2008), or the poor (Bartels, 2008). Rather than looking at one single group, this project examines a larger category of groups – those that are at a systematic disadvantage in society. By expanding beyond the study of a single group, this project is able to present a general theory for when and why members of Congress choose to serve as advocates for disadvantaged groups more broadly.

2.1.2 What Does It Mean To Be Represented?

The next critical aspect of research into relationships between a member of Congress and their constituents focuses on the means by which representation occurs. This question has motivated a large number of studies. Each of these studies puts forward some concept of relevant constituent issues or beliefs and some measure of member actions or positions relevant to those issues or beliefs. Identifying the interests of constituent groups is challenging, with most previous studies taking one of two approaches. The first approach is to use aggregated survey responses to

questions about specific policy or ideological preferences. Policy preferences tend to be determined either by questions that ask about the relative
levels of spending that are preferred or by questions that describe a bill
that came up for a vote in Congress and then ask whether the survey
respondent would have liked their representative to have voted yes or no
(Alvarez and Gronke, 1996; Wilson and Gronke, 2000; Hutchings, 2003;
Clinton and Tessin, 2007; Ansolabehere and Jones, 2010). Those that use
ideological preferences rely on measures asking respondents to self-
identify their own ideological position on a seven-point Likert scale
from very conservative to very liberal (Stimson, MacKuen, and Erikson,
1995; Stimson, 1999, 2003; Griffin and Newman, 2005). The second
approach is to make assumptions about what policies would be in the
best interests of the group, given the primary challenges that the group
tends to face (Thomas, 1994; Bratton and Haynie, 1999; Reingold, 2000;
Swers, 2002, 2013; Bratton et al., 2006; Burden, 2007; Carnes, 2013).

Each of these methods has advantages and disadvantages. Using survey
responses alleviates the pressures of having to make assumptions about
what is in a constituency's best interests, but it also asks a great deal of
respondents in terms of political knowledge and awareness. A large number of studies, extending back to Campbell, Converse, Miller, and Stokes'
The American Voter (1960), highlight the degree to which the average
American struggles to think in ideological terms, while others emphasize
the low levels of political sophistication displayed (Converse, 1964; Delli
Carpini and Keeter, 1996). The second method sidesteps these know-
ledge-related concerns, but it relies upon assumptions about what
a particular group needs.

Predetermining from the top-down what is or is not in a group's best
interest is not inherently a bad thing from a research design perspective, if
the goal is to reasonably reflect the means by which a member of Congress
might go about determining group interests. While members of Congress
do engage in some of their own internal polling, they are not able to do so
on every issue, and their results are just as likely to be plagued by the
information asymmetry present in external polling. Given the amount of
time and effort put into getting to know their districts, it seems highly
likely that members of Congress would trust their own instincts when it
comes to group interests, and when uncertainty exists, consult with an
interest group advocating on the group's behalf. Because this project is
rooted in member behavior and member assumptions, I allow members to
set their own determination of what it means to represent a constituent
group. This insures that each of the different iterations for how members

may choose to represent a given group can be captured, without artificially restricting what "group interests" should be.

When it comes to the member behavior side of the equation, most studies evaluating the congruency between member actions and constituent preferences focus on roll call votes (Miller and Stokes, 1963; Wright, Erikson, and McIver, 1987; Bartels, 1991; Clinton, Jackman, and Rivers, 2004; Griffin and Newman, 2005). These votes are unquestionably important, as they determine policy outputs – the laws that actually end up being passed and affecting people's lives. But they also necessarily require collective action. A bill being passed cannot be attributed to the actions of a single representative responding to their constituents. Moreover, most bills never make it to this stage. The bills that are voted on for final passage are, in most cases, acceptable to the majority party and its leadership (Cox and McCubbins, 2007). Thus, to have a more complete picture of the ways in which a member of Congress can represent their constituents, actions further upstream in the policy-making process must be taken into account (Schiller, 1995; Canon, 1999; Bratton and Haynie, 1999; Swers, 2002, 2013; Carnes, 2013).

These behaviors, including bill sponsorship and cosponsorship, committee work, and speeches on the floor of the chamber, are particularly consequential for representation, because they are either actions that members can take entirely of their own volition or actions that require the cooperation of a limited number of colleagues. For example, any member can decide to sponsor whatever bill they so choose, regardless of what other members are doing. To cosponsor a bill, it is only required that one other member have proposed it first. Working on a bill in committee requires the consent of the committee chair, but the preferences of the broader chamber do not always need to be taken into account. Releasing a statement to the press or using social media, on the other hand, is something a member can choose to do without consulting any other members of Congress. Similarly, members have various opportunities to speak on the floor on topics of their choosing.

A recognition of the assortment of actions that members can take and the varying importance of each are crucial to developing a holistic picture of the means by which representation happens. That said, representation is by its very nature an interplay between elected officials and their constituents back home. Lawmakers are aware of the fact that their constituents are hardly watching their every move and will frequently have little to no idea about the day-to-day activities within the legislature. Knowing this, legislators must consciously work to develop an identity and a reputation that can penetrate down to the constituent level, even if most of their actions themselves remain unknown. Therefore, to really understand a member's representational focus, one must examine the reputation that they craft and the group interests that are central to it.

Reputation is broadly considered to be important, and legislative scholars widely acknowledge that lawmakers strategically hone a reputation that is advantageous to them. However, there has not been an attempt to quantify reputation separate and apart from actions like voting, bill sponsorship, or constituent communication. These actions doubtless influence a member's reputation but do not give the whole picture. Reputation is something that a lawmaker works at by engaging in certain behaviors and rhetoric, but it is through middlemen like the press that constituents actually get a sense of member reputation (Schiller, 2000a, 2000b). This study departs from the trend of focusing on behavioral outputs alone, instead choosing to evaluate member reputations as filtered through a third-party source – allowing for member reputations to be evaluated through the use of a medium that reflects the primary means by which constituents gain information about their member of Congress. Chapter 3 is devoted to providing a detailed accounting of precisely what a legislative reputation is, explaining why members concentrate their energy upon cultivating these reputations, and demonstrating how many legislators actually have reputations as disadvantaged-group advocates across both chambers of Congress.

Previous work has examined the effort that members put in to being perceived as effective lawmakers (Frantzich, 1979; Fenno, 1991; Schiller, 1995; Volden and Wiseman, 2012, 2018), and how well that effort is reflected in their reputations as members who can get things done. However, as highlighted earlier, to be effective in the legislature – to actually move legislation through the chamber and pass it – is necessarily a collective act. Therefore, a member's individual reputation must be more than just effectiveness; it is also based in the groups on whose behalf they focus their efforts. Not all efforts, of course, are created equal. Thus, to truly understand the representation a member offers, one must recognize which group a member is working on behalf of, as well as the extent of those efforts, particularly relative to their other work within the legislature. Though not done through the explicit lens of legislative reputation, a number of studies have sought to address this third component of the representational equation: What is the quality of representation provided, and how does this vary across important group divisions in American society?

2.1.3 Inequalities in Representation

The next piece that must be determined, then, is who reaps most of the benefits from the representational efforts of members of Congress. To a large degree, the same groups that are advantaged in American society broadly are also more likely to see their interests and preferences reflected in the acts of their members of Congress. White Americans (Griffin and Newman, 2008), men (Griffin, Newman, and Wolbrecht, 2012), and the wealthy (Bartels, 2008; Gilens, 2012; Miler, 2018) are far more likely to see legislators working on their behalf. While it is well established that disadvantaged groups in society, such as the poor, racial and ethnic minorities, and women,[1] tend to receive less attention to their interests, there is a noticeable void in the literature when it comes to examining the instances in which disadvantaged groups *do* receive representation, and the conditions under which members of Congress choose to act as their advocates.

An exception to this literature gap are the studies in which researchers have investigated the advantages (or disadvantages) of increasing the number of representatives who are themselves members of a disadvantaged group. In most cases, this work focuses on female (Dolan, 1997; Swers, 2002, 2013; Lawless, 2004; Dodson, 2006); African American (Canon, 1999; Gamble, 2007; Minta, 2009); Latino (Hero and Tolbert, 1995; Bratton, 2006; Minta, 2009); blue-collar (Carnes, 2013); or, more recently, lesbian, gay, or bisexual members of Congress (Haider-Markel, 2010).[2] Burden (2007) demonstrates that personal experiences can impact and shape legislative priorities. Descriptive representation scholars, in turn, argue that the experience of being a part of a disadvantaged group – which includes confronting systemic barriers in society that those outside of the group have not faced – provides

---

[1] An important caveat to this are the findings by Griffin, Newman, and Wolbrecht that while men's interests are better represented by Republican members of Congress, Democrats tend to be closer to their female constituents, at least on measures of roll call voting and ideological scoring. To my knowledge, there are no studies specifically evaluating whether or not men's interests receive a higher level of attention when it comes to bill sponsorship, committee participation, or other activities further upstream in the policy-making process.

[2] An exception to this is the small but robust literature exploring an intersectional framework, most frequently by focusing on Black or Latina women in Congress (Crenshaw, 1995; Gay and Tate, 1998; Hawkesworth, 2003; Bratton et al., 2006; Smooth, 2010). While outside the scope of the current project, these studies move beyond the contention that individuals are defined by a single identity. They find that intersectional identities manifest in behaviors that cannot be explained by the assumptions of a purely additive framework alone, offering an important level of nuance to the study of representation.

a unique perspective that is unlikely to be matched by a representative who has not shared a similar experience (Williams, 1998; Mansbridge, 1999; Dovi, 2002). What these scholars find is that descriptive representatives are more likely to try to get group interests on the legislative agenda (Canon, 1999; Swers, 2002, 2013; Bratton, 2006) and to raise group priorities in committee markup sessions (Swers, 2002), floor speeches (Canon, 1999; Swers, 2002; Osborn and Mendez, 2010), and hearings (Ellis and Wilson, 2013) more often than other members.

2.2 REPRESENTING THE DISADVANTAGED

This project develops a broader theory of when and why members of Congress choose to advocate for disadvantaged groups. This theory centers on the pivotal role that a group-centered legislative reputation plays in the representation that groups receive, and integrates the important and differential impacts of constituency effects, descriptive representation, and institutional differences within the House and the Senate. The sections that follow lay out a clear definition for what counts as a disadvantaged group and argue for the important distinctions among these groups in terms of how deserving of government assistance they are perceived to be. Then, I introduce the concept of the advocacy window as a means of understanding how group size and group affect within a state or district can drive the representational decisions that members make, and highlight how these effects are conditioned by perceptions of group deservingness. Finally, the chapter illustrates how the institutional differences between the House and the Senate can alter the calculus behind members' reputational decision-making.

2.2.1 The Group-Centric Nature of Representation

Members of Congress put a great deal of effort into cultivating a political and legislative reputation as a senator or representative. This reputation is derived from focused actions that the individual takes within Congress and is reinforced through interactions with constituents and with the media. For some members, these reputations are built exclusively on policy, as with someone who is known for being an expert on health care or taxation. For select members, reputation is built on politics and strategy, as is often the case with members who hold positions in party leadership. For most others, reputation comes as an advocate for a constituent group, such as farmers, women, or organized labor. For many members, reputations are multifaceted and may contain more than one of these elements, though overarching priorities are often readily apparent. This project focuses on members who develop a reputation as a group advocate.

Groups and group affiliation are and have been a critical component of American political thinking. For decades, research has consistently shown that most Americans do not think in constrained ideological terms and instead make political decisions based upon group identities and group conflicts (Campbell et al., 1960; Green et al., 2002; Lewis-Beck et al., 2008). Thus, it makes sense that members of Congress would seek to develop reputations based upon advocating for specific groups in society, as that is one of the primary ways in which individuals make political evaluations. Understanding how the formation of a reputation as a group advocate serves as one of the central means by which members of Congress are able to communicate their priorities back to their constituents can provide important insight into the representation of many groups in American society.

Although this conceptualization of members as conscious builders of reputations as group advocates has broad utility, this book is focused on the specific choice that members make to build reputations as advocates for disadvantaged groups. Reputation formation in the context of the representation disadvantaged groups receive is particularly consequential and worthy of further study. The very real challenges faced by members of disadvantaged groups, as laid out in Chapter 1, are undeniable. The government has repeatedly recognized that marginalized and disadvantaged groups face additional barriers relative to non-group members, and thus require additional protections. Given this, in the aggregate, it is intellectually and morally desirable that these groups are represented within the legislature, and that their needs are not ignored. But at the level of an individual member, the circumstances under which this representation would actually occur are much less clear.

2.2.2 The Crucial Puzzle behind Disadvantaged-Group Advocacy

Members of Congress do not have infinite time, and their constituents do not have an infinite capacity to process every detail of their work within the legislature. For this reason, all members must make choices about the groups on which they are going to focus the bulk of their attention. Most districts (and nearly all states) contain a vast assortment of constituent groups: small business owners, suburban families, racial/ethnic minorities, farmers, veterans, women, manufacturers, seniors, and a great many others. It is impossible for a single member to create a legislative reputation as an advocate for all of these groups. Thus, they must make explicit decisions about which groups to prioritize as a part of their reputation, frequently with an eye toward the greatest potential electoral benefit. It therefore seems intuitive that members' best approach to winning elections would simply be to spend all of their time working on behalf of the largest and most popular groups in their district or state.

In practice, however, this is not a hard-and-fast rule. While large and popular groups – like the middle class – do receive a lot of attention (both rhetorical and substantive) from members of Congress, some members *do* sometimes choose to develop reputations as advocates for groups that are not necessarily the biggest or most well regarded within a state or a district. The select group of members who make the decision to incorporate disadvantaged-group advocacy into their legislative reputations tends to be a prime example of this dynamic at work. So what drives them to do this?

While it certainly has normative appeal for members of Congress to advocate on behalf of disadvantaged groups, why they would choose to do so has not been adequately explained. Again, in an ideal world, a legislator may very well want to equally represent all groups present in their district. But in reality, choices have to be made, particularly when some group interests are seen as being at odds with others. For this reason, the calculus around deciding to become an advocate for disadvantaged groups can become especially complicated. Because of the precarious position held by a number of disadvantaged groups in society, members must draw a balance between seeking to draw in voters who are themselves members of a disadvantaged group or who view that particular group sympathetically and those voters who look upon assisting these groups with dismay.

Some preliminary evidence of this important relationship between public opinion and constituency presence comes from Hansen and Treul, (2015). Though they focus solely on the representation of lesbian, gay, and bisexual (LGB) Americans, the authors make a new and important contribution to our understanding of group representation by showcasing the interplay between district opinion and group size on the quality of representation a group receives. They find that while the size of the LGB population in a district has a positive effect on the substantive representation (measured through bill sponsorship) the group receives, the impact of constituency size on symbolic representational actions (measured as caucus membership and position taking) is conditioned by public opinion on same-sex marriage.

However, there are some idiosyncrasies to studying the LGB community that limit how broadly these findings can be applied. In particular, the LGB community is fairly unique among disadvantaged groups in having a single, uncomplicated policy – legalizing same-sex marriage – that has often been used as a proxy for opinions regarding the group itself.

This project expands upon these ideas in three important ways. First, I argue that it is not constituent feelings toward specific policies that matter most in reputation building, but rather the feelings toward the disadvantaged group more broadly. Given that most constituents have little specific knowledge of policy, the nuances between various policy proposals are likely to be lost. Thus, I make the case that the level of hostility or affinity toward a group within a district shapes whether or not serving that group's interests are actively incorporated into a member's reputation. Second, by using a member's reputation as a group advocate as the measure of representation, I can more cohesively incorporate a variety of substantive and symbolic actions. Third, I examine a number of different disadvantaged groups that have varying levels of societal esteem, allowing for a generalized theory of how district opinion impacts the representation of disadvantaged groups.

2.2.3 Disadvantaged Groups in the United States

Disadvantaged groups are those groups that face additional societal bar-riers, particularly a history of discrimination. The groups I examine in this book are: (1) the poor, (2) women, (3) racial/ethnic minorities, (4) veterans, (5) the lesbian, gay, bisexual, transgender, and queer (LGBTQ) community,[3] (6) seniors (Americans over age 65), (7) immigrants, and (8) Native Americans. Nearly all of these groups are members of particular classes afforded nondiscrimination protections by United States federal law.[4] The one group that is included in this project but excluded from federal nondiscrimination laws is the poor. However, though protections

---

[3] Though any discussion in Congress over the last few decades has largely focused on lesbian and gay individuals, the needs of transgender individuals has recently begun to enter into important debates within the legislature.

[4] These laws include the Civil Rights Act of 1963 (Title VII), the Civil Rights Act of 1991, The Equal Pay Act of 1963, the Age Discrimination in Employment Act of 1967, the Vietnam Era Veterans' Readjustment Assistance Act, and the Immigration Reform and Control Act of 1986. In 2020, the Supreme Court also declared in *Bostock* v. *Clayton County, Georgia* that sexual orientation and gender identity were protected under Title VII of the Civil Rights Act.

for people in poverty are not currently enshrined in federal law, many states, counties, and cities include statutes prohibiting discrimination on the basis of income level. The presence of these nondiscrimination protections at the state and local level, as well as the challenges facing those in poverty with regard to food security, safe housing, quality education and adequate healthcare merit the inclusion of the poor within the category of "disadvantaged groups." Altogether, this provides a clear case for why each of these groups are included under the banner of "disadvantaged," as the purpose of these federal and state laws is to offer legal protection to groups that are at risk of receiving unequal treatment by non-group members.

This is not to say that all disadvantaged groups are the same, or even that all members of the group are disadvantaged to an equivalent degree. In no way does this project make the claim that, for example, veterans are as equally disadvantaged in American society as racial and ethnic minorities, nor does it attempt to create a hierarchy of disadvantage, which would be impossible (particularly given that these group identities are not exclusive to one another). Rather, the use of the term disadvantaged makes the assumption that an average group member faces a higher degree of systemic challenges than the average non-group member. Disadvantaged groups, then, are a broad category that implies that as a result of the group trait, additional barriers to success in American society are in place that are not present for non-group members.

The inclusion of veterans as a disadvantaged group, for instance, is an important example of this. Veterans may be frequently venerated at ballparks and Veterans' Day parades, but still must navigate special obstacles to integrating back into civilian life and finding appropriate employment when compared to the average American who did not serve in the military. They also face higher instances of physical disabilities and mental health conditions such as post-traumatic stress disorder, which can place additional barriers on their path to success relative to non-veterans. Again, this acknowledgement that veterans can be subjected to these additional societal barriers is not to paint with a single broad brush and declare that all hardship is created exactly equal. Not all veterans deal with the same challenges, and even their treatment by society at large has not remained constant over the course of the last three-quarters of a century. Service members returning from World War II received a different kind of welcome from those who returned home from the Vietnam War, which is yet different from those coming back from Iraq and Afghanistan.

The other groups analyzed in this project also exhibit varying degrees of heterogeneity both within and across groups when it comes to the form of additional societal barriers they face. But in all cases, it remains true that the average member of a disadvantaged group must overcome challenges that the average American who is not a member of that disadvantaged group need not address. The primary concerns of a middle-class Black family in suburban Atlanta may be quite different from those of a single, young, Black man in Indianapolis. But nonetheless, each must still combat additional barriers stemming from racial discrimination and the vestiges of centuries of systemic segregation that do not negatively impact white Americans in a comparable way. As another example, a married woman with children may not feel the impacts of the gender wage gap as strongly as a single woman with children, but neither is immune from the negative consequences of gendered expectations or sexism.

In sum, people belonging to each of these groups (seniors, veterans, racial/ethnic minorities, LGBTQ individuals, immigrants, Native Americans, women, and the poor) face challenges above and beyond those faced by non-group members that serve to put them at a disadvantage relative to other members of American society. The federal government (or in some cases, state and local government), in recognition of these disadvantaged positions, offers unique protections to members of these groups. In doing so, they acknowledge the need for the government to intervene to at least some degree on their behalf to provide them with a more equivalent opportunity to be successful in American society. But, while the presence of some form of relevant disadvantage is consistent across all of these groups, as discussed in the preceding paragraphs, the exact nature and intensity of the barriers facing these groups can vary widely. The next section explores the extent to which these groups face different levels of receptivity from the public at large regarding the government's assisting them in overcoming the barriers they face, and the impact that this perceived deservingness can have on the representation group members receive.

2.2.4 Perceived Deservingness of Government Assistance

Not all disadvantaged groups in the United States are held in the same level of esteem. Among the groups examined here, there are clear differences in how different groups are perceived, and in the extent to which they are broadly considered to be deserving or undeserving of government assistance by the public at large. This section lays out a categorization scheme based upon how deserving of government assistance a disadvantaged group is generally considered to be. These disadvantaged groups fall into three broad categories: groups with a high level of perceived deservingness of government assistance, groups with a low level of perceived deservingness of government assistance, and groups for which the perceived level of deservingness is more mixed.

These perceived categories of groups are rooted in broader societal beliefs regarding the extent to which a group has sacrificed and thus earned assistance from the government, or whether the group is perceived as seeking something extra from the government. Veterans who have trained and/or fought on behalf of the US are largely seen as being owed not just gratitude, but actual benefits in exchange for their service. Similarly, seniors are considered to be deserving of a government safety net as a reward for a lifetime as a hard-working American taxpayer.

At the same time, resentment and lack of willingness to acknowledge historic (and current) discrimination also play into these impressions, particularly for groups that are less favorably regarded. Discrimination against racial and ethnic minorities and corresponding feelings of racial resentment among white Americans in both political parties results in a context where a considerable portion of US citizens consider further government assistance to these groups to be undeserved and unnecessary. Despite the considerable increase in the support for equal treatment of LGBTQ individuals in the last few years, they are still regarded with suspicion or animosity by a significant percentage of the country.[5] This was even truer in the 2000s, when *the* cultural wedge issue of the 2004 election was a constitutional amendment banning same-sex marriage.

For other groups, such as women, immigrants, Native Americans, and the poor, the public's sense of deservingness is more mixed. Feelings toward the poor are pulled by the competing values of providing equal opportunity (this is particularly true for programs serving poor families and children) and lionizing the power of hard work. These dynamics were front and center in the debate over changes to the Medicaid program in the proposed Republican health-care bill during the summer of 2017, where some members made the case for protecting the most vulnerable, while others argued that poor life choices were the cause of health problems.

---

[5] As an example, according to GLAAD's 2018 Accelerating Acceptance survey, about 1 in 5 non-LGBTQ Americans did not agree with the statement "I support equal rights for the LGBT community," and 39 percent reported that they would be uncomfortable to learn that their child had "a lesson on LGBT history in school." (GLAAD, 2019)

Similarly, opinions about immigrants revolve around both the positive personal connections to being a "nation of immigrants" and the fears of demographic change in the US. Competing views about government assistance for women are present in the dual popularity of "girl power" initiatives and concerns that men are in fact being disadvantaged or treated unfairly. Finally, going back to the nation's founding, a fictionalized version of Native Americans has held a venerated place as an important symbol in American culture, while the actual suffering of native people has consistently been ignored or attributed to personal failing.

Support for this broad categorization scheme can be seen in Figure 2.1. Though there is no survey data available that directly asks about how deserving of government assistance each of these disadvantaged groups is perceived to be, this figure shows a close approximate for at least one of the groups in each of the three deservingness categories. Figure 2.1 utilizes the American National Election Study (ANES) time series data to show the varying levels of support for increasing government funding for the poor, blacks,[6] childcare, and Social Security. For the purposes of this example, support for additional government funding for childcare is taken as a rough proxy for government assistance for women, while support for additional Social Security funds are taken as a proxy for government assistance for seniors. Spending on the poor and Black Americans (as well as questions asking about government aid to blacks without specifying spending levels) are a more straightforward approximate of support for the government doing more to help these groups, with Black Americans operating as a proxy for racial/ethnic minorities more broadly.

As seen in Figure 2.1, support for government assistance to Black Americans is consistently lower than the other groups evaluated. This is in accordance with the expectation that racial/ethnic minorities will mostly be seen by the general public as less deserving of government assistance. Government support for seniors, seen through the proxy of support for increased government funding for Social Security, is consistently at the highest levels of perceived deservingness of government assistance. This demonstrates that classifying seniors as being generally seen as worthy of government help is appropriate based on the data available. Women and the poor, however, both see levels of support that fall somewhere between that for racial/ethnic minorities on one end and seniors on the other.

---

[6] Since 1964, "blacks" has been the specific term used in the ANES survey question.

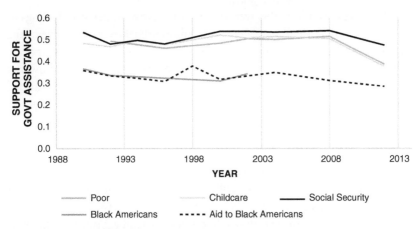

FIGURE 2.1 Average national support for increases in government spending For the Poor, Childcare, Social Security, and Black Americans, 1990–2012.
Note: Figure shows the average level of support by year for increasing government spending on behalf of the poor, blacks, childcare, and social security. Also included in the figure is the average level of support for the government doing more to help Black Americans (as opposed to Black Americans being left to help themselves). This measure follows almost exactly the same trajectory as the level of support for increased funding for Blacks, but was asked in a greater number of years. All data come from the American National Election Study's time series data, and is weighted to be nationally representative.

Categorizing these groups on the basis of their perceived deserving-ness of government assistance offers important insight into how public opinion about a group can affect the quality of representation that group members receive. These broad, national-level feelings about different disadvantaged groups' deservingness of government help are important because they shape the environment in which representa-tives make decisions about which groups to incorporate into their legislative reputations. Groups that are generally considered to be less deserving of assistance represent a riskier selection for a member of Congress, especially compared to those groups that are considered to be highly deserving of help from the government, because their constituents are more likely to angered by their representative expend-ing so much energy on behalf of a group that has not "earned" it.

In the next section, I use this categorization scheme to offer important insight into the quality of reputation that a group will receive, and the ways in which public opinion can condition the impact of group presence within a state or district. Specifically, I introduce the concept of the advocacy window to explain how the average level of positive or negative feelings in a state or district toward a group can condition the effects of the size of the disadvantaged group within the constituency, and discuss the specific hypotheses that can be derived from this theory. I also discuss how the advocacy window is expected to work differently for disadvantaged groups with varying levels of perceived deservingness of government assistance.

2.3 REPRESENTATION AND THE ADVOCACY WINDOW

Broadly speaking, the size of a group within a district should increase the likelihood that a representative will choose to include advocacy on behalf of that group as an important component of their legislative reputation. I will refer to this as the *group size hypothesis*. Members must be strategic in their choices about which groups on whose behalf to advocate. Thus, having a larger group presence in a state or district (and thus a greater potential electoral benefit to offering visible representation of this group) should make a member much more likely to prominently include this group in their legislative reputation than a member representing an area with a small group presence.

Similarly, as feelings toward a group within a state or district – the ambient temperature – become warmer, members should also be more likely to incorporate group advocacy into their reputation. This, I will subsequently call the *ambient temperature hypothesis*. Though there is expected variation in the effects of ambient temperature based on how deserving of government assistance a group is perceived to be, on average, reputations for group advocacy should be more common in states or districts with higher ambient temperatures than lower ambient temperatures. For a closer look at the nuanced ways in which group size and ambient temperature can interact with one another to drive the choices members make about which groups to advocate for, I next introduce and explain the concept of the advocacy window.

2.3.1 The Advocacy Window

The advocacy window is a means by which to conceptualize the amount of discretion that a representative is able to exercise in terms of how much of their reputation they wish to devote to a particular disadvantaged group, once group size and ambient temperature are taken into account. The percentage of group members in a district or state essentially acts as a floor, where members of Congress are expected to provide at least that

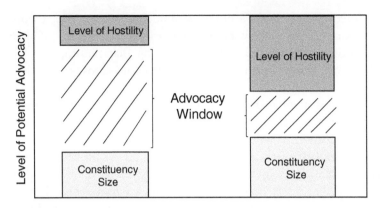

FIGURE 2.2 The advocacy window
Note: This figure demonstrates the conceptualization of the advocacy window. The advocacy window can be understood as the degree of latitude that a member of Congress has to incorporate group advocacy into their legislative reputation without suffering clear electoral damage once the size of the group within a district have been taken into account.

much representation (which, below a certain point, is unlikely to influence the reputation that member chooses to cultivate). Public opinion regarding a group in a district, however, acts as a ceiling – if the group is well regarded, there are no limits to the amount of effort that could acceptably be put in on behalf of group members, but if the group is poorly regarded, the level of advocacy that would be accepted without putting the member in electoral danger is tamped down. Figure 2.2 demonstrates this relationship.

The space in between the floor and the ceiling is what I am referring to as the *advocacy window*. The advocacy window is essentially the potential amount of acceptable, additional work that a member can do on behalf of a disadvantaged group, if they so choose, without damaging their chances electorally.[7] If the level of public disdain for a group is low, then even if the constituency group within a district is small, a member of Congress would still have a great deal of discretion over the degree to which they integrate group advocacy into their legislative reputation. But if public disdain for a group is high, the advocacy window is likely to be small, even if the

[7] Electoral damage in this context refers solely to any backlash that a member of Congress may receive for advocating on the behalf of a disadvantaged group, and not the opportunity cost that would come from spending legislative energy working on the issues of one group rather than another.

constituent group within a district is moderately sized. This theoretical framework is in line with the empirical findings of Hutchings, McClerking, and Charles (2004), indicating that the impact of Black constituency size on congressional support varies across areas with high levels of racial tension.

While this analogy holds for the vast majority of cases, there are instances in which group size can actually exceed the ambient temperature within a district. Much like a house in which the roof has collapsed, members in these districts find themselves in a treacherous space without a perfect solution. I expect that in these rare cases, the damned-if-they-do, damned-if-they-don't nature of the district environment will result in other factors such as member characteristics or partisanship taking precedence.

2.3.2 Perceived Deservingness of Assistance and the Advocacy Window

To this point, this chapter has highlighted both the district/state specific ambient temperature toward a group as well as a broader, more national sense of how deserving of government assistance a group is perceived to be as each having an important impact on the representation a group receives. While these two elements may be related to one another, it is important to note that these are in fact distinct concepts. Regardless of the group being evaluated, there is going to be some variation from district to district when it comes to the ambient temperature toward this group.[8] These changes are what are captured by the ceiling of the advocacy window. The broader conceptions of the deservingness of a group when it comes to government assistance, on the other hand, are a shaping force across all districts. These more general categorizations essentially describe the risk environment, and help to dictate how a member will respond to the advocacy window they face within their district.

Groups that are somewhat universally considered to be deserving, like military veterans or seniors, will find more ready advocates within the legislature, with variations in ambient temperature having less impact on constituency size effects. This is not to say that having more members of this group does not increase the likelihood of a member being an advocate, but that smaller numbers and changes are required for that to happen. For a disadvantaged group widely considered to be deserving, there may exist a potential boost to a member of Congress who firmly integrates

---

[8] Further evidence is provided in Chapter 4, and can be clearly seen in Figure 4.1.

providing for the group's needs into their legislative reputation. For example, constituents may be more likely to support a member who focuses on serving the needs of veterans, because they consider it to be a worthwhile use of government time and effort, even if they are not veterans themselves. Because of this potential boost, being a descriptive representative should be less necessary for a member to formulate a reputation as an advocate.

For groups where the sense of deservingness of government assistance is more mixed or party dependent, such as immigrants or the poor, I expect that constituent group size would have a large impact on whether or not a member becomes an advocate,[9] but that this effect would be minimally mitigated by its interaction with district ambient temperature regarding that constituent group. Unlike with those groups deemed widely deserving, if feelings toward a group are fairly mixed or of a more neutral variety, I would expect that the group's presence within a district or state would be the driving factor behind advocacy. Given the more neutral level of public regard, where advocacy is not seen as a clear electoral positive or negative, I expect that a member's party or experiences as a descriptive representative will be a large contributor to a member cultivating a reputation as a group advocate.

In the final category, for groups that are considered to be markedly less deserving of assistance, I expect that ambient temperature toward the group puts in place a large barrier to advocacy that is only cleared when a very large percentage of group members are present within a district. If public regard for a group is low, then members advocating for this group will receive no electoral boost or additional benefit from individuals who do not belong to the group. In fact, if a disadvantaged group is actively disliked, advocating for that group's needs could even backfire on a member so as to reduce the electoral support they might otherwise have received.

2.3.3 Party Effects

A key theoretical expectation for this project is that this reputation building on the part of disadvantaged groups should not be the exclusive

---

[9] Group size should not have a large effect on whether or not a member of Congress chooses to become an advocate for women. This is because of the unique place that women hold among the disadvantaged groups studied – there is minimal variation across states/districts in the percentage of women within the constituency, with these percentages consistently holding steady at around 50 percent of the population.

purview of members of only one political party. Both Democrats and Republicans will have at least some disadvantaged group members in their states and districts, and thus some level of representation is expected. Reputations for group advocacy are also not bound by particular means that may be sought to address the challenges facing disadvantaged groups, but rather by the act of seeking to address those needs in and of itself. This means that policy strategies preferred by Republicans and those preferred by Democrats each could be used in service to building a reputation as a disadvantaged-group advocate.

However, while potential reputations for disadvantaged-group advocacy are not explicitly tied to one party or another, there are some reputations that may be more common among one party than another. This is particularly true when considering advocacy on behalf of Black Americans. As Katherine Tate explains in her book *Concordance*, since the 1970s, the needs of Black Americans have gradually moved from being the primary focus of sometimes radical advocates within the Congressional Black Caucus to being firmly within the mainstream agenda of the Democratic Party. Given these changes over time, I expect that reputations for the advocacy of racial/ ethnic minorities are more likely to be found among Democrats than Republicans.

2.3.4 Descriptive Representatives

In all cases, I expect that being a descriptive representative of the group is a factor that will make a representative more likely to foster a reputation as an advocate for that group. I expect, however, that this effect will be the most readily apparent for members who represent a district with a large advocacy window. Given that a descriptive representative's knowledge and affinity for the group tends to exceed that of non-group members, I anticipate that they will more likely aim for the ceiling when facing a broad advocacy window and base their reputation in advocacy for that marginalized group. In accordance with Mansbridge's (1999) predictions about when descriptive representation should be most important, a member's own personal experience with discrimination or marginalization will make them more likely to risk any negative consequences that come from being a group advocate. Thus, given this potential risk, descriptive representatives should be more likely to take advantage of an expanded advocacy window to cultivate a reputation as an advocate.

2.4 LEGISLATIVE REPUTATIONS IN THE HOUSE AND THE SENATE

Given the institutional distinctions between the House and the Senate, there should be some differences in how members make decisions about which groups to include in their legislative reputations. Members of the House are considered to be specialists, at least compared to senators. Being a part of a 435-member body means that members are prone to develop narrow legislative identities and address very specific issues, groups, and policies. House districts also tend to be more homogeneous than those of the Senate (though this is not true in all cases).[10] This means that House districts are more likely to be spaces in which members of disadvantaged groups are concentrated. Coming from a more homogeneous district also minimizes the likelihood that advocating for one group in particular will provoke conflict. For these reasons, I expect that members of the House are more likely to formulate a reputation around being an advocate for a marginalized group than a member of the Senate, and that they will devote a larger portion of that reputation to advocating for the group.

In the Senate, members have far more freedom to be entrepreneurial in their legislative approach. Not only do they serve on more committees than House members, it is not unusual for senators to propose legislation outside of their specific committee-driven areas of expertise. The ability to offer non-germane amendments to legislation assists in this. Because members of the Senate tend to be generalists, this gives them a lot more latitude in the groups that they choose to represent. As a result, senators have a high level of discretion to hone their legislative reputation strategically, which provides incentives to incorporate as many "safe" groups into their legislative reputations as possible. Therefore, it is expected that Senators will more likely opt for a more superficial form of group advocacy, rather than devoting a large share of their energies toward working on behalf of any particular group.

---

[10] Small and rural states may be more homogenous than the typical House district, and there are seven states that are equivalent to House districts in population. However, when comparing the average House district to the average state, states do tend to be larger and more heterogeneous. The inclusion of these smaller, less diverse states could serve to bias the Senate sample to look more like the House sample, making it more difficult to detect differences in representational decision-making, and thereby serving as a more conservative test of the importance of representing larger and more heterogeneous areas.

For a large portion of American history, political theorists regarded the Senate as the protector of minority groups against the popular majorities in the South. Those assumptions that minority interests are somehow linked with the interests of smaller states, however, are highly problematic, particularly where racial/ethnic minorities are concerned (Dahl, 1956; Lee and Oppenheimer, 1999; Leighley, 2001). Compared to the House, senators are more likely to be running scared – the electoral margins tend to be smaller for senators, and their seats more competitive. So, there also are more risks for senators in developing a reputation as an advocate for an unpopular group, especially if the group's members are not sufficiently numerous to compensate for any losses to the senators' electoral coalition that might result from that advocacy. Given this, I hypothesize that the increased electoral vulnerability of most senators relative to most members of the House will make senators less likely to become advocates of disadvantaged groups in general, and that this will be particularly acute for groups who are not considered to be broadly deserving of government assistance, such as racial/ethnic minorities.

2.5 CONCLUSION

This chapter reviewed the ways that previous research has understood the representational relationship, and offered a more realistic conceptualization of representation that takes into account the type of information that members of Congress and their constituents could actually be expected to know. It presented a new, integrated theory of when and why members choose to represent the groups that they do, with a special focus on disadvantaged groups. In doing so, it recognizes that not all members of disadvantaged groups are considered to be equally deserving of assistance from the government by society at large, and that those different categorizations of deservingness have an impact on which members of Congress are willing to develop a reputation as a group's advocate.

Each state or district has an advocacy window, which represents the degree of latitude that a member of Congress has in making decisions about how extensively to incorporate disadvantaged-group advocacy into their legislative reputations. After the size of a group within a district or state is taken into account, members rely upon their own discretion to determine the level of group representation to offer, which is conditioned by the ambient temperature toward a group within that state or district. For all but those disadvantaged groups that are held to be the most highly deserving of assistance, such as seniors and veterans, cross-state or district variations in how favorably the rest of the district feels toward a group is expected to have a conditioning effect on how likely it is that a member will choose to include advocacy on behalf of that group into their legislative reputation. This should be most acutely felt for disadvantaged groups such as the LGBTQ community or racial/ethnic minorities that are viewed as less sympathetic by broad swathes of the American public.

The next chapter examines the critical role that legislative reputations play in the ways that groups are represented in Congress. It makes a case for legislative reputation as one of the primary conduits of representation, and offers a clear definition and operationalization for what legislative reputations are, as well as what they are not. Finally, it demonstrates the incidence of members with legislative reputations for serving the disadvantaged across a sampling of Congresses. It highlights the variation in the primacy of each group to a member's reputation, and showcases the partisan and House-Senate differences in the types of reputations members form.

3

Member Reputation

Claude Pepper had a long career in the US Congress, serving as a Florida senator from 1936 to 1951 and as a representative of Miami from 1963 until his death in 1989. The very first line of his obituary in the *New York Times* referred to him as a "former United States Senator from Florida who became a champion of the elderly in a career that spanned 60 years." These sorts of characterizations continued throughout, both in memorializing quotes from others as well as in descriptions of his work within the legislature:

"Claude Pepper gave definition and meaning to the concept of public service," the President [George H.W. Bush] said. "He fought for the poor and the elderly in his own determined way."

Horace B. Deets, the executive director of the American Association of Retired Persons, said it would be difficult to find an advocate for the rights of older Americans who could replace Mr. Pepper. "There really isn't anyone on the American political landscape who could step into Claude Pepper's shoes," he said. […]

From 1929, when he first entered politics, until his death, Mr. Pepper fought for the rights of the elderly. One of his first acts in the Florida House of Representatives was to sponsor a bill that allowed older residents to fish without a license. And as he grew older Mr. Pepper continued to wage war against those he considered willing to take advantage of the elderly. At the age of 78 he voted for a law that raised the mandatory retirement age to 70 from 65. […]

In 1977 Mr. Pepper was named chairman of the House Select Committee on Aging, soon becoming known as 'Mr. Social Security' for his ardent defense of Social Security and Medicare. He built a national reputation as the primary Congressional advocate for the elderly, introducing legislation to fight crime in housing projects for the elderly, to cut Amtrak fares for senior citizens and to provide meals to invalids. […]

Mr. Pepper's stands on behalf of the elderly did not hurt him in his own district, where 30 percent of adults are at least 65 years old. Over the last decade, he consistently won re-election with more than 70 percent of the vote.

In the special election following his death, the 18th District of Florida elected Ileana Ros-Lehtinen to be the first Latina to serve in Congress. She subsequently won all of her reelection battles, and in the spring of 2017 announced her intent to retire at the end of the term. A piece in the Miami Herald describing her tenure in Congress discussed her consistent emphasis on foreign affairs, particularly in regards to Cuba, as well as her longtime advocacy for the LGBTQ community. The author writes:

"For years, Ros-Lehtinen represented the Florida Keys, including gay-friendly Key West, and advocated for LGBTQ rights – far ahead of much of the GOP. Eventually, her transgender son, Rodrigo Heng-Lehtinen, made his way into the public spotlight; last year, he and his parents recorded a bilingual public-service TV campaign to urge Hispanics to support transgender youth."

In both cases, these individuals are described in terms of their legislative reputation. In particular, their work in Congress is defined by their broad efforts on behalf of specific disadvantaged groups. Describing a member's reputation is used as a way of summarizing a member's work within the legislature in a way that is easily understandable. Notably, member reputation is used as a concept that is distinct from any one particular action such as bill sponsorship, and distinct from group presence within a district. When specific actions are mentioned, such as Sen. Pepper's efforts to allow seniors to fish without licenses or to address crime in housing for the elderly, they are included to give examples of the work that went into building this reputation, rather than the critical factors in and of themselves. Additionally, while the importance of district composition is made clear by emphasizing the relatively high level of senior citizens and the presence of the Key West's large LGBTQ population within the district, sizeable district presence alone is not synonymous with legislative reputation. If it were, one would expect both members to have formed very similar reputations, as Reps. Pepper and Ros-Lehtinen represented roughly the same district, but this is not the case.

This book seeks to deepen our understanding of the representation that disadvantaged groups actually receive in the US Congress. Specifically, it pursues an understudied conduit of representation by exploring when and why members of Congress seek to build legislative reputations on behalf of disadvantaged groups. But before the *when* and the *why* can be explored, one must first focus on the what. Chiefly, *what* exactly is a legislative reputation? In this chapter, I lay out a specific definition for what a legislative reputation is, along with its requisite characteristics. I then make a case for why legislative reputations are so important for representation, and why members seek to craft them. Finally, I describe the source material and coding scheme for my original measure of member reputation, and present descriptive statistics on the members that do cultivate reputations as advocates of disadvantaged groups.

3.1 WHAT IS A LEGISLATIVE REPUTATION?

The concept of a reputation is one that is familiar and frequently used in common parlance, but the precise elements that make up a reputation can be hard to pin down. Despite this, scholars and journalists alike tend to treat a member's reputation as an important way of understanding their behavior within the legislature. Much like the terms "maverick" or "political capital," member reputations are commonly referenced but rarely thoroughly defined.

There are a few exceptions that make notable contributions to a holistic understanding of what a legislative reputation really is. Swers (2007) highlights the benefits conferred upon members with a reputation as an expert in national security in the post-9/11 world and explores the gender-based differences in where members focus their reputation-building efforts. Fenno (1991) explains that to establish reputations as effective legislators, senators must work both within the legislature to pass bills and on the campaign trail to bring it to constituents' attention. Schiller (2000a) argues that "the requirements for successful reputation building ... [are] media attention and constituent recognition."

Each of these authors offers important pieces to the broader puzzle of what makes a legislative reputation. Fenno emphasizes that reputations come from intentional efforts on the part of members that depend upon their communication to constituents, while Schiller develops this further by conceptualizing member reputation as part of a two-way communication with media as an essential arbiter. Swers highlights the nuanced differences in how members craft their reputations, even within the same issue area. She also offers insight into the linkage between a member's descriptive characteristics and attempting to build credible reputations.

At its simplest, a member's legislative reputation is what they are known for prioritizing and spending their time working on while in Congress. This is a definition that leaves a great deal of latitude, both in terms of the subject matter and the means of acquisition. For example, in considering the applicable subject matter for this project, I am particularly interested in reputations that are crafted around advocating for particular constituent groups. However, reputations can also be built around other aspects of legislative work, such as being a deficit hawk or attending to foreign affairs in Eastern Asia. Similarly, there are a vast number of different ways that members can "work on" issues they consider to be important. So, if legislative reputations are not just set lists of topics or behaviors, what are they?

I contend that a reputation has three essential components. First, reputations must be greater than the sum of the individual actions that contribute to them. Second, there is no single action that is required for a reputation to be formed. And third, reputations are the result of the observation and interpretation of others.

3.1.1 Emergent Properties

When biologists seek to define some of the principal characteristics of living organisms, one of the most important of these is that it possesses what are referred to as emergent properties. Emergent properties are present at all levels of biological structure and are responsible for important characteristics of life such as responsiveness to stimuli, reproduction, and evolutionary adaptation. Biological organisms are made up of an enormous number of different components that have various functions, but these elements then interact to fulfill something more than just their individual roles – the whole is greater than the sum of its parts. So too when thinking about what makes a legislative reputation. It is not simply votes cast, bills proposed, or speeches given. It is the distillation of what this individual is about and what is most important to them.

A reputation cannot simply be taking specific actions or saying specific words. Rather, it is the culmination of a number of different actions that then interact to form a broader picture. One can step outside of the political realm to get an intuitive sense of how this works. You do not have to know where Mother Teresa practiced her ministry or be able to name any of her works of mercy to know of her reputation for working to serve the poor and the sick. To give an example familiar to children and parents of children from the 1990s, one need not remember any specific storylines or plot twists to feel confident in stating that Captain Planet's top priority was protecting the environment. These reputations are built from a consistent series of actions that signal dedication to a particular cause or service to a particular group, that then take on a life of their own.

They are connected to specific behaviors, but can also be broadly understood apart from them.

Member reputations take on a life of their own and stand for something more than just individual actions in and of themselves. They hold symbolic value as well, and can serve as a mark of trust and understanding that goes beyond that of other members. In the mid-2000s, Republicans created a commission to explore ways to reform Medicare and ensure its fiscal solvency. When they went to sell their proposed reforms, one of the most important things that they relied on was not a detailed recounting of their policy proposals, but rather the support of Michael Bilirakis (R-FL9).[1] Bilirakis was known as someone who looked out for the best interests of seniors, and Republicans argued that if he believed that their proposed Medicare changes would benefit older Americans, they could believe it too. His reputation as an advocate for seniors had value in and of itself, above and beyond any individual act.

3.1.2 Reputation Is Not Synonymous with Any Specific Action

This second property is related to the first – in the same way that a reputation is more than the specific actions and signals that go into its crafting, it also does not directly imply that any particular action on behalf of a group has been taken. There are a variety of ways that a member can represent the groups within their district, and all of them feed into a member's reputation. But no one specific action – be it sponsoring a bill, speaking on the floor, or cosponsoring a number of bills to benefit the group – guarantees that a member has a reputation for advocating for the group more broadly. Similarly, knowing that a member has a reputation as a group advocate does not mean that you can predict with absolute certainty what legislative actions they will have taken.

This is a critical definitional element of a reputation for two main reasons. First, it takes into account the amount of discretion members have in terms of what they do, and how they do it. Reputations build over time as the result of a conglomerate of actions. But depending upon the member's seniority, committee membership, position in the chamber, and their other group and issue priorities, they enact their group advocacy in different ways. For example, some members of Congress sponsor hundreds of bills in a given Congress, while others may introduce less than five. By not assuming that reputation means any one specific action, it

---

[1] Politics in America: 2004.

takes into account this variation in the preferred means of representation. Second, it highlights the fact that members can take some of the same actions, with no guarantee that it will impact their respective reputations in exactly the same way. Just because members have similar cosponsorship records, for instance, does not mean that each will have the same reputation for group advocacy.

A member's reputation goes beyond a set list of specific, predetermined actions. Reputation does not have inherent transitive properties. Members who engage in bill sponsorship or cosponsorship benefiting a particular group, or who serve on a committee with the potential to address their needs may have a reputation as a group advocate, but group advocates do not have to serve on particular committees or introduce some particular set of measures. While it may be true, for example, that someone who sponsors several bills pertaining to women's health has built a broader reputation as an advocate for women, this does not mean that having a reputation for women's advocacy is synonymous with just sponsoring a bunch of bills intended to help women.

In over three decades of time spent serving in Congress, first in the House and then in the Senate, Barbara Boxer cultivated a reputation as a formidable advocate of women, with a particular focus on women's health. The vast majority of the bills she sponsored, however, came in other arenas, including national security, international affairs, public lands, environmental protection, and government operations.[2] Of the forty-one measures signed into law over the course of her career for which she was the primary sponsor (an impressive total), only five were directly related to women. Four of these were joint resolutions from the mid-to-late 1980s designating Women's History Week and then Women's History Month, and the last came in the 114th Congress, in the form of a bill designed to enhance suicide prevention efforts for women veterans. But this rather narrow record of formal legislation sponsored and enacted to benefit women does not mean that her reputation was unfairly bestowed, or that this reputation for advocacy had limited substantive effect. Instead, her impact came in ways that could be missed if one only looks to routine measures like bill sponsorship alone. She fought against any efforts to restrict women's access to preventative medical care and abortion access, offering amendment after amendment to this effect during her tenure. Boxer also engaged in less traditional or easily counted forms of representation, including frequently speaking out in defense of

---

[2] www.govtrack.us/congress/members/barbara_boxer/300011

Planned Parenthood, publishing op-eds on women's healthcare with other female lawmakers, pushing for the resignation of members credibly accused of harassment against women, and, most famously, leading a group of women Representatives from the House in a march over to the Senate side of the Capital in protest of the treatment of Anita Hill during the Clarence Thomas hearings.

Members of Congress can be creative in the ways that they choose to represent their constituents. This is particularly true when considering the representation of disadvantaged groups, especially those who are less well regarded by the public as a whole. Majority coalitions can be difficult to build for measures seen as benefiting less popular groups. Thus, representation for these groups may be less likely to take the form of trying to pass immediate, big ticket legislation and more focused on the overtime work of coalition building and elevating disadvantaged-group members' real lives and concerns. Rep. Shirley Chisholm, whose words opened the first chapter of this book, saw her role in this way. In discussing her time in Congress in her book, *Unbossed and Unbought*, she argued that her job was to help disadvantaged and marginalized people to "arouse the conscience of the nation and thus create a conscience in the Congress" whether by traditional legislative means or by any other avenue her platform and the resources available to her could provide.

3.1.3 The Eye of the Beholder

Finally, one of the primary characteristics of a reputation is that it inherently must be interpreted by others. There are a variety of things that can be done to shape a reputation, but ultimately, it is in the eye of the beholder. In the political world, that beholder most commonly is the media. Even the most politically engaged tend not to spend copious amounts of their time scouring the *Congressional Record* for every action their member took on the floor that day, or tuning in to endless hours of committee hearings on C-SPAN. Instead, individuals depend upon a variety of media sources to keep them updated on what their member is up to, with only occasional specifics. This can take a number of different forms: who the media quotes on a particular topic, pieces that do a deep dive into actions that have been taken on a salient policy topic, reports on a member's town hall, or candidate biographies and descriptions that are published to prepare voters for an upcoming election. These are distilled down from a huge quantity of member actions and positions, and once a reputation is established, it tends to be reinforced by other members of the media as well.

In the lead-up to the 2012 election, Mitt Romney declared that he had been a "severely conservative governor" of Massachusetts. The former presidential candidate was widely mocked for this statement, as it did not comport with the narrative surrounding his time in office, where he was generally described as compiling a moderate record. He did take a number of what could be considered "conservative" actions while serving as governor, but that was not the interpretation that had been drawn by the media and others who had examined his history. Conversely, in the Democratic primary campaign of 2015 and 2016, Bernie Sanders routinely described himself as the candidate of the working class, with very little pushback. This self-assessment was congruent with how the Senator tended to be described by the news media, and thus served to reinforce the reputation that had already been developed.

These examples illustrate the fact that one's reputation cannot simply be declared to be whatever one would like it to be – it must be drawn by the consensus of others who observe that person's behavior over time. Obviously, this is not to say that a person has no control at all over their own reputation, because they most certainly do. Individuals can take any number of actions in an attempt to craft and shape their own reputation. Many of the behaviors that a member of Congress engages in are designed to send important signals about their priorities and the work they are doing. But these behaviors must be interpreted by others – primarily the media – rather than simply claimed by the member themselves.

Because reputations rely upon outside determinations, they are also self-reinforcing. This can happen in two ways. First, if some members of the media repeatedly reference a member of Congress in particular ways, this can get picked up by other reporters and other news outlets as well, until there is a broad understanding of what the big pieces of a member's reputation generally are. Second, when reporters are seeking comment on particular issues, they generally want to ask a member who has experience and expertise on the topic. If a member gives an interview in which they spend a good deal of time discussing the challenges facing immigrants in this country or how pending immigration legislation might affect that group, they will get to be known as someone who can speak with authority on the issue, prompting other journalists to seek them out as well. This then has the effect of further bolstering a member's reputation as an advocate for immigrants.

Because the reputation that is communicated to constituents is dependent upon this outside party assessment, it ensures that it will have at least a base level of face validity. Members of the media and other outside observers will only coalesce around a particular understanding of a member's reputation if it is seen to be reasonably credible. Credibility generally requires that a member be considered to have a relatively high level of expertise, that they have taken at least some actions related to an issue, and that they have not taken actions considered to stand in opposition to an issue or group.

Strom Thurmond was one of the longest-serving politicians in American history, representing South Carolina in the US Senate for forty-eight years. Some of what he is best known for is his run for president in 1948 under the banner of the anti-civil rights States Rights Democratic Party, staging the longest filibuster in history against the 1957 Civil Rights Act, opposing all civil rights legislation over the next two decades, and changing parties in 1964 to protest the Democratic Party's embrace of civil rights. In his later years in the Senate, he did make some overtures to his Black constituents, who by that time made up a sizable portion of the electorate in South Carolina. These small actions had little to no effect on his general reputation as someone who was certainly not an advocate for Black Americans and other communities of color, as they did not comport with the decades of strong evidence to the contrary.

A member's credibility is most frequently considered to come from the study of issues under a committee's jurisdiction, but it also goes beyond this. Some members also take reputation-building actions on issues that are not specific to their committee assignments. This is particularly common in the Senate, where senators are expected to be generalists, but can be true in the House as well. These instances also speak to the differences between legislative effectiveness and a legislative reputation. Working on issues relevant to the jurisdiction of the committees a member is on doubtless increases their chances of moving legislation through the process. But reputation formation does not rely upon success alone. Legislators can gain reputations as "squeaky-wheel" advocates, even if their proposed changes are rarely enacted.

A person's personal, descriptive characteristics can also serve as a shortcut to credibility even without a committee-specific tie. For example, being a female member of Congress lends additional credence to their status as an advocate for women and women's issues. This then makes it more likely that members of the media will approach them on these issues, thereby serving to amplify this component of their reputation.

However, there are some instances, as demonstrated by Swers (2007), in which personal characteristics or demographics can make it a tougher climb to reach credibility. Jay Rockefeller, for instance, spent three decades representing West Virginia in the United States Senate. But, as a member of a famously wealthy family, Rockefeller had to put great effort into demonstrating his understanding of and compassion for the challenges facing the poor and elderly in West Virginia.

In summary, a legislative reputation is defined by three important characteristics. First, a reputation is essentially an emergent property – it is more than the sum of individual actions. Second, a reputation cannot guarantee that a member will have engaged in any one particular behavior. And third, reputations are translated through third-party observers. Next, I turn to why legislative reputations are important, and what drives members to attempt to craft them.

3.2 WHY DO MEMBERS OF CONGRESS SEEK TO BUILD LEGISLATIVE REPUTATIONS?

Members of Congress attempt to cultivate legislative reputations for a number of reasons, rooted in both their electoral concerns about communicating their priorities and achievements back to their constituents as well as the advantages that are conferred within the legislature itself. First, members want their constituents to know what they have been doing to represent them, but recognize that the vast majority of their constituents have extremely limited political knowledge about a member's specific actions day to day. Working to craft a clear legislative reputation is a way to demonstrate a broad picture of their efforts, without counting on the transference of specific facts. Second, much of politics is rooted in group-based understandings, making reputations for group advocacy a common denominator of communication between members and constituents. Finally, to be effective in Congress, members know they have to play the long game. By cultivating reputations, members make it easier to claim legislative turf and build coalitions over time.

3.2.1 Limited Political Knowledge

At its most basic, the idealized representational relationship consists of an elected representative diligently working within the legislature to promote actions in the best interests of their constituents. These constituents then take careful note of the member's behavior over the course of their term, and, if they feel that they have done a good job of working on behalf of the constituency, reward them with another term in office. In practice, this relationship is considerably more complicated. Despite an increase in transparency since the reforms of the 1970s, constituents do not have full information about what their representative is doing available to them. Even only considering the (still considerable) information that individuals can access, most nonetheless have extremely limited knowledge.

A member's constituents tend to have no idea what their member is doing from day to day. This is not inherently a criticism – they cannot be expected to follow everything that a member does. Most citizens have lives and priorities that leave little time for in-depth explorations of what their member of Congress has been up to each day. Given the high cost of this information gathering and the limited personal incentives for any one person to engage in this process, it ought not to be surprising that levels of political knowledge and information are fairly low. Thus, in a political reality in which fewer than one-third of Americans can name one of their state's senators (Breitman, 2015), it is unlikely that any given constituent will be aware of a specific action that a member of Congress takes. That said, even if a member cannot count on a sizable portion of their constituency to be up-to-date on the most recent amendment they proposed in mark-up or the bill they signed on to as one of the first cosponsors, it is reasonable to expect that those individuals paying at least some amount of attention to what's going on in Congress and the political world will pick up on some of the broader trends about what their member is doing.

It is this general picture of themselves that members of Congress seek to control. As described in the previous section discussing reputation as inherently in the eye of the beholder, members of Congress do not have absolute control over their reputations. That said, they are very far from helpless. Members of Congress are exceedingly conscious of how their actions are perceived by others, and work to create a cohesive pattern of behavior. Members seek to build these reputations because of their simplicity and power to penetrate down to the constituent level. The likelihood of any one vote, hearing, speech, or bill introduced becoming widely known is extremely slim, but members are able to cultivate a broader reputation by repeatedly taking actions that contribute to the larger picture of advocacy for a specific group or toward achieving particular goals.

This is then reinforced by the media, both in the way that a member is described and in who the media seeks out for comment on particular issues. Given that member reputation is filtered down to constituents through the media, this reinforcement is particularly important. Once a member begins to develop a reputation with some sources within the media as an advocate for a particular group, this understanding will be repeated. This is true at the national level and at the local level. Members of Congress place a great deal of value on local news outlets, as they are frequently the sources that constituents pay the most attention to. But given that few local media outlets are able to send staff to Washington, there is a considerable amount of member action for which local media look to previous national reporting to shape their stories. Additionally, reporters and broadcasters sometimes actively seek out members to comment and speak to specific issues. Those who have a reputation as group advocates and experts on those issues are likely to be those who are sought out. This in turn further emphasizes that reputation, as media appearances are an important piece of the narrative.

3.2.2 Group-Based Understandings

While politics at the elite level are frequently talked about in terms of political ideology, at the individual level, people are far more likely to see politics as rooted in group identities (Converse, 1964). This means that a large percentage of people think about politics as coalitions of different groups, and their issue positions or partisan identification is directly related to what groups they support or feel connected to, and which groups they oppose or see as undeserving (Green, Palmquist, and Schickler, 2002). Members of Congress also frequently see their districts as composed of groups and factions (Fenno, 1978). They pay close attention to district demographics and other subgroup divisions when conceptualizing their districts and deciding what actions to take.

Member reputation as a group advocate, then, is a particularly helpful way of thinking about representation. It acknowledges the emphasis on group-based understandings that many constituents use when evaluating their representatives but also reflects one of the principal ways that members make decisions and take action within the legislature. This is not to say that all of politics is rooted in group affinity, or that group considerations are the only means by which members of Congress make decisions. But, it is one of the most common means that constituents and members alike use to think about the political world and political decisions, creating a place of overlap in how both representatives and the represented conceptualize representation.

3.2.3 Playing the Long Game

Member reputations also provide a boost to members over the long term when it comes to getting things done within the legislature. It is extremely rare that issues are raised, problems are understood, and solutions are proposed and adopted in the two years of a single Congress. Issues can take years to enter into the public consciousness, and some never will. Single pieces of legislation are introduced over and over, some with various tweaks but the legislative intent remaining the same. Members will give speeches addressing the same issues year after year. Hearings on issues left unaddressed in the prior Congress will be revamped for the next. In the overwhelming majority of cases, if members want to actually accomplish anything in Congress, they have to be prepared to play the long game. Working to establish legislative reputations assists members in that goal in two ways: aiding coalition building and establishing legislative "turf."

Coalitions can be thought about in two ways. The first is of a majority coalition within the legislature. This involves bringing on board half of the members of the House or the Senate to legislation that is favored by a group or is meant to serve a group. These coalitions can be established either by getting other members to agree to act on behalf of a given group's cause or by adding in provisions that would serve other groups or favored issues as well.

The second way of thinking about a coalition is one of affected parties and stakeholders outside of the legislature itself, either nationally or within a district. Coalitions of this sort are necessary both to determine what sorts of services or actions groups want and require, and also to gain buy-in from important entities that can communicate to other constituent group members. Building coalitions with groups in the district that work to end hunger, provide housing for the homeless, raise awareness of the EITC, or provide job training opportunities for struggling communities helps a member stay in touch with issues that are most important to low-income individuals, but also bolsters their own reputation as an advocate for the poor. In turn, having a strong reputation on these issues can serve as a signal to other potential community partners that a member can be trusted to work diligently on their behalf.

Members also seek to establish their own legislative "turf" as a means of communicating expertise and gaining prestige within the legislature. Specializing in particular issue areas has been a long-standing tactic in both the House and the Senate to increase a member's influence within the legislature, and to reflect constituency needs (Grant, 1973; Gaddie and Kuzenski, 1996). Establishing a reputation as an expert and important operator on a specific issue increases the likelihood that a member will be able to play a major role in important legislation and gain higher visibility in the media on that issue. This then reinforces that reputation and boosts the likelihood that their efforts will be recognized by their constituents.

Having now defined legislative reputation as a concept, made a case for why reputation is an important means of understanding representation, and explained why members seek to cultivate a legislative reputation, I next turn to a discussion of how reputation can be measured.

3.3 MEASURING REPUTATION

For this project, I have developed an original variable of reputation that quantifies which members cultivate a legislative reputation as an advocate for disadvantaged groups. As previously indicated, the disadvantaged groups under consideration are the poor, women, racial/ethnic minorities, the LGBTQ population, veterans, seniors, immigrants, and Native Americans. I created this legislative reputation variable by systematically coding the written member profiles found in Congressional Quarterly's *Politics in America* for the 103rd, 105th, 108th, 110th, and 113th Congresses, all of which lie between the period from 1993–2014.[3] Utilizing these member profiles allows me to construct a reputation variable that takes into account the critical characteristics discussed earlier in the chapter – namely, that reputation is more than just a set of specific actions, and that it relies upon the interpretation of an outside observer. In the remainder of this section, I provide a description of *Politics in America*

---

[3] Written member profiles can also be found in National Journal's *Almanac of American Politics*. But the *Almanac* profiles are less systematic in the way they are laid out, with tremendous variation in length and attention paid to legislative activity (as opposed to *Politics in America*, where profiles follow a fairly consistent layout). Additionally, earlier versions of the *Almanac* (particularly the 1980s and early 1990s) have very little in the way of profiles for House members, with at most a few paragraphs almost entirely devoted to information about the congressional elections. That said, as an additional robustness check, I did code the *Almanac* for the 113th Congress, examining all Senate profiles and a random sampling of 100 of the House profiles. For Senate members, 90 percent of the 800 variables coded were in agreement between the *Almanac* and *Politics in America*. In only 1.4 percent of cases would including the *Almanac* profiles in coding have resulted in additional members being coded as primary or secondary group advocates. For House members, there was even higher agreement, with 93.5 percent of variables being coded the same between the two sources, and including the *Almanac* would have created less than one percent more primary or secondary advocates being included.

and its member profiles, make a case for using an "inside the beltway" resource like *Politics in America* to develop an innovative new measure for reputation, and give a precise detailing of how this reputation metric is operationalized.

3.3.1 CQ's Politics in America

Congressional Quarterly's *Politics in America* is a compendium of profiles of all members of Congress and their districts, published every two years with each new incoming Congress, starting in the 1970s. Each profile contains approximately two pages of text in addition to a sidebar listing biographical information such as place and date of birth, military service, education, and previous political office. The profile sidebar also contains several of the member's interest group scores and record on key votes.[4] The heart of these profiles, however, comes in the two page narrative description of who a member is, and what a member has done. These narrative profiles are a combination of biographical information, descriptions of legislative priorities, highlights of past work within the legislature, and a short concluding section covering their electoral histories. The primary emphasis in these profiles is to give a robust sense of a member's identity in Congress.

The relatively short length of these profiles is important, because it ensures that they are not simply a listing of all of the actions a member has taken on each and every issue position. Rather, they are a concise distillation of the most important elements of what a member has done, said, or intends to do. Though each profile does devote one or two paragraphs to narrating some biographical backstory or electoral intrigue, the vast majority of the profile is spent discussing what the member is known for within the legislature. Any additional biographical information that is included serves the purpose of explaining why advocating for particular groups or issues is so important to a member. This can range from highlighting how (now former) Rep. Mike Ross' (D-AR04) career as a pharmacist drove him to push for controls on prescription drug prices for seniors to describing Rep. Ruben Hinojosa's (D-TX15) experiences in

---

[4] The format has changed slightly over the last few decades. In the 2000s, the structure became much more uniform, with two pages devoted to each member (the only exception being brand new members of the House, who receive only a single page for the description of the member and their district). Prior to this, profiles averaged around two pages, but were sometimes extended for members with particularly long tenures or who held a senior leadership position.

segregated schools as a Spanish-speaking child as the catalyst for his work to promote educational equality for minority students.

It is common for members of Congress to serve for a number of terms. An important element of these profiles is that they account for the ways that a member's reputation can change over the course of their career. While there is clear overlap in some of the content that is discussed in a member's profile from Congress to Congress (as would be expected), the profiles are revisited and written anew for each term. This is important for three reasons. First, this is essential for ensuring that the information presented is up-to-date as of the contemporaneous Congress. Reputation building frequently takes time and is developed over a number of years, and this allows for new actions to be taken into account. Second, member profiles tend to be more heavily weighted toward recent actions, allowing for reputations to evolve over time. While members frequently exhibit a high level of consistency in the groups they advocate for, as discussed above, there are also instances in which members can shift their priorities or take up new causes. By updating for each new Congress, these changes can be incorporated. Finally, this also allows for the continuity for an individual member across sessions of Congress to be more organically derived. While each new writer undoubtedly references what has been written in the past, they are also at liberty to select new information to include or old information to drop based upon their interpretation of how best to describe a particular member. This process in and of itself also mirrors the process by which a member's reputation is built, evolved, and reinforced through the eyes of the media.

In the introduction to the 13th Edition of *Politics in America* (detailing the members of the 109th Congress, which was in session from January 2005 to 2007), Editor and Senior Vice President David Rapp describes the process of compiling these profiles in the following way:

Congressional Quarterly, which has been the "bible" on Congress since 1945, sets out every two years to compile the definitive insider's guide to the people who constitute the world's greatest democratic institution. The book is organized so that each member's "chapter" provides a full political profile, statistical information on votes and positions and a demographic description of the state or district a member represents.

We evaluate every member by his or her own standards. We do not try to decide where a politician ought to stand on a controversial issue; our interest has been to assess how they go about expressing their views and how effective they are at achieving their self-proclaimed goals.

The 125 reporters, editors and researchers at CQ cover Congress and its members on a weekly, daily, and even hourly basis, through the pages of CQ Weekly and CQ Today, and our online news service, CQ.com.

Under the direction of editors Jackie Koszczuk and H. Amy Stern, they have produced the most objective, authoritative and interesting volume of political analysis available on this fascinating collection of people.

In constructing these profiles, CQ writers draw upon prior reporting on the day-to-day actions in the House and the Senate, member interviews, campaign materials, and media appearances, among other sources.

3.3.2 Advantages of an "Inside the Beltway" Measure

Building a reputation measure based on the efforts of expert congressional journalists offers clear benefits on the grounds of realism, consistency, and objectivity. As discussed in greater detail in Chapter 2, very few Americans actually keep tabs on specific bills their member introduces or cosponsors, or particular votes their member takes. And the few legislative actions that do trickle down to constituents tend not come via diligent C-SPAN viewing or personal investigation, but rather from the media. By using a media-derived measure of reputation, I am able to approximate the representational relationship as it actually exists. The vast majority of information that people have about the representation they are receiving comes from media reports, so it is reasonable to operationalize reputation as it is filtered through a media lens.

Using a national media-derived measure is also beneficial when seeking to evaluate senators and members of the House from all states and all districts. Not all members of Congress have clear, single media markets in which they operate. Some members represent areas with an array of competing local stations and newspapers, while others may only have one, or sometimes none at all. Similarly, not all media outlets are created equal. While some outlets may have a correspondent in Washington, DC to monitor the behavior of their representative, many must rely on national coverage from the *Associated Press* and others, particularly as budgets for smaller newsrooms have declined over the past few decades. Given this, a national media source is useful as a broad-based measure, because it provides relatively consistent coverage across states and districts.

A national, "inside the beltway" media resource like *Politics in America* thus offers tremendous benefits when it comes to realism and consistency, but it also has clear advantages when it comes to objectivity and expertise. *Politics in America* is written by professional journalists, trained in the norms of objectivity and balance, who are on Capitol Hill day in and day out. These individuals specialize in understanding what is happening in the legislature, building relationships with members and their staff, and then synthesizing and communicating their findings in clear and objective ways. Haynie (2002), for example, in his study of legislative effectiveness in the North Carolina state legislature, found that while lobbyists and other legislators offered evaluations of the effectiveness of Black lawmakers that were tainted by bias, the journalists did not.

3.3.3 Operationalizing Reputation

For each group of interest, reputation is measured on an ordinal scale that ranges across four levels: no advocacy, superficial advocacy, secondary advocacy, and primary advocacy. Primary advocates are either those members who are most known for their reputation as a disadvantaged-group advocate or those who are equally well-known for their work on behalf of one disadvantaged group as they are an additional issue or group, with neither clearly predominating.[5] Secondary advocates are those who do invest time and energy building a reputation as a disadvantaged-group advocate, but it is not clearly their top priority. Superficial advocates are those who are known to take at least some occasional actions on behalf of a particular disadvantaged group, while non-advocates do not include working to benefit a disadvantaged group as any part of their legislative reputation. These classifications are made on the basis of both the specific and implied legislative actions on behalf of the group that are enumerated in the profile as well as the representational statements that are used to characterize the member.

3.3.3.1 Legislative Actions and Reputational Statements
Legislative actions are any member-initiated steps that a member of Congress takes – within their purview as a legislator – to advocate on

---

[5] Allowing for this flexibility for members to have more than one primary reputation is crucial, particularly for members who view politics through a more intersectional lens. If a member really focuses on serving the needs of low-income Hispanic Americans, or promoting opportunities for women of color, then they have primary reputations as one who serves the poor and racial/ethnic minorities, or women and racial/ethnic minorities. Both of these reputations are intimately tied together, and neither is clearly more foundational or important than the other.

behalf of a particular disadvantaged group. To allow members that creativity and flexibility discussed in the sections above, this project was not started with a finite, a priori list of legislative actions. Instead, legislative actions are any behaviors detailed in a member profile that meet two conditions: actions must be specifically instigated by the member themselves and thus inside the realm of their control, and actions must pertain to their work in the legislature rather than being purely electoral. Next, I consider a key element to understanding what constitutes a legislative action – clearly distinguishing what it is not.

Roll call voting, for example, is not included as a legislative action because it does not require any initiative on the part of the member. Reaching a roll call vote requires collective action within the chamber and/or a decision by party leadership to bring the measure to the floor. As this project is focused on consciously constructed legislative reputation, only actions that are firmly within a member's control and require a member-initiated choice to actively advocate on behalf of a group are included. Likewise, simple statements that a member "supports" or "opposes" a relevant issue are also not included (unless there is additional, more specific description) because it is unclear what action – if any – the member has actually taken.

Similarly, actions taken earlier in a member's life, before they made it to Congress, are not included, nor are actions taken in the purely electoral arena, as these do not meet the legislative threshold required for a legislative action. Prior experience as an immigration attorney or running a veterans' nonprofit is likely correlated with the decisions that a member will make when they go about forming their reputation, but it does not constitute a specific action taken within the legislature as a part of the conscious, intentional reputation formation process. Additionally, because this project is focused on the legislative reputations that a member builds within the institution of Congress, purely electoral actions, like running campaign advertisements or selecting a campaign debate strategy are not included. Again, these electoral choices are likely to be related to a member's work within the legislature, but they are themselves distinct concepts. For example, a member may make promises while on the campaign trail about how they are going to serve particular communities, but then not actually take action to make good on that pledge.

Legislative actions can be specific and explicit, or they can be implied. For instance, a profile may specifically mention that a member offered an amendment to increase the minimum wage or sponsored a bill to protect

TABLE 3.1 *Legislative actions in the 103rd, 105th, 108th, 110th, and 113th Congresses*

• Sponsoring a bill	• Cosponsoring a bill	• Offering amendment
• Giving a speech on the	• Public demonstrations	in committee
floor	• Shepherding bill	• Offering amendment
• Caucus chair/co-chair	through committee	on floor
• Public speaking in offi-	• Publishing op-ed about	• Holding a hearing
cial capacity	legislation	• Opposing a hearing
• Leader of task-force	• Letter to president	• Creator of congres-
• Leading negotiations		sional caucus
on bill		

Legislative actions employed on behalf of disadvantaged groups by members of Congress.

women entering abortion clinics from being blocked by protesters, either of which would be examples of explicit legislative actions. These specific legislative actions can range from holding a hearing on a topic relevant to a disadvantaged group to cosponsoring a relevant measure to shepherding a bill through committee to staging a public demonstration (such as a talking filibuster or the 1991 march over to the Senate by women in the House during the Clarence Thomas hearings). Table 3.1 provides a thorough accounting of the variety of specific legislative actions attributed to members of Congress throughout all of the profiles evaluated.[6]

Implied legislative actions are instances in which a member is described as being a "stalwart defender of veteran benefit programs,"[7] or a "longtime proponent of social programs that confront issues facing the poor,"[8] or having "promoted legislation to help his district's substantial population of American Indians."[9] Statements such as these clearly demonstrate that the member is recognized as having taken noticeable legislative actions on behalf of a group, even if those actions are not specifically laid out. Profiles can also contain broader reputational statements about members. These are more expansive than the implied legislative actions, and come in the form of a claim that a member advocates on behalf of a particular group, without tying it to any specific policy

[6] For a specific listing of the topics considered relevant to each group, please see Appendix A.
[7] Rep. Gerald Solomon's profile (NY-22) in *Politics in America: 1994.*
[8] Rep. Patsy Mink's profile (HI-02) in *Politics in America: 1994.*
[9] Rep. J. D. Hayworth's profile (AZ-05) in *Politics in America: 2004.*

measure. Representational statements give a sense of the member's legislative priorities, such as "Conyers has championed the causes of civil rights, minorities, and the poor,"[10] or "Green often works on behalf of people on the poorer end of the economic spectrum."[11] These statements most commonly refer to a member as "serving," "working on behalf of," "prioritizing," "advocating," or "championing" the needs of a particular disadvantaged group.

3.3.3.2 *Differentiating the Levels of Reputation for Group Advocacy*
As described above, reputations for disadvantaged-group advocacy can take on one of four levels: primary advocates, secondary advocates, superficial advocates, and non-advocates. After reading each member profile, members were coded into the appropriate categories based upon three criteria.[12] The first of these criteria were the number of relevant legislative actions or reputational statements attributed to the member. The second consideration was the amount of space within the profile devoted to reputational statements or legislative actions advocating for disadvantaged groups. Third, members were placed according to the degree of attention paid to disadvantaged-group advocacy relative to other issues described in the profile. These coding decisions were made independently for each disadvantaged group under consideration. In the remainder of this section, I will discuss the application of these criteria for each of the potential levels of reputation for group advocacy in turn, beginning with the lowest level, non-advocates, and working up to the highest level, primary advocates.

A member rated on the lowest end of this ordinal scale, a non-advocate, is someone with a legislative reputation entirely unrelated to serving a given disadvantaged group. Either these members are never mentioned in conjunction with a disadvantaged group or the group's legislative concerns or they are noted to be someone who has actively worked against a group or its interests. Non-advocates have zero reputational statements or legislative actions on behalf of a particular disadvantaged group attributed to them. This non-advocacy can take several different forms. For example, a member whose profile focuses primarily on their efforts to reduce climate change, with no mention of any disadvantaged groups or

---

[10] Rep. John Conyers' profile (MI-14) in *Politics in America: 2004*.

[11] Rep. Al Green's profile (TX-09) in *Politics in America: 2014*.

[12] All member profiles were coded by the author using the coding scheme laid out in the subsequent section, so intercoder reliability scores are not applicable.

their relevant issues, would be coded as a non-advocate for all of the disadvantaged groups under consideration. Similarly, a member whose profile devotes considerable space to their work to address the needs of women, but references no advocacy behavior on behalf of other groups, would be coded as having a reputation for women's advocacy, and as a non-advocate for each of the other groups. Likewise, a member who is noted as having fought against the reauthorization of the Voting Rights Act would be coded as having a reputation for non-advocacy when it comes to racial/ethnic minorities, but they could still be considered an advocate for veterans as a result of their efforts on behalf of that group.

The next step up, superficial advocacy, is the category for members whose reputations are largely based on other issues or groups, but whose profile does contain one sentence discussing a single instance of their work on behalf of a disadvantaged group. This sentence can include a reputational statement or a brief mention of a single legislative action taken on behalf of the disadvantaged group of interest. Most commonly, superficial advocates are noted to have taken one legislative action, like offering an amendment providing tax credits to businesses that hire unemployed veterans or cosponsoring a bill to repeal Don't Ask, Don't Tell. It is less common that profiles of superficial advocates contain a reputational statement, but it does occur. In these instances, a profile might state that a member is a defender of protections for senior citizens, but not include any further details beyond that single sentence about what the member has done to gain that reputation.

The next two categories, secondary and primary advocacy, represent the band of members for whom advocating on behalf of a disadvantaged group forms a considerable portion of their legislative reputation.[13] A member is coded as having a reputation as a secondary advocate if two conditions are met: first, if the profile includes two or more legislative actions and/or reputational statements pertaining to a disadvantaged group (totaling at least two sentences) *or* if the profile describes a single legislative action in great detail (occupying up to one paragraph); and, second, there are other groups or issues that receive a greater relative share of attention in the narrative. In the 113th Congress, Sen. Jack Reed of Rhode Island would be an example of a secondary advocate. Over the course of his long career, he has worked on a number of bills and provisions specifically intended to assist poor

---

[13] A list of all members included in the sample with reputations for primary or secondary disadvantaged group advocacy can be found in Appendix B.

Americans, including measures to help low-income renters and provide assistance to people experiencing homelessness. His overall legislative reputation, however, is much more focused on foreign affairs and military conflicts in the Middle East.

Primary advocates are members who are profiled as having demonstrated strong reputational connections to a group by taking multiple legislative actions on that group's behalf. It is not a requirement that these profiles *must* contain a specific reputational statement, but nearly all do – they tend to be explicitly mentioned as being an advocate with a strong focus on this group, usually within the first few paragraphs. The profiles of primary advocates devote at least one to two paragraphs worth of content to their efforts on behalf of the group, and there is no other issue with which they are more strongly associated (though, as highlighted earlier, another group or issue may receive equal billing, as would be the case for members focusing on the needs of women veterans). Rep. Frederica Wilson, of Florida's 24th District, is a primary advocate for the poor. From the very top, her profile describes her as one who "prioritizes the needs of the underprivileged," and cites her own words as further proof. She says "I've always advocated for children, for seniors, and for poor people. Not the middle class. Poor people. And I call it just like that. I don't say that I'm trying to strengthen the middle class. I am trying to help people who are poor." The profile goes on to describe her further actions in service to this goal, noting that Wilson has been a strong supporter of federal spending for unemployment and economic hardship, and advocated for the creation of a program to improve worker training efforts.

3.4 REPUTATION FOR DISADVANTAGED-GROUP ADVOCACY IN CONGRESS, 1993–2014

In each Congress evaluated between 1993 and 2014, a sizeable number of legislators formulated at least some portion of their reputation around representing disadvantaged groups. As seen in Figure 3.1, between 37 and 57 percent of members of Congress have a reputation as a primary, secondary, or superficial advocate for a disadvantaged group in any given term. The highest percentage of members with a reputation for disadvantaged-group advocacy was in the 108th Congress, with the lowest coming in the 113th Congress.

Consistently, across all Congresses, there were higher percentages of superficial advocates than primary or secondary advocates, with the

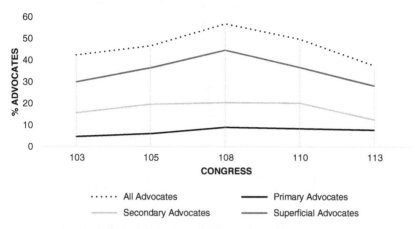

FIGURE 3.1 Disadvantaged-group advocacy in Congress
Percentage of members of Congress with a reputation for group advocacy in the
103rd, 105th, 108th, 110th, and 113th Congresses.

smallest percentage of members having a reputation for primary advocacy. The percentage of members with a reputation for superficial group
advocacy largely follows the trajectory seen across all advocates, peaking
in the 108th Congress and then declining over time. The rates of primary
and secondary advocacy remained largely constant across the sample of
Congresses studied. This demonstrates that while there is a small but
consistent block of members who root a considerable portion of their
reputation in serving disadvantaged groups, bigger changes over time are
driven by those who exhibit superficial advocacy.

3.4.1 Variation in Reputations for Advocacy across Groups

There has also been variation over time in the percentage of members with
a reputation for advocacy on behalf of any given disadvantaged group.
Figure 3.2 shows the group-specific breakdown in advocacy in each of the
sampled Congresses. In each Congress, more members incorporate advocacy
on behalf of the poor into their legislative reputations than that of any other
group, but there have been large swings in how many members have taken
on this advocacy role. Given the centrality of economic concerns to the work
within Congress, it makes sense that advocacy on behalf of the poor would
be consistently at the top among other disadvantaged groups. Additionally,
for much of the last century, there has been a broad consensus in Congress

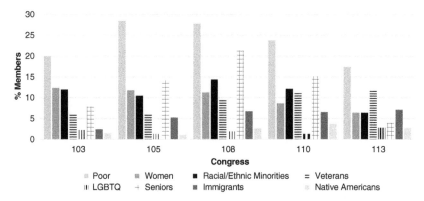

FIGURE 3.2 Members of Congress with reputation as disadvantaged-group advocate Percentage of members of Congress with reputation as an advocate for the poor, women, racial/ethnic minorities, veterans, seniors, the LGBTQ community, immigrants, or Native Americans in the 103rd, 105th, 108th, 110th, and 113th Congresses.

that the federal government should play at least some role in assisting those who are economically disadvantaged (even if the scope and means of that assistance has been fiercely debated).

Behind the poor, veterans and seniors tend to be the groups that members of Congress are the next most likely to cultivate a reputation around serving.[14] Veterans, seniors, and the poor are largely viewed sympathetically by the American public at large, so it is in line with theoretical predictions that higher percentages of members would choose to base at least some part of their legislative reputations around serving these groups. Native Americans and the LGBTQ community have tended to see the lowest percentages of group advocates within Congress.

Despite this consistency in which groups have the highest and the lowest percentages of members of Congress with reputations advocating on their behalf, there is considerable jostling among the middle ranks. This variability, in conjunction with the changes in magnitude across Congresses, demonstrates that there is considerably more to be understood about when members of Congress choose to cultivate a reputation

---

[14] The exception to this is the 103rd Congress. This was the Congress elected during 1992, frequently referred to as the "Year of the Woman." Women's issues were at the forefront following the harsh treatment of Anita Hill by an all-male Judiciary Committee during the Clarence Thomas confirmation hearings, and the number of women serving in Congress surged dramatically following the 1992 election.

around working on behalf of disadvantaged groups. It also highlights the importance of determining which groups are most likely to be the beneficiaries of these advocacy efforts, and what other factors can affect this over time.

It is also important to note that advocacy on behalf of these disadvantaged groups does not always exist in isolation. Rather, there are a number of members with reputations rooted in the advocacy of a number of different disadvantaged groups, sometimes with equal intensity and sometimes not. Twenty percent of sampled members who have fostered reputations for serving one disadvantaged group also have a reputation for advocating for another. Table 3.2 displays the correlations between member reputations as advocates on behalf of different groups.

This table shows the linkages between reputations for advocacy across groups. The strongest significant relationship exists between advocates for the poor and advocates for racial and ethnic minorities, implying that it is not uncommon for members with a reputation as an advocate for one to also have a reputation as an advocate for the other. This is in line with Miler's (2018) findings that champions of the poor tend to be those who also focus on the intersections of poverty with gender and race. There are also notable ties between reputations for advocating for the poor and reputations for advocating for women and seniors. A reputation for advocating for women is also linked to reputations for LGBTQ advocacy. Additionally, there is a statistically significant relationship between reputations for advocating for racial and ethnic minorities and those for advocating on behalf of immigrants.

3.4.2 Party Affiliation and Reputation for Group Advocacy

Given the bonds between many of these disadvantaged groups and the general Democratic Party coalition, it is tempting to dismiss the formation of a reputation as a group advocate as a purely Democratic phenomenon. But in fact, these reputations are held by both Democratic and Republican members of Congress. While Democrats are considerably more likely to formulate such a reputation, with 59 percent of the Democrats sampled holding reputations at least partially based on advocating for disadvantaged groups, a non-negligible percentage of Republicans do as well. About a third of the Republicans sampled (33%) had primary, secondary, or superficial reputations for working on behalf of the disadvantaged. Figures 3.3 and 3.4 show the breakdown by group of the reputations for advocacy among Democrats and Republicans.

TABLE 3.2 *Correlations between reputations for advocacy of disadvantaged groups*

	Poor	Women	Racial/Ethnic Minorities	Veterans	LGBTQ	Seniors	Immigrants	Native Americans
Poor	1.00	0.12	0.22	0.05	0.05	0.18	0.06	<0.00
Women	0.12	1.00	0.13	<0.00	0.12	0.09	0.06	<0.00
Racial/Ethnic Minorities	0.22	0.13	1.00	-0.01	0.07	0.07	0.14	<0.00
Veterans	0.05	<0.00	<0.00	1.00	0.01	0.03	<0.01	0.06
LGBTQ	0.05	0.12	0.07	0.01	1.00	0.02	0.07	-0.02
Seniors	0.18	0.09	0.07	0.03	0.02	1.00	-0.02	-0.01
Immigrants	0.06	0.06	0.14	<0.01	0.07	-0.02	1.00	<0.01
Native Americans	<0.00	<0.00	<0.00	0.06	-0.02	-0.01	<0.01	1.00

Pairwise Pearson correlation coefficients showing the relationship between holding reputations for advocacy across different disadvantaged groups. Statistically significant correlations (alpha=0.05) are in bold face. $N=2,675$.

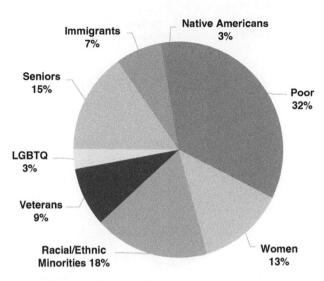

FIGURE 3.3 Disadvantaged-group advocacy among Democrats, 1993–2014
Breakdown by group of all instances of reputations formed around advocating for
disadvantaged groups among Democrats.

These figures are interesting for revealing both the variation between
the parties as to which groups members seek to incorporate as a part of
their legislative reputation, as well as the similarities. Again, Democrats in
the sample are nearly twice as likely to have advocated for at least one
disadvantaged group as a part of their reputation than Republicans. But
among just those instances in which some portion of a member's legislative reputation is devoted to advocating for the disadvantaged, there are
a surprising number of similarities. Roughly the same percentage of
Democratic and Republican advocates focus their efforts on behalf of
women, the poor, and seniors, with Democrats slightly more likely to
have reputations around advocating for the poor, and Republicans
slightly more likely to advocate for seniors. There is also almost no
difference in the percentage of Democrats and Republicans with reputations for advocating for Native Americans, immigrants, and the LGBTQ
community.

Given the large differences between the Republican and Democratic
coalitions and their corresponding policy agendas, this level of agreement
is somewhat surprising. Among those who advocate for disadvantaged
groups, there is a considerable amount of cross-party agreement in terms
of which groups are incorporated into some portion of a member's

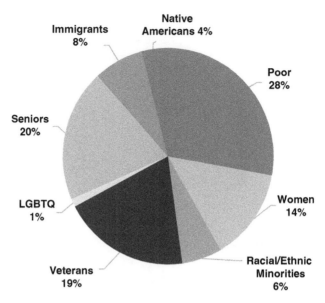

FIGURE 3.4 Disadvantaged-group advocacy among Republicans, 1993–2014
Breakdown by group of all instances of reputations formed around advocating for
disadvantaged groups among Republicans.

reputation. This demonstrates some of the advantages of using a method
of operationalization that focuses on intent, rather than means.
Democrats and Republicans may have very different approaches to how
best to advocate on behalf of these disadvantaged groups, but the efforts
of each are still recognized.

There are also some noteworthy points of departure between the two
parties. The biggest difference in reputation formation comes in the
advocacy on behalf of racial and ethnic minorities. While for
Democrats serving as an advocate for racial and ethnic minorities is
the second most common reputation to hold, among Republicans it is
one of the least common. When it comes to Republicans, however,
a considerably higher portion of Republicans who choose to build
a reputation as a disadvantaged-group advocate incorporate advocacy
on behalf of veterans into their legislative reputations than is true of
Democrats.

Finally, there are additional differences in the levels of advocacy
that Republicans and Democrats tend to engage in. Nearly

21 percent of Democrats with a reputation for disadvantaged-group advocacy are primary advocates, while this is true for only 6 percent of Republicans. Democrats are also more likely to be secondary advocates, with 45 percent of Democrats with reputations for advocacy meeting this criteria, compared to only 26 percent of Republicans. Republicans are slightly more likely than Democrats to have reputations for superficial advocacy alone, by a margin of 80 percent to 73 percent.

3.4.3 Reputations for Advocacy in the Senate and the House

Distinctions in the number of members with reputations for group advocacy exist not only between members with different party affiliations, but also between members serving in the House of Representatives and the Senate. Figure 3.5 shows the percentage of members in each chamber with reputations for disadvantaged-group advocacy for each of the five Congresses in the sample. Generally speaking, there are a higher percentage of senators possessing these reputations in any given Congress than members of the House of Representatives. On average, 53 percent of senators form some portion of their legislative reputation around serving the disadvantaged, while the same is true for only 45 percent of members of the House. This general difference in the percentage of members in each chamber with reputations as disadvantaged-group advocates matches with the general understanding of senators as generalists, while House members tend to specialize. But how does this break down across levels of advocacy?

Figure 3.6 shows the percentage of members in the House and the Senate with a reputation as primary, secondary, and superficial advocates for disadvantaged groups. Here, too, the general divergences between the two chambers tend to comport with expectations around the percentage of their reputations that senators devote to a single group or issue relative to members of the House. A higher percentage of senators have a reputation of superficial advocacy than House members, with their profiles making note of only a single action or general representational statement on behalf the group. This matches with the picture of senators as more likely to weigh in on a broad array of issues, and less likely to devote high proportions of their representational energy to a single group. Reputations for secondary advocacy are roughly the same across the two chambers, while a higher percentage

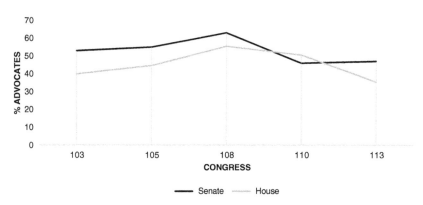

FIGURE 3.5 All disadvantaged-group advocates across chambers
Percentage of members of the House and Senate by Congress with a reputation for primary, secondary, or superficial advocacy on behalf of disadvantaged groups.

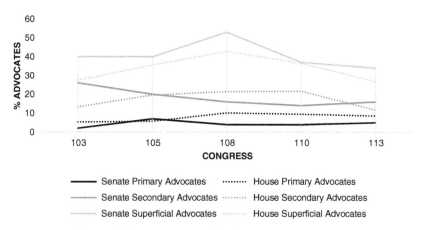

FIGURE 3.6 Types of advocates across chambers
Percentage of senators and members of the House of Representatives with a reputation for primary, secondary, and superficial disadvantaged-group advocacy in the 103rd, 105th, 108th, 110th, and 113th Congresses.

of House members hold reputations as primary advocates for disadvantaged groups.

To this point, differences between the House and the Senate largely align with what would be expected just given broad tendencies toward specialization or generalization respectively within those chambers. But this story changes somewhat when considering reputations for advocacy broken down by group, as seen in Figure 3.7. Across a number of these groups, the same general patterns hold, with the Senate tending to have more members with reputations for advocacy in total, but most of that boost coming from superficial and secondary advocates. Similarly, for most disadvantaged groups, higher percentages of members with primary reputations for advocacy are found in the House.

It is the deviations, however, that stand out the most. The most glaring of these is the difference between the House and the Senate in the percentage of members with reputations for advocating on behalf of racial and ethnic minorities. There are considerably more members with a reputation for primary advocacy in the House, but the discrepancy goes well beyond this. Members of the House also outstrip senators in terms of reputations for secondary and superficial advocacy as well. In addition to this, there are also more members of the House with reputations for advocating on behalf of veterans, immigrants, and the poor, but the bulk of the differences are accounted for by higher numbers of primary advocates in the House. However, there are a few groups with a higher percentage of advocates in the Senate than in the House. Women, Native

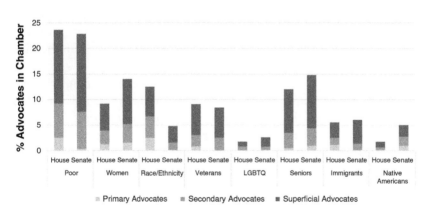

FIGURE 3.7 Reputations for advocacy in each chamber across groups
Percentage of members of the House and Senate with reputations for primary, secondary, and superficial advocacy broken out across disadvantaged groups. Data include members of the 103rd, 105th, 108th, 110th, and 113th Congresses.

Americans, and seniors have had a larger percentage of senators with a reputation for working for them than House members.

3.4.4 Unpacking Reputation

This chapter opened by describing the three central characteristics of a legislative reputation: it is something more than just the sum of its parts, it is not reliant on any one particular type of action, and it must be perceived by an outside observer. The third characteristic of reputation is clearly achieved in the construction of this reputation variable, because it relies upon the perspectives of the journalists authoring the *Politics in America* member profiles. But what of the first two? To what extent does this construction of reputation exist as a stand-alone concept that can be separated from singular actions?

I evaluate how well my measure of reputation achieves these requisite criteria by considering the correlation between the measure of reputation introduced in this chapter and the most common legislative proxies used in past research, bill sponsorship and cosponsorship. If member reputation does not constitute an emergent property in and of itself, and instead is simply a reflection of a journalist's dutiful accounting of the bills that a member introduces, there should be an extremely high and consistent correlation between these metrics and this new reputation variable. On the other hand, if reputation is a unique, separable concept wherein bill sponsorship or cosponsorship are just two examples of the many tools and tactics a member can use to build a reputation, correlations between a member's reputation and the sponsorship and cosponsorship measures should not be consistently high, and instead exhibit a considerable level of variation.

Table 3.3 shows the correlations between a member's reputation for advocacy of a particular group and the number of relevant bills on behalf of that group that the member sponsored or cosponsored in a given Congress.[15] The relationship between a member's reputation and their bill sponsorship and cosponsorship activity varies widely when advocates for different groups are considered. This ranges from a fairly strong

---

[15] Bills are coded as being about a topic relevant to a particular disadvantaged group using the topic codes from Baumgartner and Jones' *Policy Agendas Project*. For a full listing of which topic codes were included for each group, please see Chapter 6. As discussed in greater detail in that chapter, the issue codes do not include separate categories for LGBTQ issues, so these correlations are not included in the analysis.

TABLE 3.3 Correlation between reputations for advocacy of disadvantaged groups and sponsorship and cosponsorship activity in the US House and Senate

	Poor	Women	Racial/Ethnic Minorities	Veterans	Seniors	Immigrants	Native Americans
House of Representatives							
Sponsorship	**0.25**	**0.38**	**0.30**	**0.26**	0.12	**0.21**	**0.38**
Cosponsorship	**0.43**	**0.31**	**0.39**	0.15	0.12	**0.26**	**0.47**
Senate							
Sponsorship	**0.27**	**0.23**	−0.01	**0.24**	**0.21**	**0.25**	**0.36**
Cosponsorship	**0.30**	**0.26**	−0.03	0.18	0.12	**0.22**	**0.49**

Pairwise Pearson correlation coefficients showing the relationship between holding a reputation for advocacy for a given disadvantaged group and the percentage of member sponsorship and cosponsorship activity devoted to that group (measured using the issue codes from the Policy Agenda Project.) Statistically significant correlations ($\alpha = 0.05$) are in bold face.

correlation between these particular legislative actions and those with reputations as advocates for Native Americans in both chambers to an entirely insignificant relationship between bill sponsorship and cosponsorship and building a reputation for the advocacy of racial/ethnic minorities in the Senate. For advocates of other disadvantaged groups, the extent to which their reputations are tied to their sponsorship and cosponsorship activity falls somewhere between these two poles.

These results clearly demonstrate that a member's legislative reputation is not simply synonymous with their sponsorship and cosponsorship activity. Reputation is related to these actions, as would be expected, given that introducing and cosponsoring legislative proposals are important tools in a member's arsenal when seeking to build a reputation as a disadvantaged-group advocate, but they are neither all-inclusive nor equally applied on behalf of different groups. Chapter 6 evaluates which members are likely to select bill sponsorship and cosponsorship as the key tactics for their reputation building efforts and develops new theories regarding the circumstances under which this is more or less likely to occur for particular groups. The preliminary analysis is presented here, however, to emphasize the validity of this original and innovative measure of reputation, and to further demonstrate its success in meeting the three criteria laid out above.

3.5 WIELDING INFLUENCE AS A DISADVANTAGED-GROUP ADVOCATE

Representing the disadvantaged through building a reputation as someone who advocates on their behalf offers important symbolic benefits to these groups, but it also has real substantive effects. Frequently, these effects do not immediately take the shape of monumental legislation, but rather the steady, over-time work to create persistent incremental change, protect progress that has already been won, and continue to push the conversation and build coalitions to be ready to take advantage of moments when big change is possible. Each advocate works to provide for their group in different ways, and they may vary in their success (just as all legislators do). But they can have an important, substantive impact on Congress and the lawmaking process, even if that impact is not always measurable over the lifetime of a single Congress. In the sections that follow, I trace two short examples of how different members of Congress with reputations for advocacy have played an important role in creating substantive change for two different disadvantaged groups.

3.5.1 Rosa DeLauro and the Fight for Pay Equity for Women

In 2009, Congress passed the Lilly Ledbetter Fair Pay Act. This measure, the first signed into law by President Barack Obama, amended the Civil Rights Act of 1964 to say that pay discrimination occurs not just the first time that an individual is unfairly compensated, but rather reoccurs for every subsequent paycheck. This law was a response to the 2006 Supreme Court case, *Ledbetter* v. *Goodyear Tire and Rubber Company*. In this case, the Court ruled that under the existing law, salary discrimination cases could not take into account prior discriminatory behavior outside of the 180-day statute of limitations, even if past discrimination impacted current salary. The 110th Congress (elected in 2006) first attempted to pass a corrective bill, but the bill stalled out in the Senate.

The law that finally passed in 2009 came out of the Education and Labor Committee in the US House, and was sponsored by that committee's chair, California Rep. George Miller. There was, however, another member's fingerprints all over the bill – Connecticut Rep. Rosa DeLauro.[16] Over the course of her career, Rep. DeLauro had been known as a relentless advocate for women, with a tireless focus on pay equity. Since 1997, DeLauro has pushed for and proposed a pay equity bill in every Congress. In the original 2007 hearings to consider what became the Lilly Ledbetter Fair Pay Act, Rep. DeLauro was called as an expert to testify on the bill (despite not being a formal member of the committee), as well as an additional paycheck fairness measure that she had introduced. In her speech celebrating the passage of the Lilly Ledbetter Fair Pay Act, Speaker Nancy Pelosi spoke about the important contributions of Rep. DeLauro, saying, "I want to salute Congresswoman Rosa DeLauro for being a relentless advocate. Ten years ago, she introduced the Paycheck Fairness Act and has been working on it for a long time. Over the years, our ranks have grown with those who recognize the importance of this legislation."[17]

Even in the wake of the successful passage of this bill, Rep. DeLauro felt that there was more to be done, and has continued to push on the issue and to advocate for the needs of women. In the 111th Congress, her Paycheck Fairness Act (which put the onus on employers to prove that gender-based

---

[16] Rep. DeLauro is coded as having a reputation as a primary advocate for women in the 113th, 110th, 108th, and 105th Congresses, and a reputation as a secondary advocate for women in the 103rd Congress.

[17] Nancy Pelosi's speech on the House floor on January 9, 2009. (www.speaker.gov/news room/pelosi-house-passage-lilly-ledbetter-paycheck-fairness-act-priorities)

pay discrepancies were *not* a result of unlawful gender discrimination) was originally a part of the Lilly Ledbetter Act that passed the House, but it was stripped out of the Senate version. Despite this setback, she has continued to work in every subsequent Congress to get this further advancement passed into law. Her efforts have been recognized by Lilly Ledbetter herself, who stated in 2019 on the tenth anniversary of the passage of the eponymous law that "it was never intended for [the Lilly Ledbetter Fair Pay Act] to be passed as the only fix for the ongoing pay disparity between men and women. Women across the country still need the tools in the Paycheck Fairness Act to ensure they get equal pay for equal work. I applaud Congresswoman DeLauro for her leadership in this fight since 1997[.] . . . Now is the time to get this done."[18]

In the 116th Congress, the Paycheck Fairness Act passed the House again on March 27, 2019, with a bipartisan vote and 239 cosponsors, though it did not receive a vote in the Senate. This marks an impressive trajectory from when the bill was first introduced in 1997, when it garnered ninety-five cosponsors and did not make it past the committee referral stage.[19] Through Rep. DeLauro's efforts within the institution over the course of over two decades, the push for pay equity has moved from a frequently frustrated, sometimes lonely struggle to a key priority of the Democratic Party.

3.5.2 Rick Renzi and the Push for Native American Housing Reform

In 2004, the House Financial Services Subcommittee on Housing held a hearing on the state of housing on Native American reservations for the first time. The person pushing for this historic hearing was a Republican representative from Arizona, Rick Renzi.[20] Rep. Renzi had a reputation as a strong advocate for Native Americans, who made up a considerable portion of his congressional district. To create support for this hearing, Rep. Renzi organized a tour of the Navajo reservation in his district, so

[18] US Senate Committee on Health, Education, Labor, and Pensions press release from January 30, 2019. (www.help.senate.gov/ranking/newsroom/press/murray-delauro-reintroduce-paycheck-fairness-act-to-close-gender-wage-gap)
[19] www.govtrack.us/congress/bills/105/hr2023
[20] Rep. Rick Renzi is coded as having a reputation as a primary advocate for Native Americans in the 110th Congress. His first term was in the 108th Congress, so he had not yet developed a clear legislative reputation. Renzi's advocacy work did not extend into the 111th Congress, as he chose not to run for reelection in 2008 after being investigated for a corrupt land swap. He was later sentenced to three years in prison.

that other members could see first-hand the dire state of the housing situation. Members of the committee who went on the trip "credited Renzi with opening eyes," and said that there is "more congressional awareness of Indian [sic] housing problems since the Arizona visit" (Wayne, 2004).

Between October of 2004 and December of 2005, Rep. Renzi saw two of his bills seeking to address housing challenges for Native Americans signed into law. The first of these, the Homeownership Opportunities for Native Americans Act of 2004, amended the Native American Housing Assistance Act of 1996 to provide federal repayment guarantees for tribal housing.[21] The second and more substantial bill also amended the Housing Assistance Act to provide greater access to housing grant programs.[22] After the passage of this bill, Rep. Renzi pushed for its provisions to make a substantive impact for his Native American constituents, with the *Navajo-Hopi Observer* reporting that he had secured an additional seven million dollars in funds for the White Mountain Apache Tribe.[23]

3.6 CONCLUSION

In this chapter, I describe legislative reputations and make a case for why they are important, and introduce my original measure operationalizing reputation. A member's legislative reputation offers a concise way of summarizing their work within the legislature, and provides a realistic way of understanding the representational relationship between a member and their constituents. I argue that all legislative reputations have three key characteristics: it is more than just the sum of individual actions, it does not require any one specific, singular action to have occurred, and reputations are formed through the observation and interpretation of others. Members have strong incentives for seeking to craft their own legislative reputations, which can serve as both a means by which members can communicate their efforts to constituents, as well as a mechanism for substantive change over time.

For this project, I created an original variable that utilized member profiles from Congressional Quarterly's *Politics in America* to determine

---

[21] www.govtrack.us/congress/bills/108/hr4471
[22] www.govtrack.us/congress/bills/109/hr797/summary
[23] From the August 22, 2007 online edition of the *Navajo-Hopi Observer*. (www .nhonews.com/news/2007/aug/22/renzi-announces-7-million-for-white-mountain-apac/)

what portion of a member's legislative reputation is rooted in advocacy on behalf of disadvantaged groups. Between 40–50 percent of members tend to incorporate disadvantaged-group advocacy into some portion of their reputation in a given Congress. The highest percentage of these advocates have a reputation for superficial advocacy, with the smallest percentage serving as primary advocates. There are some changes over time in where different disadvantaged groups tend to rank in levels of representation, but the poor consistently have the highest percentage of members offering at least superficial advocacy. While more Democrats craft reputations around serving disadvantaged groups, a considerable number of Republicans do as well. Generally speaking, senators have higher levels of disadvantaged-group advocacy overall, but it is driven by higher percentages of superficial advocates, while the House has considerably more members with reputations as primary advocates. An important break in these patterns comes in members who advocate for racial and ethnic minorities – this is considerably less common in the Senate, across all levels of advocacy.

In the next two chapters, I analyze when and why a member of Congress would make the decision to build a reputation as a disadvantaged-group advocate. In this analysis, I consider both district and member characteristics to evaluate the implications of the advocacy window when it comes to the representation of disadvantaged groups. Chapter 4 is focused on reputation building in the House of Representatives, while Chapter 5 considers this behavior in the Senate. The penultimate chapter of the book builds upon one of the key insights from this chapter, that reputations can be developed through an array of tactics, and these tactics are not deployed in the same way in all circumstances, or by all members. Chapter 6 also investigates when two of the legislative actions most commonly assumed to be the primary mechanism of representation, bill sponsorship and cosponsorship, are actually likely to be the reputation-building activity of choice for members of the House and Senate.

4

The Choice to Be a Disadvantaged-Group Advocate in the House of Representatives

Members of Congress cultivate legislative reputations as a means of signaling to their constituents what their representational priorities are and the type of work that they have been doing during their time in Congress. As shown in the last chapter, there are certain members of Congress that choose to build these reputations around serving disadvantaged groups in particular. While these reputations can vary in terms of which group on whose behalf a member chooses to act or exactly how central a particular disadvantaged group is to that reputation, there are a select group of members that make that choice consistently, across time and party lines. So, why do members do this? What factors contribute to a member's choice to devote at least some notable portion of their legislative reputation to serving the disadvantaged?

In this chapter, I explore what drives members of Congress to form reputations as advocates for the disadvantaged. In particular, I investigate the influence that disadvantaged group size within a district, the district ambient temperature toward a group (the general group affect), and personal experience as a group member have on a member's choice to cultivate a reputation as a disadvantaged-group advocate. To start, I will describe in greater detail the construction of these primary explanatory variables of interest. Next, I analyze their effects using a series of generalized ordered logistic regression models. In this analysis, I determine the impact of group size, ambient temperature, and other relevant variables on member reputation for different levels of disadvantaged-group advocacy, both individually and in a comprehensive model. Finally, I use these models to evaluate the role of the advocacy window, as described in Chapter 2.

4.1 GROUP SIZE

As discussed in Chapter 2, one of the primary hypotheses is that a large group presence in a district will make it more likely that a member will form a reputation around serving that group. This hypothesis is derived directly from a basic understanding of how a democratic republic *should* work; members of Congress are elected by people back in their districts, and thus it is their responsibility to work on their behalf. And as demonstrated in the previous chapter, this work frequently takes the form of developing a reputation around serving the groups in their district.

4.1.1 Measuring Group Size

Group size in a state or district is measured for each decade using state and district census totals. This is determined at the unit of district/state decade to consistently account for population shifts and changes in the number and size of districts over time. For nearly all groups, this is a straightforward measure of the percentage of group members in a state or district at the time of the census. Veterans are the percentage of civilian veterans over the age of 16, seniors are the percentage of residents aged sixty-five or older, immigrants are the percentage of for-eign-born individuals, women are the percentage of the total population that identify as female, the poor are the percentage of individual residents whose income is at or below the poverty line, and racial/ethnic minorities are the percentage of residents in a district that do not identify as non-Hispanic whites.

Determining the size of the LGBTQ population in a state or district is considerably more complicated, and a perfect measure simply does not exist. The Census has never included any questions about sexual orienta-tion or gender identity at the individual level, but it does provide data about the percentage of same-sex unmarried-partner households within a state or district. The way that the Census Bureau has determined this, however, has undergone important changes over the course of the last several decades. In 1990, the Census added the category of "unmarried-partner household" for the first time and also recorded whether that household contained an opposite-sex couple or a same-sex couple. Because same-sex marriage was not recognized at the national level until the 2013 US Supreme Court decision in *United States* v. *Windsor*, no formal Census report included same-sex married couples prior to the 2020

Census, and households that classified themselves as same-sex married couples had their relationship type changed to unmarried partner.[1]

Using the percentage of unmarried-partner households in a district is certainly an imperfect proxy for the percentage of LGBTQ individuals, but the lack of a superior alternative has made it the preferred measure used by social scientists (e.g., Warshaw and Rodden, 2012; Hansen and Treul, 2015). For this same reason, I also utilize this measure as an approximation of the percentage of LGBTQ Americans in the state or district, but acknowledge that it has two important shortcomings.[2] First, by definition, this measure leaves out a count of LGBTQ individuals who are not in a same-sex coupled household and offers no insight into the percentage of transgender individuals or bisexual individuals partnered with a person of the opposite sex in a district. This undoubtedly results in an undercount relative to the actual percentage of LGBTQ individuals in a district. Second, the percentage of same-sex unmarried-partner households is likely to be highly correlated with the feelings of warmth or hostility toward a group. While LGBTQ individuals exist everywhere in the country, the likelihood of being part of an "out" same-sex couple that also feels comfortable enough to identify as such on a government form is assuredly higher in a less-hostile environment. I expand further upon the consequences of this expected strong correlation in Section 4.3 discussing the relationship between group size and group ambient temperature.

4.2 AMBIENT TEMPERATURE

Though most Americans do not conceptualize their political beliefs and decisions on strongly ideological grounds, a large percentage of

---

[1] For the 1990 Census, it was assumed that individuals who returned Census forms that indicated a same-sex married couple household had made an error in recording their gender, and the Census Bureau instead recorded them as an opposite-sex married couple, rather than a same-sex unmarried partner household. This likely led some legitimate same-sex households to be improperly characterized as opposite-sex spousal households.

[2] There is an important difference of note in one component of my calculation of this variable relative to previous work. While other studies have used the Census data from the 2000s and the 2010s, they have not attempted to extend this calculation back to the 1990s. For the 2000 and 2010 Census, calculations of the percentage of same-sex unmarried-partners were made at the state- and congressional district-level, while for the 1990 Census, this data is only provided at the state and selected county level. However, the data provide the number of same-sex unmarried households according to their status as an urban or rural household. Thus, for the 1990s, I approximate the percentage of same-sex married households using state-wide urban and rural percentages weighted by the rural-to-urban composition in the district.

individuals do use group identities and intergroup dynamics as a way of understanding politics (Campbell et al., 1960; Green et al., 2002; Lewis-Beck et al., 2008). Given this centrality of group-based political attitudes, intergroup dynamics within a district can play an important role in understanding the reputations members of Congress choose to form. In particular, feelings toward different disadvantaged groups can shape the likelihood that a member will work on their behalf.

A crucial component of a representative's job is to act in accordance with their constituents' wishes. Or, at the very least, for a member to weigh constituent preferences against other considerations like partisan pressures, individual beliefs, and national interest. Most conceptions of this representational relationship thus require that constituents be able to communicate their policy preferences to their member of Congress. For especially salient issues, particularly those coming up for a major vote, this communication can take place in a way that follows in line with these theoretical expectations. Under these circumstances, constituents are more likely to call or write in to congressional offices and show up at town halls to express their opinions, and members may even have access to internal or external polling indicating how the public feels about an issue. But when a member is considering a new policy proposal, or preparing for a vote on an issue that has not received a great deal of public attention, it is far less likely that members have a clear, specific sense of their constituents' opinions to guide their actions.

Members of Congress have markedly less formal information while making legislative decisions than is commonly assumed (Curry, 2015). Members have ever-increasing demands on their time, but limited resources. When deciding whether or not to engage in a particular legislative action, they frequently must depend upon either their own intuitions or general cues from others about how important constituencies within a state or a district are likely to be impacted. In this low-information decision-making environment, a member's trust in their own perceptions about their districts can take on paramount importance. Members of Congress pride themselves on how well they know their districts (Fenno, 1978), and their perceptions of the subconstituencies within their districts impact their work within the institution (Miler, 2010). Even if members may not have all of the information they might wish they had, they likely do have a sense of how popular certain groups of people are back home in their district. Members do not need to have specific polling data on how constituents feel about a pilot program promoting minority-owned small businesses or bill to eliminate food deserts in poor communities to have a sense of whether or not there is political risk or political benefit to supporting such a piece of legislation.

This limited information environment and reliance on the perceptions of a groups' relative popularity within a district influences not only member decisions on individual legislative actions but also their reputation formation more broadly. Making decisions based on the feelings of warmth or hostility toward a particular disadvantaged group can serve as a helpful shortcut that does not require the allocation of additional resources. Representatives must make choices about what issues they will devote their time and energy to working on, and each of these specialization decisions pulls resources away from other prospective issues. Members of Congress are risk-averse. If members feel that there is a potential for negative backlash from a considerable portion of their constituents if they were to work on behalf of a particular disadvantaged group, they will simply direct their reputation-building efforts in another direction. After members have taken into account the size of groups within their states or districts, considering the general feelings toward that group within their constituency is a reasonable heuristic when deciding whether or not to build a reputation as an advocate for that group. In the next section, I describe the operationalization of these feelings of warmth or hostility toward a particular group – what I refer to as the group ambient temperature.

4.2.1 Measuring Group Affect

For this analysis, I utilize feeling thermometer scores as a measure of how the average district resident feels about members of a particular disadvantaged group. A feeling thermometer is a commonly used survey tool that asks respondents to rate, on a scale from 0 to 100, how warmly they feel toward a particular societal group. Highly regarded and long-running political survey projects like the American National Election Study (ANES) have relied on feeling thermometer questions for decades, with some variation in the salient group identities included over time.

Feeling thermometers are a simple, readily understandable way for individuals to articulate how warmly they feel toward a particular group without needing much in the way of political knowledge or sophistication. For this reason, feeling thermometer ratings are preferable to other, more complex ways of attempting to determine group-specific representational preferences. Compared to more intricate undertakings like expressing a definitive opinion on a particular policy or political action, rating a group on a feeling thermometer is a much more manageable task for respondents across levels of political information. This makes it less subject to top-of-the-head influences and inconsistencies than other measures. As an example, a question asking individuals to identify which groups they most want their representative to work on behalf of or asking how they would want them to allocate their time is extremely complicated, and invites greater opportunity for respondents to misunderstand the question and its intent.

One potential downside to using feeling thermometers is the influence of social desirability bias. The very existence of social desirability bias as a possible issue, however, is also evidence that respondents have a keen understanding of the task set before them when presented with a feeling thermometer. Social desirability bias exists when respondents answer a question in a way that they feel is most likely to be acceptable and gain the approval of others (such as the person administering the survey) rather than in accordance with their genuine sentiment. As an example, in the United States, being racist is generally considered by society at large to be a bad thing, at least over the time period studied here. Thus, if an individual gives "Black Americans" a higher feeling thermometer rating than might actually be true out of a fear of being perceived negatively, that respondent clearly understands that the fundamental task of a feeling thermometer is to rate their own personal level of affinity toward members of different groups.

The range of disadvantaged groups I evaluate in this analysis runs the gamut in terms of expected social desirability bias. For instance, the poor and the LGBTQ community provoke very different levels of public support and affection, with the poor largely being well regarded[3] and the LGBTQ community being looked on with suspicion or outright animosity (particularly during the 1990s and 2000s). This results in different amounts of social pressure to positively evaluate each group. However, because this analysis focuses on differences across districts for each group rather than within-district differences across groups, it is only the relative positioning of each group in different areas of the country that is important. Additionally, because the presence of this bias would move the ratings in a consistent direction, artificially inflating the feeling thermometer scores, it actually provides a conservative test for the hypothesis that

---

[3] This is true in spite of low public opinions of welfare spending or concerns about the effectiveness of the social safety net. As a group, the poor are relatively popular (Gilens, 2012).

a higher ambient temperature will boost the likelihood of a member crafting a reputation around advocating on behalf of a disadvantaged group.

Using feeling thermometer scores has a number of practical advantages as well. Survey designers have been using feeling thermometers for decades, allowing for the analysis of the impact of district hostility on member behavior over a broader range of time than studies utilizing the more recent Cooperative Congressional Election Study (CCES) or the National Annenberg Election Study (NAES) data, which tend to focus on more policy-specific questions. The format and measurement of feeling thermometer questions have also been remarkably consistent over time, alleviating some of the difficulties of working with specific issue questions, where a topic might be asked about while it is salient and actively being pursued by Congress, but then is dropped or replaced as other issues gain more prominence. I generate estimates of state- and district-level feeling thermometer scores using multilevel regression with poststratification (MRP).

4.2.2 Estimating State and District Ambient Temperature

MRP modeling utilizes national public opinion data and regional (state- and district-level) demographic data to estimate the opinion of relevant population sub-groups, which are then weighted and summed for the geographic area of interest. In the remainder of this section, I provide a brief overview of the data and modeling techniques used to generate the ambient temperature estimates. Additional details on the benefits of MRP and the specific modeling formulations used in this project can be found in Appendix C.

To generate estimates of state- and district-level ambient temperatures, I use feeling thermometer data from the American National Election Study (ANES) times series data from 1992 to 2016. Feeling thermometer estimates are generated for each disadvantaged group in each of the three decades included in the scope of this project (the 1990s, the 2000s, and the 2010s) to account for changes over time. In each of these MRP models, the explanatory variables are relevant demographic data pulled from the decennial US Census and the US Religion Census, while the dependent variable is the group feeling thermometer score. The ANES includes feeling thermometer questions for a number of societal groups, and close approximates for others. The models estimating the average district and state ambient temperature toward racial and ethnic minorities, the poor, and

TABLE 4.1 *Summary of estimates for district feeling thermometer ratings by group*

Group	N	Mean	Std. Dev.	Min.	Max.
Seniors	1,740	78.74	2.33	64.89	98.89
Veterans	2,175	72.66	3.88	54.14	85.80
Poor	2,175	69.35	2.96	56.91	87.05
Women	2,175	56.32	3.56	41.28	72.54
Immigrants	2,175	42.43	8.71	22.48	70.47
Racial/Ethnic Minorities	2,175	66.09	3.23	53.42	79.76
LGBTQ	2,175	47.83	7.82	25.47	77.83

Displayed are the average estimated values for the feeling thermometer scores across all congressional districts from 1992 to 2016. Estimates were generated using multilevel regression with poststratification. The estimate for racial/ethnic minorities is an average of the ambient temperature generated for each district for Black, Hispanic, and Asian Americans.

seniors are a direct match with the feeling thermometer question in the ANES, while the models estimating feelings toward the LGBTQ community, women, immigrants, and veterans utilize proxies.[4] Respectively, these proxies are lesbians and gays, feminists/women's libbers, illegal immigrants/illegal aliens, and the military.[5] Summaries of the estimated district feeling thermometer ratings by groups are given in Table 4.1.

4.2.3 Interpreting Ambient Temperature Estimates

Before moving on to the application of these measures of district and state ambient temperature, it is necessary to say a word about how these estimates should be interpreted. First, as a general note, though the mean ambient temperatures for each group do follow approximately the same pattern as might be expected by how deserving of government assistance each group is broadly perceived to be, it is important to keep in mind that these two measures are not the same. It is possible, for

---

[4] Unfortunately, the ANES has never used a feeling thermometer question asking respondents to rate their feelings toward Native Americans. Thus, the predictors of forming a reputation as a Native American advocate cannot be analyzed in this or the following chapter. Reputations for advocacy of Native Americans are brought back in, however, for the evaluation of the sponsorship and cosponsorship activity related to a particular disadvantaged group found in Chapter 6.

[5] These are the group names used in the ANES survey questions.

instance, that people could have positive feelings toward a group, but also feel that it is not the government's role to provide assistance. Conversely, people could have more negative personal feelings about the military, for example, while still feeling that the government owes particular benefits to those who served. Given this, it is expected that the ambient temperature toward a group can vary from state-to-state or district-to-district, independent of how generally deserving of government assistance the group is considered to be.

Second, and most crucial to appropriate interpretation of these estimates, the raw values for the means and standard deviations are not intended to provide a head-to-head comparison across groups. Particularly because of the use of proxy feeling thermometer scores for several of these groups, the estimated means may better represent the true latent ambient temperatures for some groups more so than others. With the exception of the use of "lesbians and gays" as a stand-in for the LGBTQ community (which could result in a slightly more positive rating by not activating biphobia or transphobia), it is likely that the proxy group measurements (described in the previous section) may result in a slightly lower average feeling thermometer score. However, because the research design of this project calls for the evaluation of the representation of each group individually, these deviations should not negatively impact the results. What matters is the relative difference within the same group's ambient temperature across districts, not the absolute value comparison across groups. Similarly, given this research design, the different degree of variation in the ambient temperature measures is not a concern, as the effects of ambient temperature on reputation for group advocacy is evaluated independently for each group.

4.3 GROUP SIZE AND AMBIENT TEMPERATURE: RELATED BUT DISTINCT CONCEPTS

Before discussing and presenting the multivariate models exploring the factors that drive members of Congress to foster reputations as advocates of disadvantaged groups, this section takes a quick look at the relationship between the two primary independent variables – group size and ambient temperature – and establishes them as related but separate concepts, each with distinct reasons for inclusion in the models to follow.

Group size and ambient temperature are expected to be related concepts. Having frequent interactions with a group, or having a high percentage of group members within a district can boost the positive feelings toward that group. However, this relationship need not only work in a singular direction; for example, some research has shown that when white Americans are confronted with information about increasing racial/ethnic minority and/or immigrant populations, negative feelings toward those groups can actually increase (Blumer, 1958; Alba, Rumbaut, and Marotz, 2005; Craig and Richeson, 2014). Table 4.2 displays the correlations between district group size and district ambient temperature for each of the groups whose representation is being analyzed here.

There is broad diversity across disadvantaged groups when considering the strength of the relationship between the size of group within a district and the general feelings toward that group. For the two groups that are broadly considered to be deserving of government assistance, seniors and veterans, there is little to no correlation between the two variables, with the correlation for seniors failing even to reach conventional levels of statistical significance. These results match with expectations – because of the high esteem these groups are held in, any variations in ambient temperature should not be related to the percentage of veterans and seniors in a district. Women also have a low correlation between ambient temperature and group size, best explained by the very small amount of variation in the percentage of women across districts. For the poor, immigrants, racial/ethnic minorities, and the LGBTQ community, there is evidence of a much stronger correlation between group size and ambient temperature. Given the higher levels of skepticism these groups face relative to groups like veterans or seniors, this relationship is expected and, as discussed above, likely is not purely linear. The correlation between the two variables for the LGBTQ community also reflects the nature of the creation of the group size variable itself, and how Census reporting for same-sex couples are likely themselves somewhat reflective of group ambient temperature. In no case, however, even for the LGBTQ

TABLE 4.2 *Correlations between district group size and group ambient temperature by disadvantaged group*

Seniors	Veterans	Poor	Women	Immigrants	Racial/Ethnic Minorities	LGBTQ
−0.0245	0.0640*	0.4477*	0.1635*	0.5334*	0.4287*	0.6319*

Note: Figure displays Pearson's *r* correlation coefficients of the relationship between group size and ambient temperature for each of the disadvantaged groups analyzed. * represents a statistical significance level of $p \geq 0.05$.

community, is there evidence of even close to a perfect correlation between the two variables, as seen in Figure 4.1.

Figure 4.1 shows the variation in the estimated ambient temperature and group size across all congressional districts in the continental United States for the 108th Congress (Jan 2003–2005). These maps showcase both the instances of overlap in the variation in ambient temperature and group size, and the discrepancies. When considering immigrants, for example, similar bright areas in Southern California and Southern Texas display the close relationship between the percentage of and general regard for immigrants in the area. Another clear example of similarities comes in the bright dot around San Francisco indicating both one of the higher percentages of LGBTQ individuals in the countries as well as one of the highest ambient temperatures. For groups like women, seniors, and veterans, however, a high level of variation in the shading between each of the two maps can be seen.

Though not present for all groups, the relatively high correlations between ambient temperature and group size for racial/ethnic minorities, immigrants, the poor, and LGBTQ individuals do have some ramifications for the multivariate models to follow. This multicollinearity will likely have the effect of slightly inflating the standard errors on these variables, making conventional statistical significance harder to achieve. Despite this, the strong theoretical reasons for including each of these measures, laid out in Chapter 2, necessitate that the models contain both of them. Group size is a straightforward accounting of the number of group members who comprise a member's constituency, while ambient temperature measures how the district constituency tends to feel about a group writ large. To truly understand what drives members to make the reputational choices that they do, the impact of each of these variables must be accounted for. Including both of these variables is also necessary to evaluate the role of the ambient window, as is done toward the end of this chapter.

4.4 MODELING REPUTATION FORMATION

As discussed in detail in Chapter 3, reputation is coded as a four-category ordinal variable, ranking from Non-Advocates to Superficial Advocates to Secondary Advocates to Primary Advocates. In the remaining sections of the chapter, I analyze how group size, group ambient temperature, and other relevant explanatory variables impact the type of reputation members of Congress form. Specifically, in this chapter, I focus on the reputation formation of members of the House of Representatives, while the reputation formation of senators is considered in the following chapter. In

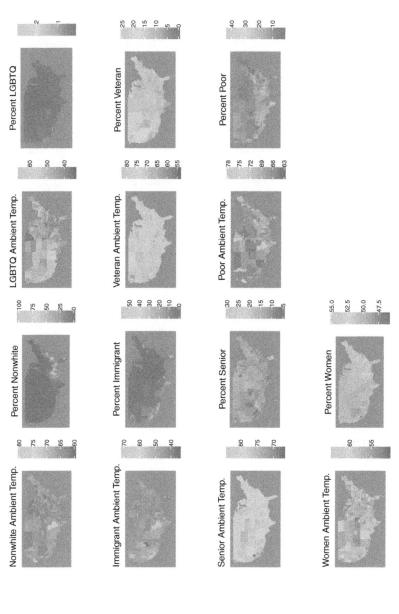

FIGURE 4.1 Average district ambient temperature and percentage of group members by district and disadvantaged group

Note: Figure displays maps of the estimated average group ambient temperature and group size by district for the 108th Congress. Groups included in the figure are racial/ethnic minorities, immigrants, veterans, seniors, the poor, and women.

each of the following sections, these relationships are modeled using generalized ordered logistic regression, or the partial proportional odds model, to account for both the ordinal character of the reputation variable and to allow for the explanatory variables to have differential impacts on primary, secondary, or superficial reputation formation.[6]

4.4.1 Alternative Explanatory Variables

In addition to my primary variables of interest, group size, and group ambient temperature, I include a number of control variables: party affiliation, whether or not a member is in their first term in Congress, the partisan leaning of the district, and whether or not the member represents a district in the South. I also include decade fixed effects and cluster the standard errors by member. Controlling for the decade fixed effects accounts for specific time-bounded changes in what drives members to form reputations around serving disadvantaged groups. By clustering my standard errors by individual member, I avoid any artificially deflated standard errors that could arise from the same person remaining in the House across more than one Congress in the sample.

---

[6] When seeking to explain the variation in an ordered dependent variable, an Ordinary Least Squares model is inappropriate, as it requires a continuous interval variable, and using multinomial logistic regression is undesirable because it discounts important information found in the ranking of the categories. Instead, I utilize a generalized ordered logit model. I make this selection over the use of an ordered logit model for statistical as well as theoretical reasons. Employing an ordered logistic regression requires that the model abide by the parallel regression assumption, or proportionality assumption (Brant, 1990). This assumption states that the relationship between each of the explanatory variables and the dependent variable cannot vary across categories of the dependent variable. In determining the primary factors involved in reputation formation, models using ordered logistic regression violate the parallel regression assumption. This violation was determined using the Brant test, which assesses both the proportionality of the effect of each independent variable across values of the dependent variable as well as the proportionality of the model as a whole.

Violations of the parallel regression assumption occur as a result of certain independent variables having an asymmetric effect on levels of reputation (Williams, 2016). Theoretically, this asymmetric effect is expected – moving from having no reputation at all for group advocacy to having a reputation for occasional advocacy is a calculation that members must make that is likely different from that of moving from a reputation for occasional action to that of primary or secondary advocacy. A partial proportional odds model relaxes the parallel regression assumption, and specifically demonstrates how the relationship between the explanatory and dependent variables can change across categories, providing insight into these important asymmetries (Williams, 2016). These models are calculated using the gologit2 program for Stata (Williams, 2006).

First and foremost, I control for the party of the representative, coded as a dichotomous variable.[7] Given the centrality of partisan concerns in the US Congress and the differences between the electoral coalitions of the Democratic and Republican Parties, understanding party-specific differences is crucial. As seen in the previous chapter, while both Democrats and Republicans do form these reputations for disadvantaged-group advocacy, the phenomenon is more common among members of the Democratic caucus. Thus, even with other factors accounted for, I expect that Democrats in Congress are going to be more likely to form a reputation around advocating for disadvantaged groups than Republicans, particularly for those groups for whom government intervention is generally viewed with more skepticism.

I include a dichotomous variable in the model indicating if a member is in their first term in the House for two reasons. First, members who have just won their first term in the House simply have not had enough time to develop a strong legislative reputation as an advocate for disadvantaged groups. Reputation building requires a pattern of behaviors and inter-actions, in which new members have not had the opportunity to engage. Second, practically speaking, *Politics in America* devotes less space to first-term members than to members that have at least one full congres-sional session under their belt, meaning there is also less available infor-mation that is written about them.[8] For these reasons, the coefficient on this variable is expected to indicate a strongly negative effect on whether a member has a reputation for disadvantaged-group advocacy.

I control for the partisan leaning of the district by including a measure of the two-party vote share that the Democratic presidential candidate received in the most recent presidential election. I expect that the more Democratic a district is, the more likely it is that a member will have a reputation for disadvantaged-group advocacy. Finally, I also control for regional effects by including a dummy variable for whether or not a district is located in the South. I define South as including the original former Confederate states, as well as states bordering the former Confederate states. These states include: Alabama, Arkansas, Delaware, Florida, Georgia, Kentucky, Louisiana, Maryland, Mississippi, North Carolina, Oklahoma, South Carolina, Texas,

---

[7] The few Independent members of the House included in the dataset are coded in accord-ance with the major party they chose to caucus with.

[8] First term members usually receive a profile of only one page in length, rather than the two that is generally standard for other members. This difference is reflective of the reality that these new members simply have not yet had the chance to fully establish themselves in the legislature in the same fashion as members with a longer tenure in the institution.

Virginia, and West Virginia. I expect that the political culture will generally make members representing districts within these states less likely to form a reputation around advocating for disadvantaged groups, and that these effects will be most acute for disadvantaged groups that are not highly regarded in the country at large.

4.5 GROUP SIZE, AMBIENT TEMPERATURE, AND MEMBER REPUTATION

In this section, I investigate the independent relationships between group size and then ambient temperature on member reputation, after taking into account all of the alternative variables listed above. Understanding each of these variables can provide valuable insight into how group size and group affect within a state or district influences the representational choices members of Congress make. Following from the basic expectations of republican governance, wherein an individual is elected by a set of constituents to act in accordance with their interests, it is expected that group size will have a positive relationship with member reputation. Members of the House of Representatives with a reputation for serving as a group advocate are more likely to come from a district with a large number of group members than a district with very little group presence. Given how inherent this is to the fundamental notion of representation, this should be true regardless of how deserving of government assistance a group is considered to be. Ambient temperature is also expected to have a generally positive effect on the likelihood of members forming reputations as group advocates. However, these effects should be the most apparent for groups that are considered to be less deserving of government assistance.

Tables 4.3–4.5 present the results of the generalized ordered logistic regression models with reputation for disadvantaged-group advocacy as the dependent variable of interest. Each group has three models (0, 1, and 2), which contain important information about how the independent variables can asymmetrically impact the likelihood of a member having a certain kind of reputation.[9] The dichotomous variable

---

[9] The exception to this are the models for LGBTQ advocacy. The exceedingly small number of cases of members with a reputation as a primary advocate for LGBTQ individuals makes the calculated coefficients for the terms demonstrating the relationship between the independent variables and the likelihood of holding a reputation as a primary advocate rather than any of the other categories unreliable. For this reason, the categories for primary and secondary advocates have been collapsed together. Thus, for the LGBTQ analysis, only Model 0 and Model 1 are presented.

indicating whether or not a member was just elected to their first term in Congress is modeled as a having parallel proportional effects,[10] while all other explanatory variables are modeled with partial proportional effects. Model 0 demonstrates how group size and the other independent variables impact the likelihood of a member shifting from having no reputation for group advocacy at all to having some kind of reputation for advocacy. The likelihood of moving from no advocacy or superficial advocacy to secondary or primary advocacy is shown in Model 1, and the shift from one of the lower levels of advocacy to primary group advocacy is presented in Model 2. Breaking the models up in this way allows for differential impacts of the explanatory variables to account for the variation in representational levels. I will next evaluate all of the groups in turn to determine the impact of disadvantaged group size and ambient temperature on the reputation a member of Congress formulates.

4.5.1 Veterans and Seniors

The impact of the percentage of veterans and seniors in a district on member reputation is presented in Table 4.3. Across nearly all levels, group size has a positive and significant effect on the type of reputation a member forms. As expected, even for groups that are considered to be broadly deserving of government assistance across the United States, members representing districts with higher quantities of group members are more likely to form reputations around advocating on their behalf. For veterans, group size has a significant impact on all shifts across levels of reputation. Seniors exhibit the same pattern when moving from a non-advocate to an advocate and when shifting to develop a reputation as a primary or secondary advocate from non- or superficial advocacy. However, a higher percentage of seniors in a district did not significantly push members from the lower levels of advocacy into primary advocacy. Florida's 5th district, for example, has consistently had one of the highest percentages of seniors in a Congressional district since the 1990s. Rep. Karen Thurman (D-FL5), who served in the 1990s, and Rep. Ginny Brown-Waite (R-FL5), who won the seat in the 108th Congress (during

---

[10] The use of parallel proportional effects for this variable acknowledges the strong negative effect of a member being in their first term on reputation formation, particularly at the two highest levels of advocacy. Because there are no incoming members with reputations for primary or secondary group advocacy, the partial proportional effects cannot be calculated.

TABLE 4.3 *Group size, ambient temperature, and member reputation for advocacy for veterans and seniors*

	Veterans						Seniors					
	0	1	2	0	1	2	0	1	2	0	1	2
Group Size	0.210 (0.00)	0.262 (0.00)	0.399 (0.00)	—	—	—	0.093 (0.00)	0.121 (0.00)	0.082 (0.54)	—	—	—
Ambient Temperature	—	—	—	0.09 (0.00)	0.17 (0.00)	0.18 (0.05)	—	—	—	−0.02 (0.66)	0.06 (0.44)	−0.10 (0.57)
Republican	−0.466 (0.02)	−0.814 (0.02)	−1.148 (0.13)	−0.157 (0.41)	−0.425 (0.20)	−0.262 (0.63)	−0.830 (0.00)	−1.123 (0.00)	−1.733 (0.03)	−0.721 (0.00)	−0.929 (0.00)	−1.565 (0.05)
Dem Pres Vote	0.000 (0.99)	0.018 (0.42)	0.061 (0.23)	0.002 (0.85)	0.030 (0.16)	0.072 (0.11)	−0.002 (0.86)	−0.019 (0.34)	−0.075 (0.22)	0.015 (0.20)	−0.003 (0.89)	−0.088 (0.15)
South	0.185 (0.38)	0.590 (0.19)	0.512 (0.38)	0.028 (0.91)	0.363 (0.46)	0.544 (0.42)	−0.118 (0.53)	−0.215 (0.49)	−1.550 (0.13)	0.025 (0.91)	−0.199 (0.63)	−1.586 (0.10)
1990s	−1.319 (0.00)	−1.126 (0.01)	−1.649 (0.03)	−0.346 (0.25)	0.322 (0.57)	−0.048 (0.96)	−0.217 (0.11)	−0.334 (0.24)	−1.227 (0.05)	−0.578 (0.00)	−0.770 (0.02)	−1.605 (0.02)
2000s	−0.938 (0.00)	−0.671 (0.09)	−1.594 (0.02)	0.217 (0.33)	0.941 (0.01)	0.618 (0.28)	—	—	—	—	—	—
First Term	−1.056 (0.00)	—	—	−0.920 (0.00)	—	—	−0.834 (0.00)	—	—	−1.020 (0.00)	—	—

(continued)

TABLE 4.3 (continued)

	Veterans						Seniors					
	0	1	2	0	1	2	0	1	2	0	1	2
Constant	-3.669	-6.611	-11.207	-8.595	-17.650	-21.992	-2.495	-3.143	-0.973	-0.719	-7.104	8.840
	0.00	0.00	0.00	0.00	0.00	0.01	0.00	0.01	0.68	0.80	0.26	0.56
N	2,175			2,175			2,175			2,175		
Wald's Chi²	95.6			90.1			68.9			70.3		
Pseudo-R^2	0.0651			0.0388			0.0436			0.0414		

Note: Coefficients calculated using generalized ordered logistic regression, with First Term modeled as a parallel proportional term and the rest of the independent variables modeled as partial proportional terms. Standard errors are clustered by member, and *p*-values are in gray. Model 0 represents the likelihood of a shift from no advocacy to superficial, secondary, or primary advocacy; Model 1 is no advocacy or superficial advocacy to primary or secondary advocacy; and Model 2 is any of the lower categories of advocacy to primary advocacy. Feeling thermometer questions for seniors were not included in the ANES of the 2010s, so the decade base category for seniors is the 2000s.

the 2002 elections), each developed reputations for superficial advocacy of seniors during their time in office.

Different patterns are evident when examining the role of group ambient temperature. Warmer feelings toward veterans within a district have a positive and statistically significant impact on a member having a reputation around advocating for veterans, regardless of the level of advocacy. For seniors, however, group ambient temperature has no significant effect on member reputation. In the models including ambient temperature, the role of party affiliation is also different for seniors and for veterans. Once the ambient temperature for veterans is taken into account, members of Congress from both parties are equally likely to form reputations as advocates. This is different when considering members with reputations around advocating for seniors, where Democrats still have a statistically significant advantage. Given that both of these groups are considered to have high levels of deservingness of government assistance, this discrepancy is intriguing. This difference is likely attributable to the close ties between seniors' issues and Social Security and Medicare, which in turn are also more closely bound to the Democratic Party.

When it comes to group size, for both veterans and seniors, Republicans are significantly less likely to form reputations as group advocates than are Democratic members. So, while a larger share of Republican members with reputations for disadvantaged-group advocacy are advocates for veterans and seniors relative to Democrats, Democratic members are still more likely to have formed these reputations on the whole. After other factors are accounted for, the partisan lean of the district and presence in the South do not have a significant impact on whether or not a member forms their reputation around advocating on behalf of veterans or seniors. Members of Congress were significantly less likely to have reputations for veterans' advocacy in the 1990s and 2000s compared to the 2010s, which may be due to a recent acknowledgement of the challenges facing veterans returning from the wars in Iraq and Afghanistan.

4.5.2 LGBTQ and Racial/Ethnic Minorities

The LGBTQ community and racial/ethnic minorities are disadvantaged groups that are generally considered to be less deserving of government assistance, and it is expected that both the size of the group in the district and the group ambient temperature will make it more likely that a member will have a reputation around serving as a group advocate. As seen in Table 4.4, both group size and ambient temperature do have the

TABLE 4.4 *Group size, ambient temperature, and member reputation for advocacy for racial/ethnic minorities and the LGBTQ community*

	LGBTQ				Race/Ethnicity					
	0	1	0	1	0	1	2	0	1	2
Group Size	1.824	3.805	–	–	0.051	0.064	0.054	–	–	–
	0.01	0.03			0.00	0.00	0.00			
Ambient Temperature	–	–	0.07	0.11	–	–	–	0.22	0.24	0.22
			0.01	0.08				0.00	0.00	0.00
Republican	–1.553	–2.319	–1.848	–2.270	–1.929	–2.116	–2.758	–2.522	–3.172	–3.779
	0.02	0.03	0.00	0.01	0.00	0.00	0.01	0.00	0.00	0.00
Dem Pres Vote	0.057	0.092	0.045	0.059	–0.027	–0.043	–0.041	–0.013	–0.016	–0.021
	0.12	0.04	0.20	0.27	0.11	0.05	0.07	0.38	0.43	0.40
South	–	–	–	–	–0.007	0.079	0.176	0.261	0.417	0.408
					0.98	0.82	0.66	0.29	0.19	0.27
1990s	1.014	4.552	0.429	1.421	1.148	0.943	0.098	1.641	1.402	0.684
	0.06	0.14	0.45	0.21	0.00	0.00	0.81	0.00	0.00	0.12
2000s	–0.226	2.809	0.123	1.189	1.301	1.090	0.151	1.696	1.719	0.940
	0.60	0.23	0.82	0.11	0.00	0.00	0.67	0.00	0.00	0.01
First Term	–1.348		–1.411		–1.882			–1.705		
	0.08		0.06		0.00			0.00		

(continued)

	Constant									
Constant	−7.956	−14.778	−9.861	−14.065	−2.867	−3.683	−3.752	−16.683	−18.497	−17.114
	0.00	0.00	0.00	0.00	0.01	0.00	0.00	0.00	0.00	0.00
N		2,175		2,175		2,175			2,175	
Wald's Chi²		34.7		38.1		367.4			226.1	
Pseudo-R²		0.1889		0.1335		0.3048			0.1791	

Note: Coefficients calculated using generalized ordered logistic regression, with First Term modeled as a parallel proportional term and the rest of the independent variables modeled as partial proportional terms. Standard errors are clustered by member, and *p*-values are in gray. Model 0 represents the likelihood of a shift from no advocacy to superficial, secondary, or primary advocacy; Model 1 is no advocacy or superficial advocacy to primary or secondary advocacy; and Model 2 is any of the lower categories of advocacy to primary advocacy. No LGBTQ member advocates come from the South, so the variable is excluded on the basis of perfect prediction. Because there is only a single member included in the sample with a primary reputation for LGBTQ advocacy, Model 2 cannot be reliably calculated for this group. For the LGBTQ analyses, reputations for primary and secondary advocacy have been collapsed into a single category.

expected positive and significant effect on member reputation. Unlike with seniors, where group size is not significantly related to the decision to serve as a primary group advocate and group affect has no significant determinative effect on reputation formation, decisions about advocacy for less highly regarded groups such as the LGBTQ community and racial/ethnic minorities are significantly related to these variables. When ambient temperature and group size are modeled separately, higher values of each increase the likelihood that a member will have a reputation for group advocacy. This is true across nearly all levels of advocacy.[11]

Republican members of Congress are significantly less likely to form reputations around advocating for racial/ethnic minorities and the LGBTQ community. This is in accordance with the breakdowns by party shown in Figures 3.4 and 3.5 – considerably fewer Republicans hold reputations as advocates for racial/ethnic minorities and LGBTQ individuals than Democrats. Though less common, Republican representatives are not wholly immune to the effects of group size or ambient temperature. Ray LaHood (R-IL18), for instance, began to be known as a superficial advocate for racial/ethnic minorities (particularly those of Middle Eastern descent) in the 2000s, after the ambient temperature of his district increased by nearly a full standard deviation in the wake of redistricting.

Region, however, has slightly different effects on the advocacy of racial/ethnic minorities and the LGBTQ community. When other explanatory variables are taken into account, whether or not a member represents a district in the South does not have a significant impact on forming a reputation as an advocate for racial/ethnic minorities. However, because there are zero members of Congress representing southern districts with a reputation for LGBTQ advocacy, the precise effects of region cannot be calculated, on account of perfect prediction.

There also exists an interesting difference between representation of the LGBTQ community and racial/ethnic minorities when considering the impact of the partisan leaning of the district. When group ambient temperature is taken into account, the partisan leaning of a district does not significantly impact reputation formation as an advocate of racial/ethnic minorities or LGBTQ individuals. But when group size is considered in place of ambient temperature, partisan leaning works in opposite directions for the LGBTQ community and racial/ethnic minorities. While partisan leaning does not

---

[11] The ambient temperature does meet the threshold of a one-tailed significance test when considering the shift from non- or superficial advocacy for the LGBTQ community to primary or secondary advocacy.

have a significant effect on whether or not a member shifts from being a non-advocate to having a reputation as some level of group advocate, it does have significant impact on the move from non- or superficial advocacy to primary or secondary advocacy. After controlling for the size of the LGBTQ community in a district, members coming from more Democratic districts are *more* likely to have a reputation as a primary or secondary advocate. However, members from heavily Democratic districts are *less* likely to have a reputation as an advocate for racial/ethnic minorities once racial composition of a district is accounted for.

4.5.3 Immigrants and the Poor

Immigrants and the poor are groups that hold a complicated place in the American mind. Many people are highly sympathetic to the poor while simultaneously treating with great skepticism those who access our welfare systems, and immigrants hold dual roles in the national zeitgeist of both heroic ancestor and multicultural villain. For each of these two disadvantaged groups, district group size and ambient temperature have a significant, positive relationship with the likelihood of members having a reputation for group advocacy, as seen in Table 4.5. The single apparent exception to this comes when considering members with a primary reputation for serving the poor – group ambient temperature does not have a statistically significant effect on this final move up the ladder, implying that other conditions are the driving force for this last step. Major Owens (D-NY11) is an example of someone who made the decision to form a reputation as a secondary advocate for the poor during the 1990s, pushing for increases in the minimum wage and boosts for other social programs. His district fell just outside of the top 10th percentile for the percentage of people in poverty, but had the second highest ambient temperature toward the poor of any other district in the sample.

Across all levels of advocacy, Republican members of Congress are significantly less likely to have a reputation as an advocate for those in poverty. In contrast, this effect is less consistent for members with reputations as immigrant advocates. After immigrant ambient temperature is held constant, Republicans are not significantly less likely to be primary or secondary advocates for immigrants. Particularly considering the time period under consideration, this difference fits with the general perceptions of the party identities – despite some more recent changes, immigration had long been considered to be a fairly bipartisan issue. And once

TABLE 4.5 *Group size, ambient temperature, and member reputation for advocacy for immigrants and the poor*

	Immigrants						Poor					
	0	1	2	0	1	2	0	1	2	0	1	2
Group Size	0.111	0.149	0.214	—	—	—	0.067	0.094	0.107	—	—	—
	0.00	0.00	0.00				0.00	0.00	0.00			
Ambient Temperature	—	—	—	0.09	0.13	0.16	—	—	—	0.06	0.13	0.07
				0.00	0.00	0.06				0.05	0.00	0.31
Republican	-0.635	-0.570	-2.518	-1.044	-0.551	-1.380	-1.136	-1.818	-2.037	-1.385	-2.217	-2.624
	0.04	0.22	0.00	0.00	0.36	0.51	0.00	0.00	0.00	0.00	0.00	0.00
Dem Pres Vote	-0.079	-0.080	-0.213	-0.014	0.016	-0.017	0.021	0.016	0.002	0.012	0.002	-0.001
	0.00	0.04	0.02	0.56	0.74	0.86	0.04	0.22	0.96	0.25	0.91	0.97
South	-0.325	-0.578	-2.365	-0.084	0.044	-0.689	-0.362	-0.833	-0.833	-0.311	-0.835	-0.498
	0.40	0.32	0.01	0.84	0.96	0.72	0.03	0.00	0.22	0.08	0.00	0.46
1990s	-0.055	0.004	0.241	0.367	0.248	0.623	0.582	0.582	-0.697	0.558	0.615	-0.806
	0.85	0.99	0.62	0.21	0.54	0.64	0.00	0.01	0.08	0.00	0.01	0.07
2000s	-0.001	0.200	-0.988	-0.123	-0.116	-0.583	0.735	0.659	0.176	0.708	0.810	0.057
	1.00	0.54	0.10	0.56	0.64	0.13	0.00	0.00	0.58	0.00	0.00	0.90
First Term		-2.000			-1.621			-1.222			-1.212	
		0.00			0.00			0.00			0.00	

(continued)

Constant	−0.020	−2.174	3.013	−5.697	−10.510	−10.221	−3.039	−4.204	−4.506	−5.446	−11.104	−7.545
	0.99	0.32	0.50	0.00	0.00	0.30	0.00	0.00	0.04	0.01	0.00	0.16
N		2,175			2,175			2,175			2,175	
Wald's Chi^2		307.2			122.6			257.0			212.6	
Pseudo-R^2		0.2851			0.1166			0.1229			0.1011	

Note: Coefficients calculated using generalized ordered logistic regression, with First Term modeled as a parallel proportional term and the rest of the independent variables modeled as partial proportional terms. Standard errors are clustered by member, and *p*-values are in gray. Model 0 represents the likelihood of a shift from no advocacy to superficial, secondary, or primary advocacy; Model 1 is no advocacy or superficial advocacy to primary or secondary advocacy; and Model 2 is any of the lower categories of advocacy to primary advocacy.

again, members in their first term are significantly less likely to have a reputation for disadvantaged-group advocacy.

The negative effects on likelihood of reputation formation of coming from a southern district are particularly strong when considering advocates for the poor, and more mixed for those with reputations as advocates for immigrants. Partisan lean of a district also has a different effect for each of these two groups. When ambient temperature is accounted for in the model, partisan leaning does not have a statistically significant effect on reputation formation for either group. For the poor, more Democratic leaning districts are more likely to push members to form superficial reputations for working on behalf of the group, but do not have a significant effect on reputations for higher levels of advocacy. The pattern for immigrants, however, is more similar to that of racial/ethnic minorities – after controlling for the percentage of immigrants in a district, more Democratic-leaning districts are actually less likely to produce members with reputations as immigrant advocates.

4.5.4 Women

Women are particularly unique among the disadvantaged groups studied in this project, both because of their limited variation in group size across districts, and because their size is near or above a majority of individuals in all districts. Based on size alone, one could argue that building a reputation around advocating on behalf of women would be a winning strategy for all members of Congress, and yet very few members choose to foster such a reputation. As seen in Table 4.6, the percentage of women in the district has no statistically significant impact on the likelihood of a member having a reputation as a women's advocate. Group ambient temperature does have significant effect on reputation formation, but the effect is nuanced. Higher ambient temperatures toward women have a significant impact on the shift from having a reputation as a non-advocate toward being an advocate at any level, even if superficial, but it is not a significant driving force behind the move to secondary or primary advocacy.

Chapter 3 showed that among instances of disadvantaged-group advocacy for Democrats and Republicans, each party had equivalent percentages of their members with reputations as women's advocates, but Democrats had a greater number of advocates overall. These descriptive statistics are born out here in the multivariate model. Across all of the models analyzed and all levels of advocacy, Republican members of Congress are significantly less likely to have reputations for advocacy on

TABLE 4.6 *Group size, ambient temperature, and member reputation for advocacy for women*

	Women					
	0	1	2	0	1	2
Group Size	0.016	−0.098	0.050	–	–	–
	0.78	0.29	0.81			
Ambient Temperature	–	–	–	0.05	0.03	0.01
				0.05	0.22	0.92
Republican	−0.826	−1.342	−2.135	−0.766	−1.277	−2.253
	0.00	0.00	0.01	0.00	0.00	0.01
Dem Pres Vote	0.054	0.069	0.086	0.047	0.063	0.102
	0.00	0.02	0.03	0.01	0.02	0.01
South	−0.554	−1.054	−1.612	−0.550	−1.039	−1.613
	0.05	0.03	0.18	0.05	0.04	0.17
1990s	0.704	0.272	0.062	0.702	0.306	0.374
	0.00	0.33	0.93	0.00	0.30	0.50
2000s	0.631	−0.001	−0.041	0.535	−0.040	−0.042
	0.00	1.00	0.93	0.01	0.88	0.93
First Term		−1.238			−1.246	
		0.00			0.000	
Constant	−5.993	−1.320	−10.904	−7.478	−7.818	−9.811
	0.06	0.81	0.29	0.00	0.00	0.03
N		2,175			2,175	
Wald's Chi^2		131.6			121.5	
Pseudo-R^2		0.0901			0.0902	

Note: Coefficients calculated using generalized ordered logistic regression, with First Term modeled as a parallel proportional term and the rest of the independent variables modeled as partial proportional terms. Standard errors are clustered by member, and *p*-values are in gray. Model 0 represents the likelihood of a shift from no advocacy to superficial, secondary, or primary advocacy; Model 1 is no advocacy or superficial advocacy to primary or secondary advocacy; and Model 2 is any of the lower categories of advocacy to primary advocacy.

behalf of women. Other variables also had similar effects across models. First term members are less likely to have a reputation for advocacy, as are members from the South. These regional effects are statistically significant for the shift to superficial advocacy and secondary advocacy, but do not have a significant effect on the decision to form a primary reputation around advocating for women. Members also become increasingly likely to have a reputation as a women's advocate the more Democratic the district that they represent.

4.6 THE RELATIONSHIP BETWEEN GROUP SIZE AND AMBIENT TEMPERATURE

Generally speaking, with a few exceptions, the results above demonstrate that both group size and ambient temperature have an important and positive impact on whether or not a member has a reputation as a group advocate when each is considered separately. However, as discussed earlier, while group size and ambient temperature are related, they are nonetheless distinct concepts that are expected to work in different ways depending upon the circumstance. Thus, I next explore the overall effects of each of these variables when allowed to work together in a single model.

4.6.1 Veterans, Seniors, Racial/Ethnic Minorities, LGBTQ Individuals

Table 4.7 demonstrates that when combined within a single model, the general relationship between group size, ambient temperature, and reputation follow the same general pattern, regardless of whether a group is broadly considered to be highly deserving of government assistance or less deserving of government assistance. Across levels of reputation for advocacy, group size nearly always has a positive and statistically significant impact upon reputation formation. Once again, members with primary reputations for advocating on behalf of seniors present the only exception to this, as group size is not a significant determinant of which members choose to focus the bulk of their representational efforts on seniors. That this should represent the exception is not in defiance of expectations, because members should not fear negative reprisals from their constituents for investing such a large share of their efforts into serving a group considered to be so deserving of assistance, even if seniors do not themselves make up a sizeable portion of the district.

An example of the significant impact of group size on the likelihood that a member will form a reputation as a group advocate even for groups that are generally considered to be less deserving of government assistance can be seen in Rep. Jerrold Nadler (D). Throughout the 1990s, Nadler represented the 8th District of New York, covering western Manhattan and parts of Brooklyn. During that time, he consistently served as

TABLE 4.7 Combined effects of group size and ambient temperature on member reputation for advocacy for veterans, seniors, LGBTQ individuals, and racial/ethnic minorities

	Veterans			Seniors			LGBTQ			Race/Ethnicity		
	0	1	2	0	1	2	0	1	2	0	1	2
Group Size	0.201	0.235	0.394	0.095	0.117	0.085	1.673	3.721		0.051	0.068	0.057
	0.00	0.00	0.00	0.00	0.00	0.51	0.02	0.05		0.00	0.00	0.00
Ambient Temperature	0.050	0.108	0.047	-0.012	0.078	-0.087	0.046	0.074		0.009	-0.049	-0.033
	0.091	0.071	0.589	0.744	0.358	0.622	0.126	0.243		0.778	0.229	0.649
Republican	-0.466	-0.819	-1.173	-0.775	-1.006	-1.643	-1.532	-2.316		-1.927	-2.116	-2.749
	0.02	0.02	0.11	0.00	0.00	0.05	0.02	0.03		0.00	0.00	0.01
Dem Pres Vote	0.003	0.026	0.062	0.012	-0.008	-0.088	0.039	0.068		-0.029	-0.036	-0.037
	0.80	0.22	0.20	0.33	0.70	0.18	0.29	0.17		0.08	0.09	0.12
South	0.039	0.322	0.363	-0.017	-0.317	-1.632	–	–		-0.019	0.128	0.213
	0.86	0.50	0.55	0.94	0.39	0.12				0.94	0.71	0.59
1990s	-1.015	-0.488	-1.324	-0.611	-0.802	-1.635	1.450	5.492		1.182	0.893	0.081
	0.00	0.44	0.15	0.00	0.01	0.02	0.01	0.14		0.00	0.01	0.85
2000s	-0.721	-0.210	-1.377	–	–	–	0.147	3.483		1.323	0.957	0.066
	0.01	0.66	0.06				0.77	0.21		0.00	0.00	0.88
First Term		-1.051			-0.897			-1.321			-1.892	
		0.00			0.00			0.08			0.00	

(continued)

TABLE 4.7 *(continued)*

	Veterans			Seniors			LGBTQ		Race/Ethnicity		
	0	1	2	0	1	2	0	1	0	1	2
Constant	-7.526	-14.989	-14.827	-2.003	-9.427	6.807	-9.512	-17.803	-3.408	-0.860	-1.839
	0.00	0.00	0.02	0.49	0.16	0.66	0.00	0.01	0.17	0.76	0.68
N	2,175			1,740			2,175		2,175		
Wald's Chi^2	104.6			93.2			38.2		368.2		
Pseudo-R^2	0.0678			0.0543			0.1954		0.3058		

Note: Coefficients calculated using generalized ordered logistic regression, with First Term modeled as a parallel proportional term and the rest of the independent variables modeled as partial proportional terms. Standard errors are clustered by member, and *p*-values are in gray. Model 0 represents the likelihood of a shift from no advocacy to superficial, secondary, or primary advocacy; Model 1 is no advocacy or superficial advocacy to primary or secondary advocacy; and Model 2 is any of the lower categories of advocacy to primary advocacy. Feeling thermometer questions for seniors were not included in the ANES of the 2010s, so the decade base category for seniors is the 2000s. No LGBTQ member advocates come from the South, so the variable is excluded on the basis of perfect prediction. Because there is only a single member included in the sample with a primary reputation for LGBTQ advocacy, Model 2 cannot be reliably calculated for this group. For the LGBTQ analyses, reputations for primary and secondary advocacy have been collapsed into a single category.

a secondary advocate for LGBTQ Americans. After the decennial redistricting, most of that territory was shifted into the 10th District, and the percentage of LGBTQ individuals increased by almost a full standard deviation. As the representative of the 10th District of New York in the 113th Congress, Nadler gained a reputation as a primary advocate, becoming a leader of the efforts to repeal Don't Ask, Don't Tell.

When group size is taken into account, ambient temperature is no longer seen to exert a significant effect upon the reputations members choose to form. This is not unexpected. While higher levels of group ambient temperature boost the likelihood of a member forming a reputation as a group advocate when considered independently, it should not overtake the effects of the size of a group. The other explanatory variables also largely perform as anticipated, with first termers and Republican members of Congress being less likely to have reputations as advocates for any of the four groups. Other district demographic factors such as whether or not a district is in the South and the partisan lean of a district generally have no significant impact on member reputation as advocates for these groups.

4.6.2 Women, Immigrants, and the Poor

Table 4.8 displays the results of the combined model evaluating reputations for serving women, immigrants, and the poor. For the groups that hold a more mixed position in the American psyche, such as immigrants and people in poverty, group size again has a positive and statistically significant impact on reputation for group advocacy. This can be seen through the actions of former Rep. Xavier Becerra (D-CA30/31/34). Originally known through much of the 1990s and 2000s as a primary advocate for immigrants, Becerra also began building other forms of advocacy into his reputation as redistricting moved him from a district of nearly 60 percent immigrants to one in which immigrants made up less than a majority.

Once group size is accounted for, ambient temperature does not have a statistically significant effect on member reputation for serving immigrants and the poor. Having a reputation as a women's advocate, however, is not dependent upon group size. Ambient temperature does have positive and statistically significant impact on whether or not a member chooses to form a reputation as some kind of women's advocate, though the choice to be a primary or secondary advocate is reliant upon other factors.

TABLE 4.8 Combined effects of group size and ambient temperature on member reputation for advocacy for women, immigrants, and the poor

	Immigrants			Poor			Women		
	0	1	2	0	1	2	0	1	2
Group Size	0.121	0.153	0.226	0.068	0.090	0.110	0.001	-0.110	0.058
	0.00	0.00	0.00	0.00	0.00	0.00	0.99	0.26	0.79
Ambient Temperature	-0.033	-0.005	-0.058	-0.003	0.032	-0.051	0.048	0.043	0.008
	0.118	0.866	0.517	0.918	0.482	0.481	0.046	0.118	0.919
Republican	-0.664	-0.407	-2.809	-1.136	-1.815	-2.067	-0.765	-1.286	-2.173
	0.03	0.45	0.01	0.00	0.00	0.00	0.00	0.00	0.01
Dem Pres Vote	-0.078	-0.078	-0.222	0.021	0.014	0.005	0.047	0.062	0.088
	0.00	0.03	0.02	0.04	0.33	0.90	0.01	0.03	0.03
South	-0.356	-0.595	-2.608	-0.358	-0.903	-0.597	-0.550	-1.050	-1.617
	0.35	0.28	0.02	0.05	0.00	0.39	0.06	0.04	0.17
1990s	-0.292	-0.160	-0.450	0.575	0.633	-0.749	0.713	0.257	0.091
	0.40	0.72	0.67	0.00	0.01	0.08	0.00	0.39	0.90
2000s	0.051	0.157	-1.110	0.728	0.773	-0.041	0.541	-0.094	-0.132
	0.84	0.65	0.08	0.00	0.01	0.93	0.01	0.74	0.77
First Term		-1.992			-1.221			-1.243	
		0.00			0.00			0.00	

(continued)

Constant	1.314	-2.091	6.429	-2.844	-6.296	-1.072	-7.529	-2.738	-11.806
	0.41	0.28	0.44	0.18	0.04	0.84	0.02	0.61	0.26
N		2,175			2,175			2,175	
Wald's Chi^2		359.4			266.3			156.0	
Pseudo-R^2		0.2895			0.1239			0.093	

Note: Coefficients calculated using generalized ordered logistic regression, with First Term modeled as a parallel proportional term and the rest of the independent variables modeled as partial proportional terms. Standard errors are clustered by member, and *p*-values are in gray. Model 0 represents the likelihood of a shift from no advocacy to superficial, secondary, or primary advocacy; Model 1 is no advocacy or superficial advocacy to primary or secondary advocacy; and Model 2 is any of the lower categories of advocacy to primary advocacy.

As with the representation of the groups discussed above, first term and Republican members are less likely to form any kind of reputation as advocates for women, immigrants, and the poor. Members coming from districts with a more Democratic lean are more likely to have reputations for advocating on behalf of women, but actually less likely to advocate for immigrants. Partisan leaning also has a statistically significant effect on the choice to form a reputation for at least some level of advocacy for the poor, but is not a significant determinant of primary or secondary advocacy. Members representing Southern districts are also less likely to form reputations as advocates for these groups, though it does not retain statistical significance across all advocacy levels.

4.7 DESCRIPTIVE REPRESENTATIVES AND MEMBER REPUTATION

Thus far, this chapter has demonstrated that group size and group ambient temperature can play an important role in a member's choices about the reputations they seek to foster, and which groups they do or do not wish to be known as an advocate for. But as discussed in Chapter 2, personal experiences – particularly, being a member of the disadvantaged group yourself – also contribute to these decisions, both by increasing the salience of issues facing that group and by providing an opening to be seen as a credible group advocate. In the next section, I first explore the impact of being a descriptive representative on the reputations for group advocacy that members form. Next, I take a closer look at how the effect of ambient temperature on reputation formation changes for members of Congress that are and are not descriptive representatives.

For these analyses, members are coded as being descriptive representatives of a group if they themselves can claim group membership. For women, racial and ethnic minorities, veterans, and LGBTQ members, this determination is straightforward. Members are considered to be immigrants if they themselves were foreign born and immigrated to the United States, while members with immigrant parents who personally were born in the United States are not included. Those who were first elected to the House at or above the age of sixty-five are considered to be descriptive representatives of seniors. This specific criterion is used in place of someone who has reached the age of sixty-five while serving to both acknowledge that reputations are something that are built over time and that having lived experience as a senior adult prior to entering into Congress may impact the representational choices a person may make once in the institution. This provides continuity with all other descriptive representatives in that experiences prior to serving in Congress are expected to make a difference.

Obviously, there are no members of Congress that are currently destitute – members of Congress tend to be much wealthier than the average American. However, I code a member as a descriptive representative if their CQ *Politics in America* profile describes them as having grown up in poverty (not working class, but poor), or if there was a time in their life that they relied on public assistance for those in poverty, such as welfare or food stamps. Given the popularity of "up by the bootstraps" narratives among those of both parties in Congress, members with such histories tend to place such experiences front and center in their life stories.

Table 4.9 shows the number of members who are themselves a member of a disadvantaged group who also serve as group advocates. To account for the relatively small number of descriptive representatives in the House of Representatives and ensure a sufficient number of cases across levels of advocacy, for these analyses I combine the categories of secondary advocates and primary advocates. Thus, in each of the models discussed below, there are only two sets of coefficients, rather than three. Model 0 is evaluating the relationship between the explanatory variables and the shift from reputations for non-advocacy to reputations for superficial, secondary, or primary advocacy, and Model 1 compares the impact of the same variables when comparing members with reputations for non-advocacy or superficial advocacy with primary and secondary advocates. Members with reputations as advocates for seniors are excluded from this portion of the analysis, as there are no members that were elected to the House when they were over the age of sixty-five that are secondary or primary advocates for seniors. I expand further on the significance of this lack of descriptive representatives devoting the bulk of their reputations to advocacy for seniors at the end of this section.

4.7.1 Veterans, Racial/Ethnic Minorities, and the LGBTQ Community

The first sets of results in Table 4.10 display models including whether or not a member is themselves LGBTQ, a veteran, or a racial/ethnic minority alongside all of the previous explanatory variables. Here, while many of the patterns seen earlier for these groups that have higher and lower levels of perceived deservingness remain the same, there are a few additional insights that are important. Members who are themselves LGBTQ or

TABLE 4.9 *Number of members serving as advocates of disadvantaged groups across descriptive and nondescriptive representatives*

		Seniors	Veterans	Women	Poor	Immigrants	Racial/Ethnic Minorities	LGBTQ
Non-DR	Non	1,897	1,437	1,785	1,587	2,032	1,781	2,130
	Superficial	183	76	66	284	63	57	19
	Secondary	65	28	17	128	23	10	11
	Primary	11	11	1	39	24	3	1
	Total	2,156	1,552	1,869	2,038	2,142	1,851	2,161
DR	Non	18	541	191	75	23	122	7
	Superficial	1	54	47	28	2	69	1
	Secondary	0	20	42	17	6	81	6
	Primary	0	8	26	17	2	52	0
	Total	19	623	306	137	33	324	14

Disadvantaged-group advocates in the 103rd, 105th, 108th, 110th, and 113th Congresses by disadvantaged group and member status as descriptive representatives.

TABLE 4.10 *Descriptive representatives and member reputation for advocacy for veterans, LGBTQ individuals, and racial/ethnic minorities*

	Veterans				LGBTQ				Race/Ethnicity			
	0	1	0	1	0	1	0	1	0	1	0	1
Group Size	0.195	0.233	0.195	0.237	2.010	5.072	1.974	5.058	0.033	0.015	0.016	0.032
	0.20	0.00	0.00	0.00	0.01	0.07	0.02	0.07	0.00	0.01	0.01	0.00
Ambient Temperature	0.047	0.105	0.020	0.062	0.059	0.189	0.060	0.189	-0.070	-0.018	-0.039	0.091
	0.114	0.084	0.529	0.301	0.065	0.106	0.069	0.108	0.184	0.712	0.413	0.528
Descriptive Representative	0.663	0.504	-5.725	-12.130	4.380	6.351	9.064	5.756	3.257	3.339	0.221	14.324
	0.00	0.12	0.07	0.17	0.00	0.00	0.11	0.87	0.00	0.00	0.97	0.16
Ambient Temp. & DR	—	—	0.086	0.170	—	—	-0.097	0.012	—	—	0.047	-0.167
			0.04	0.15			0.46	0.99			0.57	0.28
Republican	-0.516	-0.856	-0.521	-0.885	-1.340	-1.507	-1.387	-1.563	-1.409	-1.430	-1.435	-1.317
	0.01	0.02	0.01	0.02	0.04	0.34	0.04	0.33	0.00	0.00	0.00	0.00
Dem Pres Vote	0.004	0.028	0.004	0.028	0.011	0.013	0.013	0.014	-0.022	-0.016	-0.017	-0.019
	0.73	0.19	0.74	0.18	0.72	0.85	0.68	0.84	0.30	0.32	0.29	0.37
South	-0.015	0.291	-0.059	0.225	—	—	—	—	0.051	-0.163	-0.176	0.072
	0.95	0.56	0.80	0.66					0.87	0.53	0.49	0.82
1990s	-1.191	-0.622	-1.173	-0.525	1.845	8.757	1.783	8.713	1.039	1.492	1.511	1.025
	0.00	0.31	0.00	0.39	0.01	0.14	0.01	0.14	0.00	0.00	0.00	0.00

(continued)

TABLE 4.10 (continued)

	Veterans				LGBTQ				Race/Ethnicity			
	0	1	0	1	0	1	0	1	0	1	0	1
2000s	−0.771	−0.260	−0.802	−0.263	0.218	4.767	0.192	4.753	1.590	0.941	1.660	0.897
	0.00	0.59	0.00	0.59	0.71	0.29	0.77	0.28	0.00	0.01	0.00	0.01
First Term	−0.953		−0.953		−1.643		−1.523		−2.501		−2.512	
	0.00		0.00		0.10		0.12		0.00		0.00	
Constant	−7.413	−14.894	−5.372	−11.746	−9.304	−24.508	−9.377	−24.508	−2.181	−0.344	−0.833	−10.974
	0.00	0.00	0.04	0.01	0.00	0.05	0.00	0.05	0.50	0.92	0.80	0.24
N	2,175		2,175		2,175		2,175		2,175		2,175	
Wald's Chi^2	90.6		101.8		89.2		141.6		493.3		512.9	
Pseudo-R^2	0.0782		0.0816		0.3024		0.3033		0.4245		0.4258	

Note: Coefficients calculated using generalized ordered logistic regression, with First Term modeled as a parallel proportional term and the rest of the independent variables modeled as partial proportional terms. Standard errors are clustered by member, and *p*-values are in gray. Model 0 represents the likelihood of a shift from no advocacy to superficial, secondary, or primary advocacy and Model 1 is no advocacy or superficial advocacy to primary or secondary advocacy. No LGBTQ member advocates come from the South, so the variable is excluded on the basis of perfect prediction.

a racial/ethnic minority are considerably more likely to form a reputation for group advocacy across both levels, even while group size remains an important determinant of member reputation. Reps. Albert Wynn (D-MD4) and Joe Crowley (D-NY7), for example, represented districts with nearly the same ambient temperature and percentage of racial/ethnic minorities in moderately liberal states. But while Wynn, a Black man, had consistently served as a superficial or secondary advocate for racial/ethnic minorities, Crowley, who is not a descriptive representative for racial/ethnic minorities, prioritized other groups. For veterans, however, being a descriptive representative is significantly related to having at least some part of your reputation built around advocating for veterans, but those who have taken on the highest levels of group advocacy are driven by the percentage of veterans in their districts.

Once again, first term and Republican members of Congress are less likely to form these reputations for group advocacy, though there is some small variation in the significance of the effect of party. This is particularly true for members with reputations as advocates for the LGBTQ community – once descriptive representatives are taken into account, these other variables that have been significant in prior models drop in significance. After the principal explanatory variables and decade-specific fixed-effects are taken into account, neither the partisan lean nor representing a district in the South has a significant effect on member reputation.

4.7.2 Women, Immigrants, and the Poor

Women, immigrants, and the poor are groups that do not fit as neatly into the categories of being generally considered to be of high or low deservingness of government assistance. The effects of descriptive representation, ambient temperature, and group size on member reputations as advocates for these groups are given in Table 4.11, and a few differences from the groups discussed above can be seen. Being an immigrant is not a statistically significant predictor of member reputation as an advocate for immigrants, while the percentage of immigrants and partisan leaning of a district do have a significant impact. Additionally, while Republican members are less likely to have reputations as advocates for immigrants at any level, partisanship is not a statistically significant factor separating non- and superficial advocates from secondary and primary advocates. But while members representing Southern districts are not any less likely to have reputations for serving as advocates for immigrants, Southern members are considerably less likely to build reputations as advocates on

TABLE 4.11 *Descriptive representatives and member reputation for advocacy for women, immigrants, and the poor*

	Immigrants				Poor				Women			
	0	1	0	1	0	1	0	1	0	1	0	1
Group Size	0.123	0.155	0.127	0.160	0.066	0.089	0.064	0.088	0.098	0.009	0.089	0.008
	0.00	0.00	0.00	0.00	0.00	0.00	0.00	0.00	0.16	0.94	0.20	0.94
Ambient Temperature	−0.041	−0.020	−0.046	−0.029	−0.005	0.027	−0.017	0.025	0.016	0.016	0.045	0.077
	0.078	0.532	0.059	0.381	0.861	0.580	0.588	0.625	0.581	0.646	0.182	0.136
Descriptive Representative	0.084	0.235	5.377	−7.473	0.574	0.606	−10.239	−1.740	2.746	3.370	6.340	9.151
	0.90	0.73	0.05	0.04	0.02	0.04	0.05	0.78	0.00	0.00	0.03	0.02
Ambient Temp. & DR	–	–	−0.116	0.157	–	–	0.155	0.034	–	–	−0.063	−0.100
			0.04	0.03			0.03	0.70			0.23	0.14
Republican	−0.700	−0.587	−0.662	−0.491	−1.106	−1.773	−1.120	−1.775	−0.426	−0.942	−0.427	−0.940
	0.02	0.30	0.03	0.40	0.00	0.00	0.00	0.00	0.07	0.01	0.07	0.01
Dem Pres Vote	−0.080	−0.087	−0.082	−0.088	0.022	0.015	0.022	0.016	0.050	0.053	0.050	0.054
	0.00	0.03	0.00	0.03	0.04	0.28	0.04	0.27	0.01	0.05	0.01	0.05
South	−0.419	−0.762	−0.403	−0.750	−0.355	−0.884	−0.361	−0.855	−0.386	−0.847	−0.364	−0.803
	0.29	0.20	0.31	0.21	0.05	0.00	0.05	0.00	0.20	0.08	0.23	0.10
1990s	−0.416	−0.341	−0.469	−0.380	0.570	0.625	0.561	0.613	1.353	1.001	1.360	0.992
	0.23	0.43	0.19	0.40	0.00	0.01	0.00	0.01	0.00	0.00	0.00	0.00

(continued)

2000s	0.052	0.209	0.059	0.224	0.697	0.727	0.712	0.723	0.932	0.152	0.921	0.169
	0.84	0.55	0.81	0.52	0.00	0.01	0.00	0.01	0.00	0.65	0.00	0.60
First Term		-1.983		-1.965		-1.206		-1.203		-1.771		-1.771
		0.00		0.00		0.00		0.00		0.00		0.00
Constant	1.859	-0.861	2.074	-0.496	-2.713	-5.998	-1.896	-5.876	-12.263	-8.769	-13.501	-12.268
	0.29	0.75	0.25	0.86	0.20	0.06	0.39	0.09	0.00	0.13	0.00	0.07
N	2,175		2,175		2,175		2,175		2,175		2,175	
Wald's Chi^2	275.2		293.2		239.6		251.7		258.7		275.8	
Pseudo-R^2	0.2894		0.2928		0.129		0.131		0.2521		0.2539	

Note: Coefficients calculated using generalized ordered logistic regression, with First Term modeled as a parallel proportional term and the rest of the independent variables modeled as partial proportional terms. Standard errors are clustered by member, and *p*-values are in gray. Model 0 represents the likelihood of a shift from no advocacy to superficial, secondary, or primary advocacy, and Model 1 is no advocacy or superficial advocacy to primary or secondary advocacy.

behalf of the poor, after group size and other variables are held constant. Partisan leaning of a district is also a significant source of separation between non-advocates and members with a reputation for some level of advocacy. After these district-specific factors are taken into account, group size, ambient temperature, and descriptive representation follow now-familiar patterns. Personal experience with poverty and the percentage of poor constituents in a district each have a significant impact on member reputation, while the significance of ambient temperature drops off.

The unique situation of women among other disadvantaged groups is again revealed in these models – while group size in a district is not a driving force behind members forming reputations as women's advocates, being a woman in Congress has an enormous influence. These effects can be clearly seen in the case of Rep. Barbara Lee (D-CA13). Lee has cultivated a reputation as a primary advocate for women, serving as a vocal defender of abortion rights and a strident opponent to any cuts in the funding of women's health organizations such as Planned Parenthood. Lee was preceded as a representative of the 13th District of California by Rep. Pete Stark (D). Stark built a reputation as an advocate for liberal healthcare solutions, but did not focus his advocacy specifically on women's health or other issues directly pertaining to women.

Once descriptive representation is taken into account, the ambient temperature toward women in a district no longer plays a statistically significant role in member reputation. Members coming from more Democratic districts are more likely to craft reputations around serving women, and while Republicans are less likely to have reputations as primary or secondary advocates, conventional levels of statistical significance are not quite met when evaluating the role of party on the choice to become a superficial advocate of women. This could indicate that once a member's gender is taken into consideration, the choice to form a reputation as a superficial advocate of women is a slightly less partisan choice than that of other disadvantaged groups.

4.7.3 Interactive Effects of Descriptive Representation on Reputation

Next, I look more closely at the differences in the effect of ambient temperature on reputation for descriptive and nondescriptive members. To this point, ambient temperature has only occasionally (as in the case of women's advocates) been seen to have a statistically significant effect on member reputation once group size is included in the model. But while it is not surprising that the size of the group within a district would have a much stronger pull on member reputation than group ambient temperature, I do expect that the marginal effects of changes in ambient temperature will have different effects for members who are themselves a descriptive representative of a disadvantaged group than those who are not.

I test this by including an interaction term between ambient temperature and whether or not someone is a descriptive representative, and then examining the predicted marginal effects on the probability of a member holding a reputation as a disadvantaged-group advocate. The models themselves can be seen in the second set of columns in Tables 4.10 and 4.11. Because these are generalized ordered logistic regression models, predicted probabilities are the best means of displaying the interactive effects of these variables on member reputation for group advocacy. These predicted effects can be seen in Figures 4.2 and 4.3. For each of these figures, all other variables in the models besides ambient temperature and the dichotomous measure for descriptive representatives take on the actual values that they have in the dataset, which allows for the specific marginal effects of ambient temperature to be isolated and estimated for descriptive representatives and nondescriptive representatives.

Figure 4.2 shows the differences in the marginal predicted effects of ambient temperature on forming any level of reputation for advocacy of disadvantaged groups for members of the House who are themselves a part of that group, and members who are not a descriptive representative. One of the most interesting trends seen below is not just how the impact of ambient temperature on reputation varies depending upon the group being represented, but the differences in these predicted marginal effects for members who are and are not descriptive representatives. For nondescriptive representatives, the effects of changes in ambient temperature on the likelihood of having a reputation for group advocacy are extremely small, with slopes remaining close to constant. For members who are descriptive representatives, however, changes in ambient temperature have larger effects on reputations for group advocacy, with stronger effects for some groups than others.

For veterans, a group broadly considered to be deserving of government assistance, there is little change in the predicted effects across values in ambient temperature. The same is true for immigrants and LGBTQ members. Women in the House, though, have a clear and significant boost in the likelihood of having a reputation as a women's advocate relative to

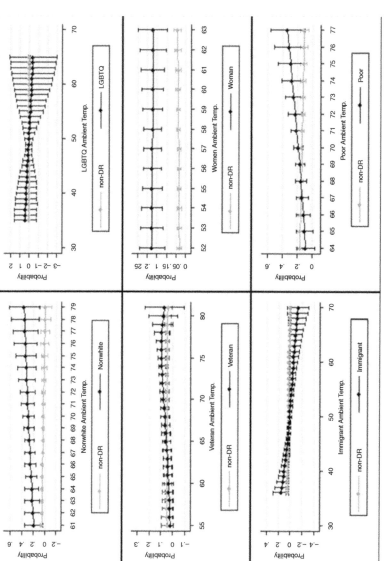

FIGURE 4.2 Predicted effects of ambient temperature for members with reputations as advocates relative to non-advocates for descriptive representatives
Note: Figures show the predicted marginal effects of ambient temperature on reputation for superficial, secondary, or primary advocacy relative to non-advocacy for members who are themselves descriptive representatives of the group and members who are not. Predicted marginal effects are calculated using Stata's margins command for the Model 1's containing interactions between descriptive representative and ambient temperature shown in Tables 4.10 and 4.11. All other variables are held to their observed values within the dataset. Clockwise from the top left, the groups whose

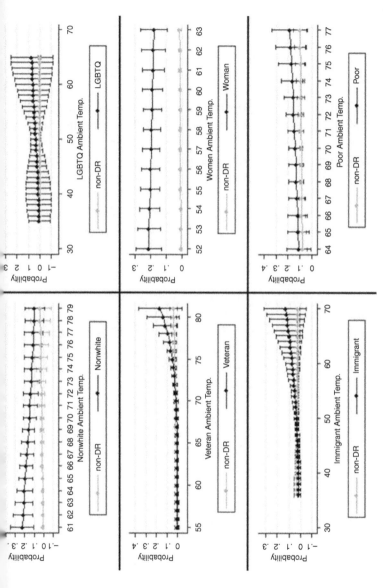

FIGURE 4.3 Predicted effects of ambient temperature for members with reputations as primary or secondary advocates relative to non- or superficial advocates for descriptive representatives

Note: Figures show the predicted marginal effects of ambient temperature on reputation for secondary or primary advocacy relative to non- or superficial advocacy for members who are themselves descriptive representatives of the group and members who are not. Predicted marginal effects are calculated using Stata's margins command for the Model 1's containing interactions between descriptive representative and ambient temperature shown in Tables 4.10 and 4.11. All other variables are held to their observed values within the dataset. Clockwise from the top left, the groups whose representation is being analyzed are racial/ethnic minorities, LGBTQ individuals, women, the poor, immigrants, and veterans.

men, but also do not see a clear shift in that likelihood as ambient temperature increases. For racial/ethnic minorities and those with a history of poverty, however, there is a clear increase in the likelihood of a member of the House who is a descriptive representative forming a reputation as some kind of group advocate – even if only a superficial advocate, as is true in the majority of cases – as the group ambient temperature of the district goes up.

The marginal effects of ambient temperature for descriptive and non-descriptive representatives when considering the difference between non- and superficial advocates and primary and secondary advocates are shown in Figure 4.3. These figures demonstrate that there are important differences in how descriptive representation and ambient temperature affects the likelihood of having a reputation that may include superficial group advocacy versus that of a reputation specifically for secondary or primary advocacy – those members that choose to cultivate a considerable amount of their legislative reputation around advocating for a disadvantaged group. The groups for which changes in ambient temperature were previously seen to do little to increase the likelihood of some level of advocacy on their behalf, regardless of whether or not a member was a descriptive representative, largely do see some effects of changes in ambient temperature when comparing those members with reputations for primary and secondary advocacy to all other members.

As before, members of Congress who are not themselves descriptive representatives experience only very small boosts in the likelihood of having primary or secondary reputations for group advocacy when ambient temperature increases. For members who are themselves part of the disadvantaged group, however, increases in the predicted effects are seen for nearly all groups. Veterans, immigrants, those with a history of poverty, and LGBTQ members see an increased likelihood of being primary or secondary group advocates at high levels of district group ambient temperature. Once again, members with reputations for advocating for women are the exception to this trend – even when only considering what sets primary and secondary advocates apart, changes in ambient temperature have very little effect once the large and clearly statistically significant boost that comes from being a woman is taken into account.

One of the most interesting trends that can be seen in Figure 4.3 is the effect of changes in ambient temperature on reputation as a primary or secondary advocate for racial and ethnic minorities. Here again, there is a clear and statistically significant difference in the effects of ambient temperature between descriptive representatives and nondescriptive representatives. However, in this instance, as ambient temperature increases, the likelihood that a member who is themselves a racial/ethnic minority will have a primary or secondary reputation for group advocacy actually *decreases*. This change in the direction of the predicted probabilities speaks to the uniqueness of the place of racial/ethnic minorities in American politics, even when compared to other disadvantaged groups. It implies that, unlike for other disadvantaged groups, members of Congress who are racial and ethnic minorities are more likely to serve as advocates for their group when the threat environment is high, rather than when it is low. I return to this point for further discussion in the conclusion.

4.7.4 The Advocacy Window

These figures showing the marginal predicted effects also allow for evaluation of the concept of the advocacy window introduced in Chapter 2. The advocacy window is the space between the level of representation that is expected based upon the size of the group in a district, conceptualized as the floor, and the high point of the amount of representation that would be tolerated given the feelings toward a particular group in a district, analogized to the ceiling. On their own, both group size and ambient temperature tend to have a positive, significant relationship with member reputation, as would be expected. But once these variables are evaluated within a single model, group size tends to take precedence, and ambient temperature loses significance. This indicates that, when making decisions about where to focus their reputations, most members tend to stay firmly rooted to the floor when considering the representation of disadvantaged groups.

A level of additional nuance is added, however, when descriptive representation is taken into account. Most other members tend not to shoot for the ceiling when creating their reputations as advocates, but descriptive representatives tend to be more likely to take advantage of an open advocacy window when it exists. This important difference in the effect of the advocacy window on members' reputational choices is on full display in Figures 4.2 and 4.3. Particularly when considering members who build reputations as primary or secondary advocates for disadvantaged groups, there is a noticeable increase in the responsiveness of descriptive representatives to changes in the ambient temperature – the opening and closing of the advocacy window. Those who are themselves a member of a disadvantaged group tend to utilize this opening of the advocacy window to boost the level of group advocacy they choose to build their reputation around.

Members who are racial/ethnic minorities, however, have an important and unique response to these changes in the dimensions of the advocacy window. For these members, reputations for primary or secondary advocacy of racial/ethnic minorities are more likely to come in districts with a tighter advocacy window. This very likely speaks to the unmatched levels of suspicion and concentrated discrimination racial/ethnic minorities have experienced relative even to other disadvantaged groups. Under such circumstances, members who have themselves experienced this may be most likely to dedicate their reputation to serving racial/ethnic minorities when the threat is high – when they feel if they do not step up for their minority constituents, no one will. Only when the advocacy window is large can they relax, and focus more of their attention on other issues.

This is very different from the situation facing members who enter Congress as a senior, for instance. Zero members of Congress who won their first election to the House of Representatives at or after the age of 65 made the choice to craft a reputation as a primary or secondary advocate for seniors. Very clearly, there is not the same sense that if they do not take these actions, no one else will. Instead, they can feel free to focus their legislative reputations around whatever issues they please, knowing that there will always be other members willing to advocate for seniors.

4.8 CONCLUSIONS

The results from this chapter demonstrate the crucial roles that group size, ambient temperature, and descriptive representation have on the legislative reputations that members choose to cultivate. Both group size and ambient temperature tend to have a positive and significant effect on member reputation when considered independently, with group size serving as the more prominent force behind reputation formation when considered together. Descriptive representatives were also more likely to take on reputations as group advocates than other members, with the exception of those disadvantaged groups considered to be most highly deserving.

This chapter also introduced group ambient temperature as a new measure for group affect in a district. It explained the process through which estimates of how positively or negatively a district tends to feel toward a group on average can be generated, making use of the multilevel regression with poststratification procedure. Maps and summary measures were used to provide face validity for these ambient temperature estimates, which were then compared to the variations in group size across districts.

In sum, this chapter provides evidence that reputations for serving disadvantaged groups are rooted both in district demographics such as group size and partisan lean and in member characteristics such as party affiliation and personal experience as a member of a disadvantaged group. Decision-making on legislative reputations in the House of Representatives is well characterized by the concept of the advocacy window, wherein group size is considered to be the floor, or baseline level of representation that would be expected, and ambient temperature serves as a ceiling the members could reach for if they so choose. For most members, this is not a favored choice, preferring instead to root their reputation for advocacy on the floor, and preserve the remainder of their representational capital for other issues.

This trend is evidence of the avoidance behavior expected of a risk-averse member reacting to a potentially unpopular group in their district. Members want to maximize their electoral prospects, and thus are unlikely to expend more than the minimum amount of effort representing groups that have any potential to create a backlash. It is not the case that these members of Congress are doing *no* work to advocate on behalf of disadvantaged groups in their district, but, as a general rule, they are not maximizing the degree to which their reputations could reflect the advocacy work on their behalf. Descriptive representatives break this pattern by being more likely to increase the part of their reputation that they devote to group advocacy when their district provides them with a wider advocacy window. Racial/ethnic minority members are the exception to this trend, instead being more likely to cultivate a primary or secondary reputation for advocacy of racial/ethnic minorities in instances when ambient temperature is lower, and the advocacy window is reduced.

In the next chapter, I turn to the United States Senate. In it, I utilize a similar framework to determine what drives a senator to form a reputation as an advocate for the disadvantaged.

5

The Choice to Be a Disadvantaged-Group Advocate in the US Senate

This chapter examines what leads someone to cultivate a reputation as an advocate for the disadvantaged in the US Senate. In particular, it will investigate how certain institutional differences between the House of Representatives and the Senate can affect how members make representational choices. Compared to members of the House, senators have considerably more individual power, and do not face the same pressures to specialize. Senators serve on more committees, are markedly less restrained in their ability to speak on the floor, and are more likely to be a pivotal vote on any given piece of legislation. This expectation that senators will be involved in a broader range of issues allows for considerably more flexibility when crafting their legislative reputations, and makes it less likely that they will solely prioritize advocating for any one particular group. Chapter 3 demonstrated this difference in the incidence of senators with a reputation for primary or secondary advocacy on behalf of disadvantaged groups relative to members of the House in Figure 3.7.

However, it is important to bear in mind that while this increased pressure on senators to diversify their representative activities may make them less likely to craft reputations as primary or secondary advocates for the disadvantaged, they are actually slightly more likely on average to serve as disadvantaged-group advocates at least at a superficial level (as seen in Figure 3.7). Thus, even if senators tend to build reputations as superficial advocates rather than primary or secondary advocates (though these higher levels of advocacy on behalf of disadvantaged groups do still exist within the upper chamber), it remains necessary to determine if the same factors driving the decisions behind reputation formation in the

House are also at work in the Senate. The sections to follow take on that task, and work to untangle the ways in which different pressures and institutional constraints can alter the reputation building calculus for members within the two legislative chambers.

In this chapter, I will analyze the impact of the size of a disadvantaged group and the ambient temperature toward a disadvantaged group on reputation formation in the Senate, and compare the effects with what was seen in the House of Representatives. Next, I will introduce and evaluate three alternative hypotheses that take into account senator electoral security and the advocacy environment within the Senate to determine their impact on senator reputation. Following that, I will investigate how the reputations of descriptive representatives in the Senate differ from nondescriptive representatives, and highlight the implications of these differences, particularly relative to descriptive representatives in the House. Finally, I return to the concept of the advocacy window, and discuss how well the concept characterizes the decision to build a reputation as a disadvantaged-group advocate in the US Senate.

5.1 CONSTITUENCY CHARACTERISTICS: GROUP SIZE AND AMBIENT TEMPERATURE

As with the previous chapter, explaining what drives members to cultivate a reputation as an advocate for disadvantaged groups starts with an exploration of the role of group size and group ambient temperature within a state. These variables are a useful place to start this discussion about when and why senators build legislative reputations because a basic understanding of how a democracy *should* work provides clear expectations. Assuming that, just as in the House, members of the Senate care both about getting reelected and about representing their constituents, one would expect that as the size of a group increases within a state, members will devote more of their efforts to working on their behalf, and be more likely to craft a reputation as a group advocate. Similarly, the more warmly the average person in a district feels toward a group, it seems reasonable to expect that a senator would be even more likely to form a reputation as a defender of that group. In the remainder of this section, I briefly review the operationalization of these two key variables. Next, I utilize models equivalent to those used to explain the formation of member reputations in the House to evaluate the extent to which these expectations hold in the US Senate.

5.1.1 Group Size

For the analysis to follow, group size is measured using the Census counts for the percentage of group members within a state. Racial and ethnic minorities within a state are determined using the percentage of individuals who do not identify as non-Hispanic whites, veterans are the percent of the civilian population that served in any branch of the armed services, seniors are the percentage of individuals over the age of sixty-five, and immigrants are the percentage of residents of a state who are foreign born. The percentage of women in a state is a straightforward count, and the percentage of poor residents are those whose household income is below the federal poverty line. The Census has never asked the sexual orientation or gender identity of respondents, and thus operationalizing the percentage of LGBTQ individuals within a state requires a proxy. Because of this lack of data, I follow the lead of prior researchers and use the percentage of same-sex households within a state to approximate the size of the state LGBTQ population (e.g., Warshaw and Rodden, 2012; Hansen and Treul, 2015).[1]

5.1.2 Ambient Temperature

The ambient temperature variable is a unique measure that conceptualizes feeling thermometer scores as a way of determining the average level of hostility or favorability toward a group within a state or district, which was introduced in detail in the previous chapter. For this analysis exploring reputation formation in the Senate, I followed the same procedure from Chapter 4 to estimate the state ambient temperature toward a group (as opposed to congressional district ambient temperature). This was done using multilevel regression and poststratification on the feeling thermometer questions from the ANES time series data, aggregated by decade.[2] Table 5.1 shows a summary of the state estimates generated for each of the disadvantaged groups analyzed.

---

[1] For further discussion of why this proxy was selected and the potential consequences of this selection, please see Chapter 4, where this issue is addressed at length.

[2] Again, for those groups that were not expressly asked about in the ANES during this time period, I use a close proxy. Veterans, women, immigrants, and LGBTQ individuals were not included directly, so instead I use the military, feminists, illegal immigrants, and gays and lesbians, respectively, as proxies.

TABLE 5.1 *Summary of estimates for state feeling thermometer ratings by group*

Group	N	Mean	Std. Dev.	Min.	Max.
Seniors	400	78.63	2.34	72.20	85.10
Veterans	500	72.37	3.82	65.23	82.34
Poor	500	68.76	2.89	61.24	77.63
Women	500	55.42	3.18	46.84	63.19
Immigrants	500	40.75	7.63	26.59	57.61
Racial/Ethnic Minorities	500	65.38	2.90	59.31	71.58
LGBTQ	500	46.25	7.75	21.85	64.57

Note: Displayed are the average estimate values for the feeling thermometer scores across all fifty states from 1992 to 2016. Estimates were generated using multilevel regression with poststratification. The estimate for racial/ethnic minorities is an average of the ambient temperature generated for each district for Black, Hispanic, and Asian Americans.

5.2 REPUTATIONS FOR DISADVANTAGED-GROUP ADVOCACY IN THE US SENATE

Chapter 3 demonstrated that legislative reputations for disadvantaged-group advocacy are common to both the House and the Senate, with over 50 percent of senators possessing a reputation for at least superficial advocacy of a disadvantaged group. Table 5.2 shows the total number of senators sampled with a reputation for disadvantaged-group advocacy, separated by group and level of advocacy.[3] Compared to their counterparts in the House, senators are less likely to have reputations as primary or secondary disadvantaged-group advocates, tending to opt for superficial advocacy instead. Given the markedly smaller number of senators compared to members of the House – 100 to 435 – these differences in the level of advocacy a senator or member of the House are known for have important consequences for selecting the most appropriate means of modeling those reputations.

Table 5.2 shows that, for five out of the seven groups under evaluation, there are fewer than two senators with a primary reputation as group advocates. Because the raw numbers for the highest category are so small, in the analysis to follow, I combine reputations for primary and secondary advocacy into a single category, to create a three-category ordered

---

[3] As described at length in Chapter 3, the sample includes all 500 senators from the 103rd, 105th, 108th, 110th, and 113th Congresses.

TABLE 5.2 *Number of senators with reputations as advocates for disadvantaged groups in the 103rd, 105th, 108th, 110th, and 113th Congress*

	Seniors	Veterans	Women	Poor	Immigrants	Racial/ Ethnic Minorities	LGBTQ
Non	426	458	430	386	470	476	487
Superficial	52	29	44	76	23	16	9
Secondary	17	13	18	36	6	7	3
Primary	5	0	8	2	1	1	1
Total Advocates	74	42	70	114	30	24	13

dependent variable. Using this combined top category allows for better estimation of the impact of relevant explanatory variables on the likelihood that a member will have a reputation for superficial advocacy or higher.[4]

5.3 GROUP SIZE, AMBIENT TEMPERATURE, AND REPUTATION FORMATION IN THE SENATE

Chapter 4 showed that both the size of a disadvantaged group and feelings toward that group play an important role in the legislative reputations that members of the House choose to form. Particularly for groups that are generally considered to be less deserving of government assistance, both group size and ambient temperature had a positive, significant effect on the likelihood that a member would form a reputation as a group advocate when evaluated independently. In this section, I examine the relationship between these variables and member reputation for the US Senate.

To gain a more nuanced understanding of how these explanatory variables impact member reputation and to account for any violations of the parallel regression assumption, I utilize generalized ordered logistic regression models.[5] Because member reputation has been collapsed into

[4] Because of the particularly small number of cases of senators with reputations as advocates of the LGBTQ community at any level, I further collapse the dependent variable into just two categories: reputation for advocacy (superficial, secondary, or primary) and no reputation for advocacy. Thus, for estimates of the likelihood of a senator having a reputation for LGBTQ advocacy, I utilize a logistic regression model, rather than generalized ordered logistic regression.

[5] A more in-depth discussion of why generalized ordered logistic regression models are most appropriate can be found in Chapter 4.

a three-category ordinal variable, each generalized ordered logistic regression model will produce two sets of estimated coefficients, referred to in each instance as Model 0 and Model 1. Model 0 shows the estimated effects of each independent variable on the likelihood that a senator will have a reputation for some level of advocacy relative to non-advocacy, while Model 1's coefficients represent the estimated effect that a variable has on the likelihood of having a reputation for primary or secondary advocacy, relative to non-advocacy or superficial advocacy. The results of these models are displayed in Tables 5.3–5.6.

5.3.1 Veterans and Seniors

The coefficients of the models evaluating how group size and ambient temperature affect the likelihood of senators building reputations as advocates of veterans and seniors are shown in Table 5.3. For these groups, with a high level of perceived deservingness of government assistance, the forces driving senators to foster reputations as advocates look relatively similar to those that were at work in the House, but with some important exceptions. The percentage of veterans and seniors in a state has a positive and statistically significant impact on whether or not a senator will have some form of reputation as a group advocate, but not on the choice to expand that reputation as a primary or secondary advocate.

This distinction is not unexpected – senators have a great deal of leeway in determining how to allocate their legislative efforts. State demographics do push senators to try to dedicate at least a small portion of their legislative reputation to serving veterans and seniors, but other factors are responsible for determining which senators choose to signal that advocating for these groups are their top priority. Many Florida senators, for instance, despite representing the state with the highest percentage of individuals over the age of sixty-five, have a superficial reputation as an advocate for seniors. People like former Sen. Bob Graham (D-FL), most known for his work on anti-crime legislation (particularly his support for the death penalty), also made sure that he could be described as a supporter of seniors by pushing for prescription drug coverage for Medicare recipients.

State ambient temperature, on the other hand, does not have a statistically significant effect on a senator's reputation as an advocate of either of these two groups. Because veterans and seniors are broadly considered to be deserving of government assistance, it is not expected that small state-by-state variations in how these groups are viewed would have a large effect on reputation. Senators can be reasonably confident

TABLE 5.3 *Group size, ambient temperature, and member reputation for advocacy for veterans and seniors*

	Veterans						Seniors					
	0	1	0	1	0	1	0	1	0	1	0	1
Group Size	0.325	0.461	—	—	0.320	0.417	0.025	0.022	—	—	0.023	-0.049
	0.00	0.04			0.00	0.11	0.04	0.32			0.05	0.72
Ambient Temperature	—	—	-0.061	0.014	-0.051	0.014	—	—	-0.018	-0.016	-0.009	0.012
			0.29	0.93	0.36	0.93			0.81	0.89	0.90	0.93
Republican	-0.677	-1.150	-0.650	-0.920	-0.696	-0.932	-0.735	-1.770	-0.723	-2.067	-0.764	-2.092
	0.11	0.08	0.12	0.37	0.09	0.36	0.04	0.01	0.05	0.01	0.04	0.01
Dem Pres Vote	0.004	-0.044	-0.007	-0.045	0.004	-0.031	-0.004	0.018	-0.012	0.012	-0.011	0.012
	0.89	0.48	0.78	0.43	0.88	0.62	0.84	0.52	0.52	0.74	0.56	0.75
South	0.052	0.465	-0.052	0.279	0.056	0.364	0.114	0.563	-0.050	0.475	-0.009	0.559
	0.90	0.48	0.90	0.72	0.90	0.64	0.73	0.26	0.89	0.42	0.98	0.31
1990s	-0.660	-0.131	-0.610	0.438	-0.956	-0.110	-0.210	-0.420	-0.477	-0.564	-0.543	-0.498
	0.18	0.91	0.31	0.73	0.12	0.95	0.42	0.31	0.07	0.20	0.04	0.31
2000s	-1.785	-1.929	-0.953	-0.403	-1.994	-1.796	—	—	—	—	—	—
	0.00	0.05	0.06	0.56	0.00	0.14						
First Term		-1.073		-1.059		-1.105		-0.655		-0.467		-0.524
		0.10		0.10		0.08		0.13		0.30		0.25

(continued)

Constant	-5.227	-5.980	3.419	-2.117	-1.280	-7.197	-1.470	-3.754	1.012	-1.690	0.018	-3.258
	0.01	0.20	0.39	0.87	0.75	0.58	0.12	0.02	0.86	0.86	1.00	0.74
N	500		500		500		500		400		400	
Wald's Chi^2	41.5		26.1		46.9		21.6		19.7		23.7	
Pseudo-R^2	0.0599		0.0419		0.0638		0.0445		0.0488		0.0563	

Note: Coefficients calculated using generalized ordered logistic regression, with First Term modeled as a parallel proportional term and the rest of the independent variables modeled as partial proportional terms. Standard errors are clustered by member, and *p*-values are in gray. Model 0 represents the likelihood of a shift from no advocacy to superficial or primary/secondary advocacy, and Model 1 is no advocacy or superficial advocacy to primary/secondary advocacy. Feeling thermometer questions for seniors were not included in the ANES of the 2010s, so the decade base category for seniors is the 2000s.

that advocating for these groups will not negatively impact them, and may even provide a boost in how they are regarded by their constituents.

As was true for members of the House, neither partisan lean nor location in the South has a significant impact on a senator's choice to build a reputation as a veteran or senior advocate. Democrats are more likely to have a reputation as an advocate for seniors, but, unlike in the House, the choice to become a veterans' advocate in the Senate is nonpartisan. One last noteworthy but not unexpected difference between the House and the Senate comes in considering the gap in reputation building between first-termers and returning incumbents. In the House, members in their first term simply have not spent long enough within the institution to have amassed the over-time pattern of behavior that is required to build a legislative reputation. Senators, with a full six years before they must face the voters again, have considerably more time in their first term to craft a reputation that reflects their legislative priorities. This also speaks to the erosion of the norm of apprenticeship highlighted by Matthews in *The Folkways of the Senate* – being in their first term does not deter a senator in the contemporary Congress from taking action to establish their legislative reputation (Sinclair, 1989).

5.3.2 LGBTQ and Racial/Ethnic Minorities

Table 5.4 displays the impact of group size and ambient temperature on the likelihood of a senator having a reputation for advocacy on behalf of the LGBTQ community and racial/ethnic minorities. These models indicate that *neither* group size *nor* ambient temperature has a statistically significant impact on a senator's choice to cultivate a reputation as an LGBTQ or racial/ethnic minority advocate. This is a crucial and telling distinction from what was seen in the previous chapter.

Of all of the disadvantaged groups being studied here, the LGBTQ community and racial/ethnic minorities are generally considered to be the least deserving of government assistance by the country at large, particularly for the time period investigated here. In the House, both the percentage of racial/ethnic minorities and same-sex households and the general feelings toward those groups within a district had a positive and significant effect on the likelihood that a member would form a reputation as an advocate. This connection is critical, because it demonstrates that if a group is large enough in a district, even if they are unpopular nationally, their member of Congress is still more likely to actively represent them within the legislature, and that this is further enhanced by improvements in district ambient temperature.

TABLE 5.4 *Group size, ambient temperature, and member reputation for advocacy for racial/ethnic minorities and the LGBTQ community*

	LGBTQ					Race/Ethnicity			
	logit	*logit*	*logit*	0	1	0	1	0	1
Group Size	-0.989	—	-1.824	0.009	-0.001	—	—	0.009	-0.010
	0.75		0.46	0.48	0.97			0.52	0.70
Ambient Temperature	—	0.047	0.055	—	—	0.081	0.076	0.070	0.303
		0.63	0.56			0.45	0.75	0.50	0.52
Republican	-0.604	-0.624	-0.618	0.410	-0.372	0.397	-0.393	0.429	-0.153
	0.55	0.55	0.55	0.41	0.60	0.41	0.69	0.38	0.85
Dem Pres Vote	0.074	0.065	0.083	0.037	0.059	0.044	0.040	0.039	0.060
	0.10	0.08	0.04	0.25	0.44	0.14	0.42	0.23	0.43
South	-0.640	-0.627	-0.669	-1.232	-14.895	-1.142	-15.884	-1.222	-16.160
	0.54	0.54	0.51	0.03	0.00	0.06	0.00	0.03	0.00
1990s	-0.823	0.282	-0.380	2.172	16.927	2.558	18.091	2.559	19.664
	0.60	0.87	0.86	0.04	0.00	0.03	0.00	0.03	0.00
2000s	-0.662	-0.269	-0.203	1.417	15.263	1.712	16.149	1.701	17.235
	0.40	0.84	0.88	0.19	0.00	0.14	0.00	0.14	0.00
First Term	-0.933	-0.997	-0.943	-1.031		-1.057		-1.013	
	0.34	0.30	0.32	0.14		0.14		0.15	

(continued)

TABLE 5.4 (continued)

	LGBTQ			Race/Ethnicity						
	logit	logit	logit	logit	0	1	0	1	0	1
Constant	-6.168	-8.869	-9.261	-6.559	-22.812	-12.288	-27.651	-11.536	-44.894	
	0.01	0.17	0.13	0.00	0.00	0.11	0.10	0.13	0.18	
N	500	500	500	500		500		500		
Wald's Chi²	8.4	9.2	8.8	2,049.2		1,105.8		1,055.6		
Pseudo-R^2	0.0814	0.0882	0.0912	0.1176		0.1155		0.1230		

Note: Coefficients for LGBTQ are estimated using logistic regression, as necessitated by the bivariate coding of the LGBTQ advocacy reputation variable. Coefficients for racial/ethnic minorities are calculated using generalized ordered logistic regression, with First Term modeled as a parallel proportional term and the rest of the independent variables modeled as partial proportional terms. Standard errors are clustered by member, and p-values are in gray. Model 0 represents the likelihood of a shift from no advocacy to superficial or primary/secondary advocacy, and Model 1 is no advocacy or superficial advocacy to primary/secondary advocacy.

In the Senate, however, there appears to be a disconnect when it comes to this expected dyadic relationship. An example of this can be seen in the senators from Rhode Island and Vermont. These two northeastern states consistently have one of the highest percentages of same-sex couples, but none of their senators included in the sample have cultivated a reputation as an advocate for LGBTQ individuals. Clearly, other factors outside of the status of the group within a state are the driving force behind a senator's choice to form a legislative reputation as an advocate for racial/ethnic minorities and the LGBTQ community. Because of this, these groups cannot feel confident that the likelihood of being represented by their own senator will increase even if their numbers or the state-wide feelings toward them as a group go up.

The insignificant impact of partisanship on the chance that a senator will decide to form a reputation as an advocate for these groups is also striking. Even in a context where few senators take on this responsibility and choose to advocate for racial/ethnic minorities or LGBTQ people, Republicans are not significantly more or less likely to take this leap, once the partisan leaning of a state is taken into account. The more Democratic a state is, the more likely it is that a senator will form some portion of their reputation around advocating for the LGBTQ community. Notably, however, the partisan leaning of a state does not impact the choice of a senator to cultivate a reputation as a racial/ethnic minority advocate. Given how closely tied racial/ethnic minorities are to the Democratic coalition, particularly for Black Americans, this relationship (or lack thereof) is stunning. One of the biggest factors influencing if a senator will have a reputation as an advocate for racial/ethnic minorities is instead whether or not they are representing a state in the South. The decade fixed effects also have a particularly strong and significant effect on reputation formation, indicating that the likelihood of having a reputation as an advocate for racial/ethnic minorities in the senate was considerably larger in the 1990s and 2000s than in the 2010s.

5.3.3 Immigrants and the Poor

The models demonstrating the effect of ambient temperature and group size on the likelihood of a senator having a reputation as a group advocate for immigrants and the poor are shown in Table 5.5. Here, too, there are some important similarities and differences in the effects of these variables on senators relative to members of the House. Both the percentage of immigrants and the poor in a district and the group ambient temperature, when evaluated independently, had a significant impact on whether or not a member of the House would craft a reputation as a group advocate. In the Senate, these patterns are different.

As seen in Table 5.5, the percentage of immigrants in a state has a significant and positive effect on whether or not a senator makes the choice to integrate some level of advocacy on behalf of immigrants into their legislative reputation. Reputations for primary or secondary advocacy, though, are not significantly affected by group size within a state. This is similar to the effects observed for senators with reputations as advocates of veterans or seniors – superficial advocacy is significantly driven by state demographics, while higher levels of advocacy in the Senate are encouraged by other factors. Variation in ambient temperature toward immigrants across states, however, consistently does not have a significant effect, even when examined in isolation.

When it comes to senators with reputations for advocating on behalf of the poor, neither group size nor ambient temperature is a significant driver of their decision. This insignificance of group size to the choice to craft a reputation as an advocate of the poor is important. It indicates, much like with advocates of racial/ethnic minorities and the LGBTQ community, that there is a disconnect between senators' reputation-building choices and what some of the basic principles of a representational democracy would predict for groups that are not generally considered to be highly deserving of government assistance.

The effects of senators' party affiliation on reputations for advocacy on behalf of immigrants and the poor have several layers of nuance. While Republican senators are less likely to form a reputation as a primary or secondary advocate for the poor, the effects of partisanship dissipate when the bar for advocacy for those in poverty is lowered to a superficial level. Conversely, partisanship has an insignificant effect on the formation of primary or secondary reputations as immigrant advocates, but Republican senators are actually *more* likely to cultivate at least a superficial reputation around advocating for immigrants. This likely speaks to the fact that, in the 1990s and much of the 2000s, issues pertaining to immigrants were considerably more bipartisan than is the case in the 115th Congress. Republicans like Connie Mack (FL) and Alan Simpson (WY) exemplified this – while advocating for immigrants was never their primary concern in the Senate, they did serve as consistent, supportive voices for a compassionate approach. This was still seen into the 2010s as well, as with the former junior and senior Republican senators from Arizona, Jeff Flake and John McCain.

TABLE 5.5 Group size, ambient temperature, and member reputation for advocacy for immigrants and the poor

	Immigrants						Poor					
	0	1	0	1	0	1	0	1	0	1	0	1
Group Size	0.104	−0.076	—	—	0.104	−0.075	0.008	0.034	—	—	−0.006	−0.001
	0.00	0.69			0.01	0.69	0.85	0.53			0.90	0.99
Ambient Temperature	—	—	0.029	0.010	0.001	−0.017	—	—	−0.068	−0.155	−0.070	−0.155
			0.61	0.95	0.99	0.92			0.23	0.11	0.24	0.12
Republican	1.014	1.927	0.790	1.455	1.014	2.018	−0.518	−0.917	−0.533	−0.915	−0.535	−0.913
	0.03	0.09	0.07	0.16	0.03	0.16	0.08	0.03	0.07	0.03	0.07	0.03
Dem Pres Vote	0.014	0.074	0.043	0.058	0.014	0.076	0.058	0.038	0.057	0.035	0.057	0.034
	0.58	0.20	0.07	0.03	0.59	0.18	0.02	0.25	0.01	0.26	0.02	0.28
South	−0.474	−16.656	−0.576	−14.331	−0.474	−16.652	−0.277	−1.095	−0.268	−0.956	−0.251	−0.962
	0.40	0.00	0.30	0.00	0.40	0.00	0.39	0.10	0.42	0.11	0.43	0.13
1990s	−0.136	−2.751	−0.233	−1.166	−0.122	−3.079	0.465	1.258	0.220	0.665	0.206	0.662
	0.77	0.25	0.79	0.66	0.89	0.40	0.16	0.02	0.56	0.31	0.61	0.31
2000s	−0.587	−0.996	−0.700	−1.119	−0.587	−1.056	0.536	0.986	0.226	0.235	0.203	0.229
	0.15	0.26	0.08	0.28	0.15	0.35	0.12	0.12	0.57	0.76	0.65	0.76
First Term		−0.459		−0.578		−0.460		−0.316		−0.329		−0.331
		0.47		0.35		0.47		0.28		0.27		0.28

(continued)

TABLE 5.5 (continued)

	Immigrants						Poor					
	0	1	0	1	0	1	0	1	0	1	0	1
Constant	-4.373	-6.529	-6.008	-7.201	-4.428	-5.837	-4.409	-5.213	0.657	6.461	0.901	6.486
	0.00	0.00	0.07	0.34	0.19	0.47	0.01	0.01	0.88	0.37	0.85	0.39
N	500		500		500		500		500		500	
Wald's Chi²	988.6		1,429.7		1,030.9		34.6		38.1		38.6	
Pseudo-R^2	0.0903		0.0536		0.0904		0.0681		0.0743		0.0743	

Note: Coefficients calculated using generalized ordered logistic regression, with First Term modeled as a parallel proportional term and the rest of the independent variables modeled as partial proportional terms. Standard errors are clustered by member, and *p*-values are in gray. Model 0 represents the likelihood of a shift from no advocacy to superficial or primary/secondary advocacy, and Model 1 is no advocacy or superficial advocacy to primary/secondary advocacy.

Senators from the South are significantly less likely to form a primary or secondary reputation as advocates for immigrants, but geography does not have a significant effect on the formation of a reputation that at least reaches the level of superficial advocacy. However, southern senators are no more or less likely to have a reputation as an advocate for the poor, which makes another departure from the dynamics of reputation formation in the House. Democratic-leaning states are more likely to produce senators that openly work to benefit the poor at some level of advocacy, though not primary/secondary advocates in particular, while partisan leaning does not have a significant effect on immigrant advocacy.

5.3.4 Women

Table 5.6 shows the estimated effects of group size and ambient temperature on the likelihood that a senator will have a reputation for advocating on behalf of women. The initial pattern that stands out in these models is that the percentage of women in a state has a significant and negative relationship with senator reputation as a women's advocate. As discussed in the previous chapter, women are the only disadvantaged group being considered here whose representation should *not* be dependent upon group size, as women consistently make up roughly 50 percent of the population in each state (give or take about two percentage points). This means that in every state, women are a strong electoral force, and the very small variation across states should have no effect on that. Thus, the fact that the percentage of women in a state has not just a significant relationship, but a significant *negative* relationship, is at first perplexing. After a more in-depth examination, however, it can be seen that this result is masking other dynamics at work.

In Table 5.6, group size essentially serves as an inadvertent proxy for descriptive representation. The states with the highest percentage of women also happen to be states that tend not to elect women to serve in the Senate. The three states with the highest concentration of women – Mississippi, Alabama, and Pennsylvania – have never elected a woman to the US Senate, as of the 2018 elections.[6] Out of the ten states included in this analysis with the highest percentage of women, six of them have never

---

[6] There have been two women that were appointed to serve in the Senate from the state of Alabama. The first, Dixie Bibb Graves, served only four months in the late 1930s after being appointed by her husband to hold the seat and did not compete in the special election. The second woman, Maryon Pittman Allen, was appointed in 1978 after her husband, Senator James Allen, died in office. Allen did run for the seat, but was defeated in the primary, and resigned immediately after the election, having only served for five months.

TABLE 5.6 *Group size, ambient temperature, and member reputation for advocacy for women*

	Women					
	0	1	0	1	0	1
Group Size	−0.115	−0.715	−	−	−0.114	−0.739
	0.69	0.05			0.70	0.04
Ambient Temperature	−	−	0.004	0.037	−0.003	0.049
			0.95	0.55	0.96	0.52
Republican	−0.273	−0.479	−0.305	−0.429	−0.276	−0.396
	0.48	0.49	0.43	0.50	0.48	0.58
Dem Pres Vote	0.059	0.129	0.054	0.098	0.059	0.136
	0.02	0.00	0.03	0.01	0.02	0.00
South	−0.364	1.364	−0.439	0.632	−0.362	1.320
	0.48	0.21	0.37	0.49	0.48	0.23
1990s	0.839	0.513	0.819	0.064	0.839	0.523
	0.02	0.41	0.03	0.90	0.02	0.39
2000s	0.159	0.096	0.138	−0.450	0.171	−0.143
	0.65	0.86	0.68	0.25	0.63	0.77
First Term	−0.690		−0.694		−0.693	
	0.05		0.05		0.05	
Constant	0.796	26.104	−4.916	−9.995	0.889	24.312
	0.96	0.15	0.17	0.02	0.96	0.18
N	500		500		500	
Wald's Chi^2	39.7		49.6		42.1	
Pseudo-R^2	0.093		0.0825		0.0946	

Note: Coefficients calculated using generalized ordered logistic regression, with First Term modeled as a parallel proportional term and the rest of the independent variables modeled as partial proportional terms. Standard errors are clustered by member, and p-values are in gray. Model 0 represents the likelihood of a shift from no advocacy to superficial or primary/secondary advocacy, and Model 1 is no advocacy or superficial advocacy to primary/secondary advocacy.

elected a woman to serve in the Senate, and one of them, Massachusetts, only elected a woman to the Senate for the first time in 2012.[7]

---

[7] The ten states with the highest percentage of women, from highest to lowest, are Mississippi, Alabama, Pennsylvania, New York, Rhode Island, Massachusetts, West Virginia, Louisiana, Missouri, and Tennessee. Elizabeth Warren is the female senator that was elected by the state of Massachusetts in 2012.

Though untangling the tantalizing riddle of why this negative relationship between the percentage of women in a state and actually electing women to the Senate exists is beyond the scope of this project, its effects are clearly visible. In the Senate, just as in the House, female representatives are markedly and significantly more likely to build reputations as women's advocates than male representatives. Once the presence of female senators is taken into account, the coefficient showing the estimated effects of group size loses significance. Though the precise effects of descriptive representation across groups are examined in more detail later in the chapter, models retaining all present variables while also adding an indicator that denotes the senator's gender can be found in Table C-1 of the Appendix.

Table 5.6 also reveals that, once again, ambient temperature does not have a statistically significant effect on a senator's choice to build a reputation as a women's advocate. Given that there is very little variation across states and districts in their gender composition, ambient temperature toward women within a state would be expected to play an even larger role in a senator's decision-making when seeking to build their legislative reputations than might be the case for other disadvantaged groups. This is, in fact, the dynamic that is present in the House, where an increase in the ambient temperature makes members more likely to have a reputation as a women's advocate, even when considered jointly with group size. But this is not the case in the Senate, where, as with the other groups analyzed here, reputations as women's advocates are driven by factors outside of the ambient temperature toward women within the state. Additionally, a senator's party affiliation does not have a significant effect on member reputation, but senators representing states that lean Democratic are more likely to have a reputation as an advocate for women.

5.3.5 Discussion

In each of these cases, when considering those who build reputations as advocates for any one of these disadvantaged groups, the nonsignificant impact of state ambient temperature on those decisions is an important and noteworthy departure from what was seen in the House. The initial hypotheses laid out in Chapter 2 indicate that in states that feel more warmly toward a particular disadvantaged group, a senator should be more likely to incorporate advocacy on that group's behalf into their legislative reputation, but this is not what these results show. Instead, ambient temperature has no appreciable effect on the reputation a senator chooses to build.

The disparity in effects of group size on senator reputation between the House and the Senate are also critically important for understanding the different forces driving the representation of disadvantaged groups in each of the two chambers. In the House, the size of a disadvantaged group in a district had a significant effect on member reputation for nearly every group (except for women). Thus, in the House, there is a strong dyadic relationship between how many of a representative's constituents belong to a disadvantaged group, and the intentional effort put in on their behalf.

In the Senate, however, the strength of this dyad appears to rest upon how generally deserving of government assistance a group is broadly perceived to be. For the two groups included in the analysis with a high level of perceived deservingness – veterans and seniors – and one of the groups with a more mixed level of perceived deservingness – immigrants – their size within a state has an important impact on the likelihood that a senator will build a reputation as an advocate on their behalf. But for racial/ethnic minorities, the LGBTQ community, and the poor – groups with generally mixed or lower levels of perceived deservingness of government assistance – variations in the size of their group within a state do not have a significant effect on a member's decision to include advocating for them in their legislative reputation.

So far, this analysis has demonstrated that while the reputations that members choose to build as disadvantaged-group advocates in the House are significantly impacted by the size and ambient temperature toward that group, senators tend to rely on other factors to make their decisions, especially for groups that are not broadly considered to be deserving of government assistance. But if group size and ambient temperature tend not to be significant elements in the decision to craft a reputation as an advocate for disadvantaged groups, what is? Next, I turn to the institutional and electoral factors that contribute to reputation formation in the US Senate.

5.4 ALTERNATIVE DRIVERS OF REPUTATION FORMATION IN THE US SENATE

In this section, I pursue three alternative explanations to explore the extent to which certain elements of the institutional and electoral environment can take precedence over constituency-specific factors for senators making decisions about whether or not to actively include disadvantaged groups within their legislative reputations. Specifically, I will evaluate the following hypotheses: the *electoral insecurity hypothesis*, the *in-state differentiation hypothesis*, and the *collective amplification hypothesis*.[8]

5.4.1 Electoral Insecurity

Almost as a rule, most members of Congress tend to be fairly risk-averse – they do not want to take actions that have a high likelihood of jeopardizing their chance at being reelected – but this caution is even stronger within the Senate (Schiller, 2000b). On average, incumbent senators have a lower probability of getting reelected than an incumbent member of the House (Jacobson, 2013). Senators are not oblivious to this fact – they know that they are more likely to face a competitive race during their next election cycle, and they make strategic choices in their legislative behavior to try to position themselves as well as possible for that fight. Given this risk-avoidant environment, it is possible that only the senators who perceive themselves to have the safest seats are willing to take the risk of focusing at least some of their legislative reputation around serving disadvantaged groups – especially those that are considered to be less deserving of government assistance.

The *electoral insecurity hypothesis* builds off of these assumptions, and predicts that the closer a senator's previous election, the less likely they are to want to be known as an advocate of the disadvantaged. Senators who survived a "close call" in their last election spend more time looking over their shoulder, and may be less inclined to take the chance of alienating constituents in their state who are less comfortable with members of a given disadvantaged group. In the next section, I evaluate this hypothesis by examining the impact of a senator's state vote share in their most recent election on the likelihood that they will have chosen to build a reputation as a disadvantaged-group advocate.

5.4.2 In-State Differentiation

In her book *Partners and Rivals*, Wendy Schiller argues that senators seek to differentiate themselves from their same-state counterparts by crafting intentionally distinctive reputations for subject-matter expertise within the institution. She demonstrates this both through case studies and by

---

[8] For a deeper comparison and to further illustrate the differences in the institutional and electoral environments between the House and the Senate, a replication of the analysis of the electoral insecurity hypothesis and the collective amplification hypothesis in the House of Representatives, as well as a short discussion, can be found in Appendix D.

comparing the legislative similarity of same-state senators across measures such as roll-call votes, committee assignments, and bill cosponsorship, and finds that the legislative pairings of these same-state senators rarely mirror one another. By this logic, same-state senators should also be less likely to form legislative reputations as advocates for the same disadvantaged group. However, the degree to which Schiller's argument can be expanded to shed additional light on a senator's decision to include disadvantaged-group advocacy within their legislative reputation is an open question.

During the over two decades that they served together, California senators Barbara Boxer (D) and Diane Feinstein (D) could be an example of this sort of differentiation when it comes to disadvantaged-group advocacy. During her time in the House, Sen. Boxer had already begun developing a reputation as a primary advocate for women, which she continued when she reached the Senate. But despite being a woman herself and coming from a state where such advocacy was clearly not discouraged, Sen. Feinstein developed a legislative reputation that did not include prominent advocacy for women's issues. This is what would be expected if same-state senators intentionally chose not to develop the same advocacy reputations. As a counter example, though, citizens of Ohio were represented in the 1990s by two senators, John Glenn (D) and Howard Metzenbaum (D), who both had developed legislative reputations as superficial advocates for women.

A primary reason for this uncertainty is that disadvantaged-group advocacy is not always a conventional subset of subject-matter expertise in the way that crime, environmental, or tax policy would be. Disadvantaged-group advocacy can span a huge range of issues and subject areas, and is only occasionally tethered to a singular committee or area of expertise. For example, during a conversation about how members think about their advocacy, one staffer for a member with a reputation for women's advocacy outright rejected the notion that there exists a single set of "women's issues." They explained that women's concerns are instead incorporated into the broader subject matter that the member focuses on, such as labor or healthcare. Former Kansas Sen. Bob Dole (R) provides another illustration of the distinction between group advocacy and subject-matter expertise. Before his time as a Republican presidential candidate or Senate Majority Leader, Bob Dole was known as an expert on agriculture policy. But within that context, he also built a reputation as an advocate for people in poverty through his concentrated efforts to expand the food stamp program.

Given these important differences between policy-domain expertise and group advocacy, it is worth investigating whether or not a senator takes into account their same-state counterpart's reputation for disadvantaged-group advocacy when making decisions about their own reputation, in the same way that they would take into account their counterpart's subject-matter specialization. The *in-state differentiation hypothesis* predicts that senators with a same-state counterpart who has integrated advocacy for a given disadvantaged group into their legislative reputation will be less likely to have one themselves. To evaluate this hypothesis, I include in the analysis a categorical variable denoting the type of reputation for group advocacy held by a senator's same-state counterpart.[9]

5.4.3 Collective Amplification

Toddlers, teenagers, and frankly most human beings, are more likely to do something if the people around them are doing it as well. This is particularly true for actions that are potentially risky. A child who has never leapt off a diving board is more likely to take the plunge after watching their friends jump and emerge from the water unscathed. Drivers on the interstate are more likely to exceed the speed limit if the cars around them are speeding as well. So too it may be for senators facing the decision to cultivate a legislative reputation as a disadvantaged-group advocate.

The *collective amplification hypothesis* predicts that as the total number of disadvantaged-group advocates within the institution increases, other senators will be more likely to incorporate at least a superficial level of advocacy for that group into their legislative reputations as well. As more senators feel comfortable crafting a reputation that includes advocating for a given disadvantaged group, perceptions of the risk associated with including such advocacy into one's legislative reputation may decline, leading others to then do the same. To evaluate this hypothesis, I add a variable for the number of other senators with a reputation for advocacy for each disadvantaged group in a given Congress.

5.5 INSTITUTIONAL ENVIRONMENT, ELECTORAL HISTORY, AND REPUTATION FORMATION

In this section, the three alternative hypotheses described above are tested by incorporating the relevant variables into the same generalized ordered

---

[9] I also performed an analysis of the impact of same-party, same-state reputation building in the US Senate, to explore the alternative possibility that the effect of same-state group advocates is conditioned by partisanship. Including this measure did not produce appreciably different results than that of same-state reputation building.

logistic regression models utilized above. To evaluate the impact of these additional variables on senator reputation relative to that of the constituency variables previously described, I estimate these effects of the institutional and electoral variables both independently and all together. The results of these models are displayed in Tables 5.7–5.10.

5.5.1 Veterans and Seniors

Table 5.7 displays the effects of these additional institutional and electoral variables on the likelihood of a senator having a reputation as an advocate for seniors and veterans. For both of these cases, a senator's vote share from their most recent election does not significantly impact their choice to serve as an advocate. This implies that, at least when advocacy for these groups is considered, the electoral insecurity hypothesis is not supported. However, because veterans and seniors are generally considered to be broadly deserving of government assistance, it is not unexpected that the negative effects of electoral insecurity would be attenuated – the positive regard with which these groups are held creates a relatively low-risk advocacy environment. Of the two variables representing the advocacy environment within the institution, only one has a statistically significant relationship with senator reputation. As the number of senators who incorporate advocacy for veterans and seniors increases, there is an increased likelihood that other senators will follow suit, at least at the superficial advocacy level. Having a same-state counterpart with a reputation as an advocate for veterans and seniors, however, has no effect on reputation formation. These models provide support for the collective amplification hypothesis, but not the same-state differentiation hypothesis. This evidence of the significance of the institutional advocacy context provides an important layer to understanding when and why senators form reputations as advocates for veterans and seniors, but it also does not eliminate the importance of the district constituency effects – group size remains a significant driver of the choice to incorporate this advocacy at least at a superficial level.

5.5.2 LGBTQ and Racial/Ethnic Minorities

Models estimating the effects of electoral insecurity and institutional advocacy context on senator reputation as an advocate for racial/ethnic minorities and the LGBTQ community are given in Table 5.8. Here too, a senator's vote share in the previous election does not significantly impact a senator's decision to cultivate a reputation as a group advocate. Once

TABLE 5.7 *Institutional, electoral, and constituency effects on member reputation for advocacy for veterans and seniors*

	Veterans						Seniors					
	0	1	0	1	0	1	0	1	0	1	0	1
Total Advocates	0.167	−0.083	—	—	0.167	−0.222	0.061	−0.003	—	—	0.062	−0.017
	0.05	0.64			0.05	0.56	0.03	0.96			0.03	0.77
Same State Advocate	0.163	−0.697	—	—	0.190	−0.585	0.086	−0.394	—	—	0.103	−0.505
	0.64	0.31			0.59	0.43	0.67	0.30			0.60	0.24
Previous Vote Share	—	—	−0.015	−0.029	−0.011	−0.063	—	—	0.014	−0.043	0.015	−0.053
			0.49	0.54	0.61	0.45			0.36	0.23	0.35	0.14
Group Size	0.313	0.369	0.316	0.379	0.310	0.295	0.023	−0.053	0.023	0.010	0.023	0.015
	0.00	0.16	0.00	0.24	0.01	0.36	0.06	0.68	0.05	0.86	0.05	0.66
Ambient Temperature	−0.051	0.087	−0.053	0.022	−0.055	0.117	−0.006	−0.008	−0.006	−0.006	−0.003	−0.036
	0.347	0.665	0.34	0.91	0.29	0.62	0.933	0.945	0.93	0.96	0.97	0.74
Republican	−0.744	−1.081	−0.690	−0.946	−0.741	−0.896	−0.687	−2.150	−0.783	−2.162	−0.690	−2.394
	0.06	0.39	0.09	0.33	0.06	0.47	0.07	0.01	0.04	0.01	0.07	0.01
Dem Pres Vote	−0.001	−0.038	0.005	−0.031	0.000	−0.025	−0.001	0.003	−0.011	0.032	−0.001	0.020
	0.96	0.64	0.87	0.63	0.99	0.79	0.97	0.94	0.53	0.46	0.97	0.65
South	0.050	0.005	0.086	0.452	0.093	−0.113	−0.010	0.757	−0.020	0.740	−0.040	1.082
	0.91	1.00	0.84	0.50	0.82	0.92	0.98	0.23	0.96	0.23	0.91	0.10

(continued)

TABLE 5.7 (continued)

	Veterans						Seniors					
	0	1	0	1	0	1	0	1	0	1	0	1
1990s	-0.391	0.208	-0.964	0.083	-0.440	0.408	-0.010	-0.418	-0.506	-0.620	0.051	-0.691
	0.53	0.91	0.12	0.97	0.48	0.83	0.98	0.59	0.06	0.19	0.89	0.37
2000s	-1.059	-1.534	-1.954	-1.569	-1.042	-1.960	–		–		–	
	0.19	0.19	0.00	0.29	0.21	0.17						
First Term	-1.115		-1.166		-1.152		-0.474		-0.473		-0.431	
	0.08		0.07		0.07		0.29		0.29		0.32	
Constant	-2.948	-10.854	-0.896	-6.971	-2.484	-10.480	-2.072	-1.163	-0.442	-2.952	-2.668	0.491
	0.46	0.52	0.82	0.59	0.52	0.51	0.73	0.90	0.94	0.76	0.64	0.96
N	500		500		500		400		400		400	
Wald's Chi²	74.0		45.7		71.4		41.1		28.9		38.1	
Pseudo-R²	0.0875		0.0659		0.0941		0.0709		0.0655		0.0832	

Note: Coefficients calculated using generalized ordered logistic regression, with First Term modeled as a parallel proportional term and the rest of the independent variables modeled as partial proportional terms. Standard errors are clustered by member, and p-values are in gray. Model 0 represents the likelihood of a shift from no advocacy to superficial or primary/secondary advocacy, and Model 1 is no advocacy or superficial advocacy to primary/secondary advocacy. Feeling thermometer questions for seniors were not included in the ANES of the 2010s, so the decade base category for seniors is the 2000s.

TABLE 5.8 *Institutional, electoral, and constituency effects on member reputation for advocacy for racial/ethnic minorities and the LGBTQ community*

	LGBTQ					Race/Ethnicity			
	logit	*logit*	*logit*	0	1	0	1	0	1
Total Advocates	0.880 (0.04)	–	–	0.902 (0.03)	0.251 (0.10)	1.249 (0.48)	–	0.188 (0.23)	3.262 (0.16)
Same State Advocate	–	–	–	-0.055 (0.92)	0.018 (0.99)	–	–	0.096 (0.84)	7.033 (0.24)
Previous Vote Share	–	-0.006 (0.81)	-0.012 (0.57)	–	–	0.040 (0.10)	-0.060 (0.58)	0.035 (0.17)	-0.369 (0.26)
Group Size	-3.251 (0.30)	-1.827 (0.46)	-3.270 (0.30)	0.009 (0.49)	0.018 (0.72)	0.009 (0.49)	-0.025 (0.38)	0.014 (0.29)	-0.069 (0.28)
Ambient Temperature	0.062 (0.50)	0.055 (0.56)	0.063 (0.50)	0.071 (0.48)	0.440 (0.38)	0.069 (0.49)	0.459 (0.52)	0.037 (0.72)	2.123 (0.16)
Republican	-0.534 (0.60)	-0.619 (0.54)	-0.544 (0.59)	0.477 (0.31)	0.751 (0.51)	0.582 (0.22)	-2.361 (0.43)	0.795 (0.11)	-6.477 (0.33)
Dem Pres Vote	0.119 (0.04)	0.085 (0.03)	0.124 (0.03)	0.052 (0.16)	0.146 (0.74)	0.045 (0.15)	0.038 (0.51)	0.052 (0.19)	0.677 (0.23)
South	-0.665 (0.52)	-0.650 (0.52)	-0.617 (0.55)	-1.155 (0.05)	-12.287 (0.00)	-1.308 (0.03)	-15.899 (0.00)	-1.151 (0.06)	-13.657 (0.00)

(continued)

TABLE 5.8 (continued)

	LGBTQ					Race/Ethnicity				
	logit	*logit*	*logit*	0	1	0	1	1	0	1
1990s	0.384	-0.393	0.400	0.837	10.763	2.580	20.795		0.929	5.612
	0.83	0.85	0.83	0.60	0.30	0.03	0.00		0.58	0.49
2000s	1.559	-0.189	1.635	0.906	10.962	1.616	15.815		0.892	0.976
	0.20	0.89	0.19	0.48	0.11	0.17	0.00		0.49	0.92
First Term	-0.803	-0.959	-0.834		-0.927			-0.817		-0.516
	0.38	0.32	0.37		0.15			0.22		0.45
Constant	-14.450	-9.236	-14.603	-12.547	-60.532	-12.591	-51.859		-11.070	-196.836
	0.01	0.13	0.01	0.09	0.27	0.09	0.31		0.13	0.13
N	500	500	500	500		500			500	
Wald's Chi^2	13.8	14.4	19.2	1,631.7		769.3			3,221.8	
Pseudo-R^2	0.1166	0.0915	0.1177	0.1577		0.1553			0.2261	

Note: Coefficients for LGBTQ are estimated using logistic regression, as necessitated by the bivariate coding of the LGBTQ advocacy reputation variable. Coefficients for racial/ethnic minorities are calculated using generalized ordered logistic regression, with First Term modeled as a parallel proportional term and the rest of the independent variables modeled as partial proportional terms. Standard errors are clustered by member, and p-values are in gray. Model 0 represents the likelihood of a shift from no advocacy to superficial or primary/secondary advocacy, and Model 1 is no advocacy or superficial advocacy to primary/secondary advocacy. Presence of same-state advocate is omitted from the LGBTQ models due to perfect prediction; there are no states for which both senators have reputations as LGBTQ advocates.

again, the electoral insecurity hypothesis is not supported. While this was not unexpected when considering advocacy on behalf of groups with a high level of perceived deservingness, the context of advocacy for groups like racial/ ethnic minorities and the LGBTQ community is where electoral insecurity should have its strongest effects. Instead, models imply that relative electoral marginality is not a pivotal factor that senators use to make decisions about the reputations they craft as disadvantaged-group advocates.

While electoral insecurity is insignificant across each of the models estimated in Table 5.8, the institutional advocacy context variables do not have the same effect on the likelihood of having a reputation as a racial/ethnic minority advocate as they do reputations for LGBTQ advocacy. The decision to craft a reputation as an advocate for racial/ ethnic minorities is not significantly impacted by the number of other senators with reputations as minority advocates nor by the presence of a same-state advocate. The decision to form a reputation as an LGBTQ advocate, however, is significantly related to the number of other advocates within the institution, providing further support for the collective amplification hypothesis.

5.5.3 Immigrants and the Poor

Table 5.9 displays the coefficients demonstrating the estimated effects of electoral insecurity and the institutional advocacy context on the likelihood of a senator having a reputation as an advocate for immigrants and the poor. Across all of these models, the effects of partisanship on senator reputation retain their significance, as does the effect of the percentage of immigrants within a state. Senators from more Democratic-leaning states also remain more likely to have at least a superficial reputation as an advocate for the poor. However, a senator's previous vote share yet again does not exhibit a significant effect on the choice to build a reputation as a group advocate.

The presence of a same-state senator with a reputation as an advocate for immigrants or the poor once again does not have a significant effect on senator reputation, and thus fails to provide support for the same-state differentiation hypothesis. Additionally, while having a larger number of other senators who are actively known as immigrant advocates does not have a significant impact on the choice to build a reputation as an advocate for immigrants, it does significantly enhance the chances that a senator will have a reputation as at least a superficial advocate for the poor, providing mixed support between these two cases for the collective amplification hypothesis.

TABLE 5.9 *Institutional, electoral, and constituency effects on reputation for advocacy for immigrants and the poor*

	Immigrants						Poor					
	0	1	0	1	0	1	0	1	0	1	0	1
Total Advocates	0.166	1.543	—	—	0.174	1.653	0.099	0.055	—	—	0.098	0.055
	0.58	0.15			0.56	0.25	0.02	0.29			0.02	0.30
Same State Advocate	0.271	0.290	—	—	0.279	0.543	0.238	0.202	—	—	0.231	0.204
	0.52	0.67			0.51	0.67	0.12	0.33			0.13	0.33
Previous Vote Share	—	—	0.029	0.042	0.029	0.047	—	—	0.008	0.000	0.006	-0.002
			0.09	0.28	0.09	0.60			0.55	0.98	0.70	0.91
Group Size	0.104	-0.108	0.114	-0.063	0.114	-0.097	-0.002	0.001	-0.008	-0.003	-0.003	0.000
	0.01	0.64	0.00	0.73	0.00	0.66	0.97	0.98	0.86	0.96	0.95	1.00
Ambient Temperature	0.002	-0.165	-0.003	-0.013	-0.002	-0.167	-0.063	-0.149	-0.069	-0.158	-0.062	-0.152
	0.98	0.36	0.96	0.93	0.97	0.35	0.30	0.14	0.24	0.11	0.30	0.14
Republican	0.984	2.423	1.075	2.035	1.046	1.978	-0.510	-0.887	-0.534	-0.900	-0.509	-0.873
	0.04	0.18	0.03	0.20	0.03	0.55	0.08	0.03	0.07	0.03	0.09	0.04
Dem Pres Vote	0.012	0.094	0.014	0.073	0.011	0.081	0.061	0.038	0.056	0.034	0.061	0.037
	0.67	0.26	0.58	0.19	0.67	0.33	0.03	0.29	0.02	0.29	0.03	0.31
South	-0.448	-16.794	-0.467	-15.305	-0.439	-16.764	-0.234	-0.905	-0.265	-0.954	-0.244	-0.893
	0.44	0.00	0.40	0.00	0.44	0.00	0.46	0.17	0.41	0.14	0.45	0.17

(continued)

1990s	0.522	−1.287	−0.085	−2.984	0.591	−0.638	−0.562	0.209	0.211	0.654	−0.555	0.201
	0.73	0.71	0.92	0.40	0.69	0.89	0.24	0.79	0.60	0.33	0.24	0.80
2000s	0.081	4.707	−0.652	−1.309	0.042	4.964	−0.476	−0.143	0.189	0.200	−0.481	−0.162
	0.95	0.26	0.12	0.30	0.97	0.34	0.34	0.87	0.68	0.80	0.34	0.86
First Term	−0.448		−0.388		−0.369		−0.247		−0.299		−0.227	
	0.48		0.54		0.55		0.43		0.32		0.46	
Constant	−5.891	−13.363	−4.875	−6.725	−6.395	−14.427	−1.670	−0.247	0.758	6.726	−1.753	5.156
	0.18	0.17	0.14	0.35	0.14	0.20	0.75	0.43	0.88	0.38	0.74	0.53
N	500		500		500		500		500		500	
Wald's Chi^2	1,247.0		970.1		1,539.6		59.4		39.6		60.1	
Pseudo-R^2	0.1053		0.0980		0.1129		0.0864		0.0751		0.0868	

Note: Coefficients calculated using generalized ordered logistic regression, with First Term modeled as a parallel proportional term and the rest of the independent variables modeled as partial proportional terms. Standard errors are clustered by member, and *p*-values are in gray. Model 0 represents the likelihood of a shift from no advocacy to superficial or primary/secondary advocacy, and Model 1 is no advocacy or superficial advocacy to primary/secondary advocacy.

5.5.4 Women

Table 5.10 presents the models demonstrating the effects on senator reputation as a women's advocate for each of the institutional, electoral, and constituency factors introduced to this point.

These models show that senators representing more Democratic-leaning states remain significantly more likely to have a reputation as an advocate for women, and that the percentage of women within a state retains its significant effect.[10] As has been the case for all groups for which advocacy on their behalf has been examined, the models also indicate that variation in a senator's vote share from their most recent election does not have a significant effect on member reputation. These models do, however, provide further support for the collective amplification hypothesis, as evidenced by the significant effect that the total number of women's advocates has on member reputation for both superficial and primary/ secondary advocacy.

5.5.5 Discussion

None of these models demonstrating the relative impact of these institutional, electoral, and constituency factors on senator reputation as a disadvantaged-group advocate support the electoral insecurity hypothesis. Regardless of the particular group that senators are known as advocating for, their vote share in their most recent election does not have a significant effect on the choice to craft such a reputation.[11] At first look, this result is surprising. Most senators face a more heterogeneous electorate than members of the House, and the average Senate election is more competitive than the average House election. Because it is less likely that a single constituent group will dominate in a state in the same way as in a congressional district, it becomes even more important to be sure that representational decisions on behalf of one group do not inadvertently raise the ire of another. But to understand the lack of support for the

---

[10] Again, this significant result is most likely due to the curious correlation between states with the highest percentage of women and states who have never sent a woman to the Senate (as discussed in more detail earlier in the chapter). Because of this, group size is essentially serving as a proxy for descriptive representation, as can be seen in Table C-1 of the Appendix and in Table 5.12.

[11] I also ran these analyses using Cook's Partisan Voter Index (PVI) as a measure of marginality in place of the senator's previous vote share, and the results are not appreciably changed.

TABLE 5.10 *Institutional, electoral, and constituency effects on member reputation for advocacy for women*

	Women					
	0	1	0	1	0	1
Total	0.167	0.276	–	–	0.167	0.265
Advocates	0.00	0.03			0.00	0.04
Same State	–0.087	–0.371	–	–	–0.114	–0.354
Advocate	0.67	0.23			0.58	0.23
Previous	–	–	–0.019	0.002	–0.019	–0.004
Vote Share			0.37	0.95	0.38	0.88
Group	–0.176	–0.953	–0.102	–0.798	–0.172	–0.950
Size	0.56	0.03	0.73	0.05	0.57	0.02
Ambient	–0.005	0.051	–0.006	0.071	–0.007	0.067
Temperature	0.93	0.55	0.92	0.36	0.90	0.41
Republican	–0.215	–0.125	–0.277	–0.579	–0.218	–0.293
	0.58	0.87	0.48	0.46	0.57	0.73
Dem Pres	0.076	0.181	0.061	0.134	0.079	0.177
Vote	0.01	0.01	0.02	0.00	0.01	0.00
South	–0.277	1.553	–0.332	1.362	–0.231	1.542
	0.59	0.21	0.50	0.21	0.65	0.18
1990s	–0.658	–1.661	0.813	0.609	–0.673	–1.539
	0.15	0.11	0.02	0.31	0.15	0.15
2000s	–0.035	–0.211	0.216	–0.249	0.008	–0.313
	0.92	0.77	0.54	0.59	0.98	0.62
First	–0.651		–0.770		–0.726	
Term	0.06		0.03		0.04	
Constant	1.588	29.493	0.689	26.228	1.640	28.898
	0.92	0.14	0.97	0.17	0.92	0.14
N	500		500		500	
Wald's Chi^2	45.7		45.9		50.2	
Pseudo-R^2	0.1132		0.0988		0.1166	

Note: Coefficients calculated using generalized ordered logistic regression, with First Term modeled as a parallel proportional term and the rest of the independent variables modeled as partial proportional terms. Standard errors are clustered by member, and p-values are in gray. Model 0 represents the likelihood of a shift from no advocacy to superficial or primary/secondary advocacy, and Model 1 is no advocacy or superficial advocacy to primary/secondary advocacy.

electoral insecurity hypothesis, it is important to keep in mind what these results do and do not show.

The insignificance of a senator's most recent vote share to the reputations they form demonstrates that close reelections themselves do not actively turn a senator off from building a reputation as a disadvantaged-group advocate, even for those groups that are generally viewed more skeptically in American society. It does not imply, however, that reelection concerns play no role in reputation formation. These models are also compatible with a circumstance in which, particularly for groups that are not considered to be highly deserving of government assistance, there is no electoral margin that is "safe" enough to push a senator to form a reputation as a disadvantaged-group advocate in the absence of incentives from other factors. This makes the lack of support for the electoral insecurity hypothesis particularly important, because it implies that a senator's decisions about the electoral risk of their reputational decisions may be untethered to the reality of their electoral situation.

These models also do not provide support for the same-state differentiation hypothesis. There is no evidence, for any of the group advocacy reputations evaluated, that senators are less likely to decide to build a reputation as a disadvantaged-group advocate on account of their same-state senator being known for similar advocacy work. This serves to demonstrate how unique disadvantaged-group advocacy is relative to more subject-matter specific specializations. These results also actually emphasize the importance of considering representation as a reputation built over time by an assortment of actions (over which a senator has a wide range of latitude), rather than a specific set of policy preferences or predetermined types of member behavior.

The collective amplification hypothesis, however, receives strong support. Women, the poor, the LGBTQ community, veterans, and seniors are significantly more likely to gain additional senators as advocates for their needs as the number of advocates within the institution increases.[12] Note that this effect was present in a model that controlled for underlying public opinion toward the group. Having higher numbers of senators who include disadvantaged-group advocacy in their legislative reputation not only provides an example to other senators that it can be "safe" to do so, it also raises the salience of issues relevant to these groups. The level of advocacy where the greatest increase is seen is superficial advocacy.

---

[12] Operationalizing other group advocates within the institution as the number of primary or secondary advocates in a given Senate produces similar results.

Superficial advocates are rarely those who take it upon themselves to insert a disadvantaged group's needs into the conversation, and instead frequently piggyback off of the actions of others, whether through cosponsorship or some other partnering. Thus, it is perfectly reasonable that as the number of other senators with reputations for advocacy goes up, more senators could be induced to join them.

Women's advocates are particularly unique in this, because the boost in the number of other senators with reputations for women's advocacy occurs both for superficial advocates as well as for primary and secondary advocates. This implies that the presence of other advocates within the Senate does not just push others to jump on board with less frequent or lower-key actions like cosponsorship, but rather encourages them to take up a greater role in pushing for the needs and interests of women. In sum, out of all three of these alternative hypotheses, only the collective amplification hypothesis is supported by these models.

5.6 DESCRIPTIVE REPRESENTATION AND REPUTATION FORMATION IN THE US SENATE

As discussed in Chapters 2 and 3, personal experiences as a member of a disadvantaged group may make a legislator more determined to address some of the challenges group members face, and can also serve as a shortcut for crafting a reputation as a credible group advocate. In the House, descriptive representatives – those who are themselves a member of a disadvantaged group – are significantly more likely to form a reputation as an advocate for nearly all disadvantaged groups under consideration (immigrants and seniors being the exceptions). It is expected that descriptive representation will boost the likelihood that a representative will have a reputation as a disadvantaged-group advocate in the Senate as well. Given the amount of leeway that senators possess relative to a member of the House in establishing their legislative reputations, those personal experiences as a member of a disadvantaged group may even have an outsized influence in pushing a senator to form a reputation as an advocate. In this section, I specifically examine that relationship, and estimate the impact of being a descriptive representative on the likelihood of a senator building a reputation as a disadvantaged-group advocate.[13]

---

[13] The coding scheme for descriptive representatives matches that used in the analysis of members of the House of Representatives, and is described in detail in Chapter 4.

5.6.1 Modeling Reputation Formation for Descriptive Representatives

Table 5.11 shows the number of descriptive representatives included in the dataset, broken down by group and level of advocacy. When looking at this table, there is one inescapable fact that must be acknowledged before moving forward in analyzing the effect of descriptive representation on senator reputation: there simply are far fewer descriptive representatives present in the Senate than in the House. This is particularly evident for descriptive representatives of groups that are considered to be anything less than highly deserving of government assistance. There are two particularly important consequences that follow from having such a small number of cases, with the first being qualitative, and the second quantitative.

First, from a qualitative perspective, these basic descriptive statistics regarding the characteristics of people present within the institution already say a great deal about some of the critical differences between the two chambers of Congress. For nearly all disadvantaged groups, descriptive representatives are less likely to successfully make it to the Senate than to the House of Representatives. This discrepancy is most egregious in the case of racial/ethnic minorities, who make up 25 percent of the sample of members of the House, but less than 5 percent of senators. While it is not a new observation that there are fewer descriptive representatives in the Senate than in the House, it has important implications for the analysis to follow.

It is beyond the scope of this current project to pin down all of the reasons for this divergence, but the fact that it exists implies that there may be systematic differences between the types of descriptive representatives that are present in the Senate relative to the House. Just under two thirds of racial/ethnic minorities in the House, for instance, have reputations as advocates for racial/ethnic minorities, compared to less than ten percent of racial/ethnic minorities in the Senate. The implication of this is that, particularly for descriptive representatives for those groups that are not broadly considered to be highly deserving of government assistance, the characteristics it takes to be successful in a Senate election may not be the same as for a House election. This important caveat is addressed in more detail below, when interpreting the results of the analysis for descriptive representatives in the Senate.

Second, from a quantitative perspective, the severely restricted number of cases changes both the best coding of the dependent variable and the type of model that is most appropriate for estimating the effects of descriptive representation. Table 5.11 shows that, among the descriptive representatives in the Senate, there are a number of types of representation for advocacy that

TABLE 5.11 *Number of members serving as advocates of disadvantaged groups across descriptive and nondescriptive representatives*

		Seniors	Veterans	Women	Poor	Immigrants	Racial/Ethnic Minorities	LGBTQ
Non-DR	Non	417	288	402	365	470	455	487
	Superficial	50	15	27	71	21	15	9
	Secondary	17	7	7	36	6	7	3
	Primary	5	0	0	2	1	0	0
	Total	489	310	436	474	498	477	499
DR	Non	9	170	28	21	0	21	0
	Superficial	2	14	17	5	2	1	0
	Secondary	0	6	11	0	0	0	0
	Primary	0	0	8	0	0	1	1
	Total	11	190	64	26	2	23	1

Senators with reputations for disadvantaged-group advocacy in the 103rd, 105th, 108th, 110th, and 113th Congress by group and descriptive representative status.

are not occupied. To account for the quantity of zeros across these individual categories, reputation is collapsed into a binary variable for the analysis of the effects of descriptive representation on reputation formation in the Senate.[14] The analysis to follow, then, uses Penalized Maximum Likelihood Estimation (PMLE) models to estimate the impact of descriptive representation on the likelihood that a member will have a reputation as a disadvantaged-group advocate at any level.[15]

5.7 THE IMPACT OF DESCRIPTIVE REPRESENTATION ON SENATOR REPUTATION

Table 5.12 presents the coefficients demonstrating the estimated effect of being a member of a disadvantaged group on the likelihood of a senator having a reputation as a group advocate. These models also include all variables incorporated in the sections above, to evaluate their relative impacts. Given the data constraints discussed above, these models should not be treated as perfect estimates, but rather as the best means available to glean important insights about the general relationship between descriptive representation and reputations for disadvantaged-group advocacy in the Senate.

---

[14] Senators with reputations as advocates for the LGBTQ community are left out of the analysis, as there is only a single LGBTQ senator included in the dataset. That senator, Tammy Baldwin (D) of Wisconsin, does herself have a primary reputation as an LGBTQ advocate. This provides anecdotal support for the contention that descriptive representatives are more likely to form reputations as advocates for the disadvantaged groups that they themselves are a part of, but there simply is not enough data to perform any statistical analysis.

[15] Even after reputation is collapsed to combine all levels of advocacy into a single category, the number of cases remains small because of the limited number of total descriptive representatives in the Senate. Given the relative rarity of the event that a senator will be a descriptive representative with a reputation for group advocacy, the data shows signs of quasi-complete separation. Quasi-complete separation occurs when, for one of the two values of a binary independent variable, the dependent variable takes on the same value. Under such conditions, maximum likelihood estimates will be biased or inestimable. Thus, for the analysis to follow, I utilize Firth's method of Penalized Maximum Likelihood Estimation (1993). This method modifies the estimate equations to reduce the degree of bias present in the model and to facilitate model convergence. Test statistics are then computed by comparing the log-likelihood values of a model in which the separated explanatory variable is constrained with the unconstrained model. (This method can sometimes result in an overcorrection of bias, which can serve to understate the substantive effects of the variable of interest.) To perform this analysis, I use Joseph Coveney's firthlogit program for Stata.

5.7.1 Veterans, Seniors, and Racial/Ethnic Minorities

The first three columns of Table 5.12 show the impact that descriptive representation in the Senate can have on the representation of groups that are broadly considered to be the most deserving of government assistance, like veterans and seniors, and those groups that are considered to be less deserving of assistance, like racial/ethnic minorities. For the highest deservingness groups, results are mixed. Veterans in the Senate are significantly more likely to form reputations as veterans' advocates, just as they were in the House. For seniors, however, entering the institution over the age of sixty-five does not make a senator more likely to serve as a senior advocate. With groups that are considered to be the most deserving of government assistance, descriptive representation is expected to be less important to a senator's decisions about the reputation they craft. The results for seniors, then, fit in with these expectations. Veterans may still be more likely to form reputations as veterans' advocates than nonveterans because of the extra credibility that is granted to them as a result of their military service. Also noteworthy is that group size remains a significant factor in member reputation as an advocate even after descriptive representation is taken into account.

For groups with lower levels of perceived deservingness of government assistance, results are vastly different from those seen in the House of Representatives. In the House, members who were themselves racial/ethnic minorities were considerably more likely to form a reputation as a minority advocate. As seen in the third column of Table 5.12, however, this significant effect is absent in the Senate. As highlighted above, this has some particularly important implications. First, this further supports the contention that there are systematic differences in the characteristics and priorities of racial/ethnic minorities who are elected to the House, relative to the Senate. Second, this difference is critical because it speaks to the representational inequalities in the Senate when it comes to racial/ethnic minorities. One of the most notable elements of Table 5.12 is that *none* of the explanatory variables included in the model have a significant, *positive* effect on a senator forming a reputation as an advocate for racial/ethnic minorities. This demonstrates that, even relative to other disadvantaged groups, racial/ethnic minorities receive especially low levels of representation, and there is not an immediately apparent means that can be pointed to of rectifying it.

TABLE 5.12 *Descriptive representatives and senator reputation for advocacy*

	Veterans		Seniors		Race/Ethnicity		Poor		Immigrants		Women	
	logit	logit	logit	logit	logit	logit	logit	logit	logit	logit	logit	logit
Total Advocates	0.160	0.160	0.057	0.056	0.234	0.242	0.092	0.092	0.144	0.144	0.208	0.216
	0.09	0.09	0.07	0.07	0.09	0.08	0.03	0.03	0.63	0.63	0.01	0.01
Same State Advocate	0.307	0.320	0.116	0.118	0.001	0.002	0.303	0.320	0.392	0.391	-0.479	-0.528
	0.37	0.35	0.60	0.60	1.00	1.00	0.08	0.06	0.31	0.31	0.10	0.08
Previous Vote Share	-0.015	-0.015	0.015	0.018	0.036	0.040	0.005	0.005	0.031	0.031	-0.007	-0.007
	0.45	0.44	0.33	0.24	0.12	0.09	0.71	0.68	0.13	0.13	0.73	0.70
Group Size	0.313	0.307	0.023	0.023	0.008	0.017	-0.002	0.000	0.098	0.098	0.142	0.117
	0.01	0.01	0.04	0.04	0.64	0.35	0.95	0.99	0.01	0.01	0.52	0.59
Descriptive Representative	0.701	6.032	0.180	115.938	0.233	48.317	-0.659	-6.126	3.883	7.615	3.688	-2.941
	0.05	0.337	0.81	0.28	0.81	0.07	0.20	0.528	0.02	0.90	0.00	0.64
Ambient Temperature	-0.048	-0.007	-0.005	0.005	0.070	0.111	-0.062	-0.069	0.006	0.006	-0.063	-0.094
	0.374	0.919	0.93	0.93	0.50	0.30	0.19	0.161	0.92	0.92	0.27	0.15
Ambient Temp. & DR	–	-0.074	–	-1.487	–	-0.739	–	0.081	–	-0.091	–	0.118
		0.40		0.28		0.08		0.57		0.94		0.30
Republican	-0.766	-0.745	-0.667	-0.659	0.512	0.578	-0.554	-0.563	0.864	0.863	0.072	0.062
	0.04	0.05	0.03	0.03	0.28	0.23	0.03	0.03	0.08	0.08	0.83	0.86

(continued)

Dem Pres Vote	-0.001	0.000	-0.001	0.002	0.052	0.055	0.057	0.057	0.000	0.001	0.054	0.055
	0.98	0.99	0.97	0.92	0.09	0.08	0.00	0.00	0.99	0.98	0.03	0.03
South	0.075	0.110	-0.003	-0.073	-1.178	-1.282	-0.218	-0.199	-0.578	-0.580	-0.714	-0.731
	0.83	0.76	0.99	0.81	0.07	0.05	0.44	0.48	0.25	0.25	0.10	0.09
1990s	-0.673	-0.614	-0.011	0.019	0.658	0.881	-0.524	-0.524	0.763	0.758	0.223	0.040
	0.30	0.35	0.98	0.96	0.64	0.55	0.29	0.29	0.58	0.58	0.79	0.96
2000s	-1.146	-1.032	–	–	0.564	0.729	-0.419	-0.420	0.018	0.012	0.543	0.431
	0.16	0.21			0.61	0.51	0.41	0.41	0.99	0.99	0.33	0.44
First Term	-0.924	-0.931	-0.345	-0.320	-0.629	-0.881	-0.156	-0.159	-0.568	-0.558	-1.518	-1.462
	0.12	0.12	0.44	0.48	0.38	0.27	0.63	0.62	0.41	0.42	0.01	0.01
Constant	-2.973	-5.993	-2.379	-3.347	-12.598	-15.860	-1.406	-0.960	-5.699	-5.701	-12.088	-9.107
	0.53	0.31	0.61	0.48	0.10	0.05	0.72	0.81	0.14	0.14	0.28	0.42
N	500	500	400	400	500	500	500	500	500	500	500	500
Wald's Chi²	20.8	21.4	18.6	18.8	18.4	20.6	43.6	43.8	23.1	25.4	78.1	79.5
Prob > Chi²	0.0538	0.0663	0.0679	0.0949	0.1034	0.0809	0.0000	0.0000	0.0267	0.0205	0.0000	0.0000

Note: Coefficients calculated using the Firth Method for penalized maximum likelihood estimation for logistic regression, using the firthlogit Stata program. *P*-values are presented in gray.

5.7.2 Immigrants, the Poor, and Women

Immigrants, women, and the poor are groups that have a more mixed position in the American psyche, and tend not to be seen as either broadly deserving or not deserving of government assistance. For these groups as well, the effects of descriptive representation are also mixed, as seen in the final three columns of Table 5.12. Senators who are themselves women and immigrants are significantly more likely to form reputations as group advocates, while those with a personal history of poverty are not. This is different from that which was seen in the House, where the impact on reputation of having personally spent time in poverty and emigrating from another country are inverted. For the poor, the lack of the significance of descriptive representation could stem from the fact that any US senator is likely to be very far removed from their days in poverty, even relative to members of the House, leaving them less connected to individuals who are currently experiencing poverty.

Immigrants, on the other hand, stand out as the only other group outside of veterans and seniors for whom group size retains its significant effect on senator reputation. Though the number of immigrants that have served in the Senate and are included in the sample is small – there are only two of them – each incorporated advocacy for immigrants into their reputations. The first, Democratic Sen. Mazie Hirono (HI), fought for benefits for Filipino service members who immigrated to the United States, and the second, Republican Sen. Mel Martinez (FL), worked to pass an immigration reform bill that included a path to citizenship for undocumented immigrants.

In both the House and the Senate, female members are significantly more likely to have a reputation as women's advocates than male members. The positive effect of more Democratic states being more likely to have a senator with a reputation as an advocate for women also retains its significance, as does the presence of additional women's advocates within the institution. Also in these models, once women in office are themselves accounted for, the percentage of women within a state loses its misleading prior significance.

5.7.3 Interactive Effects of Descriptive Representation on Reputation

As in the previous chapter, I next turn to examine the differences in the impact that ambient temperature has on descriptive representatives relative to nondescriptive representatives. As shown in the earlier analysis in this chapter, ambient temperature has not been seen to have a statistically significant effect on senator reputation, even when analyzed independently from group size or descriptive representation. Thus, the object of this analysis is to determine if ambient temperature takes on a significant role for descriptive representatives, as would be expected by the theory laid out in Chapter 2, despite these effects being masked when examining the Senate as a whole.

Figure 5.1 displays the predicted effects of ambient temperature on member reputation for senators who are themselves members of a given disadvantaged group relative to those who are not. For women's advocates, these effects in the Senate very closely resemble those of the House. Regardless of the ambient temperature toward women in a state or district, female senators and members of the House are consistently and significantly more likely to have a reputation as an advocate for women. The difference in the predicted effects of being a woman is even larger in the Senate than in the House – the predicted likelihood that a female senator will have a reputation for some level of women's advocacy is over 50 percent, compared to less than one percent for male senators.

For all other groups, the effects shown in Figure 5.1 may not be consistently statistically significant, but the trajectories of the predicted effects still provide important insight into the role of descriptive representatives as group advocates in the Senate. As can be readily seen by comparing Figures 4.2 and 5.1, for the majority of groups examined, the pattern of the effects are quite different in the Senate than in the House. In the Senate, descriptive representatives are more likely than nondescriptive representatives to build a reputation as a group advocate in instances where ambient temperature is low. However, this distinction fades when the group ambient temperature increases. This is essentially the opposite from what is seen in the House, where members who are themselves descriptive representatives become more likely to build a reputation for group advocacy as the ambient temperature in a district increases.

5.8 THE ADVOCACY WINDOW AND THE US SENATE

The analysis contained within this chapter also allows for the evaluation of the concept of the advocacy window in the context of the US Senate. The advocacy window, as introduced in Chapter 2, is a means of conceptualizing the discretion that a legislator has when making decisions about the legislative reputation they seek to cultivate. It argues that for any disadvantaged group, there is essentially a "floor" level of representation

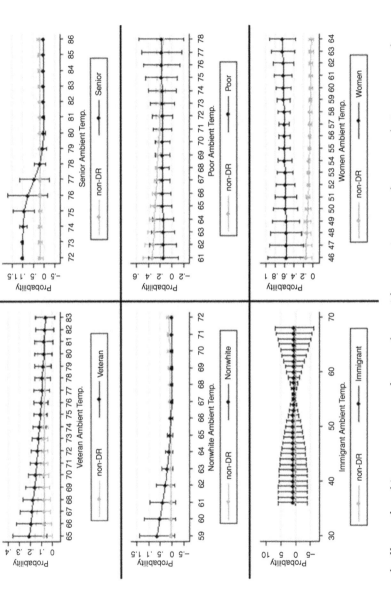

FIGURE 5.1 Predicted effects of ambient temperature for members with reputations as advocates relative to non-advocates for descriptive representatives

Note: Figures show the predicted marginal effects of ambient temperature on reputation for superficial, secondary, or primary advocacy relative to non-advocacy for members who are themselves descriptive representatives of the group and members who are not. Predicted marginal effects are calculated using Stata's margins command for the models containing interactions between descriptive representative and ambient temperature shown in Tables 5.12. All other variables are held to their mean values within the dataset. Clockwise from the top left, the groups whose representation is that is expected, and that the placement of this floor is tied to the size of the group within a state or district. There is also a "ceiling" for group representation that marks the higher end of the level of representation that will be tolerated in a given state or district, which is based on the general feelings toward a group in a state or district. If a group is popular, a legislator can devote more of their time and energy to serving the needs of those group members without provoking a negative response from the rest of the state or district as a whole (and thus without risking unnecessary electoral reprisals). If a group is unpopular in a state or district, legislators have less space in which they can exercise discretion over the amount of representation they provide without risking the ire of the majority of the state or district.

In the House, the advocacy window is a fairly effective means of conceptualizing the decisions that members make in regards to the reputations for disadvantaged-group advocacy that they choose to cultivate. For nearly all groups evaluated, the likelihood of a member having a reputation for some level of advocacy increases as the size of a group in a district increases, and as positive views toward a disadvantaged group within a district go up. Also, as per expectations, there is evidence that descriptive representatives are more likely to take advantage of a large advocacy window, especially for those groups that are generally considered to be less deserving of government assistance.

When it comes to the advocacy window, there are important differences between the House and the Senate. First, while group size played an important role in the House in determining whether or not a member would have a reputation for at least a superficial level of advocacy, in the Senate, group size plays a significant role for only a limited number of groups. Specifically, group size has the expected significant and positive effect for those groups that are broadly considered to be deserving of government assistance, like seniors and veterans. For nearly all other groups, the size of the group constituency within a state is not a significant factor.

This implies that, in the Senate, the acceptable "floor" for groups that are not held in high esteem in the country is in fact doing nothing at all. Generally speaking, there are more constituent groups that are vying for the attention of a senator than a member of the House, and any one particular group is less likely to be a dominant force in a state, compared to a congressional district. Therefore, it tends to be only the disadvantaged groups who are held in high regard who are able to command enough influence to raise the floor of their advocacy window to match their presence within the state. Other constituent groups are markedly less likely to be resentful of a senator who advocates for the veterans and seniors in their state, for example, than for other disadvantaged groups that are viewed skeptically, making it a less electorally risky choice.

Second, while group ambient temperature may well still serve as a ceiling for the potential level of representation a legislator can offer a group, hardly any senators actually aim to reach that ceiling. When evaluated independently, having a higher ambient temperature in and of itself does not make a senator more likely to form a reputation as a disadvantaged-group advocate, regardless of the group being considered. Bringing descriptive representatives into the mix, however, adds important nuance into this discussion.

In the House, descriptive representatives are generally more likely to form a reputation as a group advocate as ambient temperature goes up and the advocacy window increases in size. But in the Senate, descriptive representatives tend to invert that behavior – they are more likely to have a reputation as a group advocate when the ambient temperature in a state is low, with that advantage over nondescriptive representatives fading away as ambient temperature and the advocacy window increases. This implies that there is a fundamental difference between members of the House and the Senate in how they view their advocacy window, and when they are sparked into action.

As a general rule, for both senators and members of the House, descriptive representatives tend to be more likely to craft a reputation as a group advocate. But in the Senate, these descriptive representatives may instead be more likely to act when things feel dire – when the advocacy window is closer to closing. Senators who are themselves disadvantaged group members (especially those who are descriptive representatives for less well-regarded groups) face a constant pressure between group identity and electoral viability, and tend to be pushed into action only when they perceive the threat level against their group to be particularly high. Members of the House, on the other hand, will act when they see the greatest opportunity at the lowest risk – when the advocacy window is large.

The tale of two senators from Illinois can illustrate both the vast level of discretion that senators possess when cultivating their reputations, as well as the additional levels of risk that descriptive representatives may sometimes be willing to take on relative to senators who are not themselves a member of a disadvantaged group. Illinois is one of the more racially/ethnically diverse states in the country, and has become even more so over the course of the last few decades. During the 1990s, Illinois was also a state with one of the lowest ambient temperatures toward racial/ethnic minorities. In 1992, Carol Moseley-Braun (D) became the first Black woman elected to the US Senate. During her first and only term in the Senate, she built a reputation as a primary advocate for racial/ethnic minorities, despite the relatively low ceiling of her advocacy window in Illinois. Less than a decade after Sen. Moseley-Braun's defeat in her reelection battle, Illinois sent another Black representative to the Senate. Sen. Barack Obama (D), likely with his eyes on a national constituency rather than the state of Illinois alone, made the opposite decision, and chose not to integrate racial advocacy into his legislative reputation.

5.9 CONCLUSION

Senators tend to face additional stressors as the result of responsibilities that come with representing an entire state. Relative to the average congressional district, states contain considerably more groups that a senator must adjudicate between when making decisions about the legislative reputation they wish to cultivate. As discussed in Chapter 3, it is simply not possible to build a reputation as an advocate for all the different groups that are present within their state – they must be strategic, and they must choose wisely. This makes them much less likely to stick their neck out to represent a group that is generally viewed as being less deserving of government assistance, out of fears that it will frustrate non-group members, and diminish their chances of reelection.

This chapter has shown that, unlike in the House, the size of a disadvantaged group within a district generally does not increase the likelihood that a senator will form a reputation as a disadvantaged-group advocate, unless the group is broadly considered to be deserving of government assistance. Likewise, though group ambient temperature had a positive independent effect on member reputation in the House, in the Senate, disadvantaged group ambient temperature is not a significant driving factor in reputation formation. These distinctions also shed light on important differences in the way that senators and members of the House make use of the advocacy window.

In the House, the advocacy window holds up well as a means of representing the amount of discretion a member has in choosing the extent to which they devote their legislative reputation to serving the needs of disadvantaged group members, with descriptive representatives as the most likely to take advantage of a large advocacy window. In the

Senate, however, the advocacy window works slightly differently. Rather than having a floor of expected advocacy that is in line with the size of the group within a district, the minimum level of anticipated advocacy in the Senate tends to be none at all, unless a disadvantaged group is considered to be particularly deserving of government assistance. Additionally, given their risk-averse nature, senators only rarely shoot for the ceiling of their advocacy window, as set by the general ambient temperature toward a group in a district, unless they are themselves a descriptive representative. And if they are, unlike in the House, where descriptive representatives are more likely to take advantage of a larger advocacy window, senators feel more pressure to act in the face of an advocacy window that is especially narrow.

To account for some of the variations in the institutional and electoral environments faced by members of the House and the Senate, this chapter also introduced and evaluated three alternative hypotheses to explain reputation formation in the Senate. The first, the electoral insecurity hypothesis, argued that senators with more marginal victories in their most recent elections would be less likely to work to craft a reputation as a disadvantaged-group advocate, out of fear that it would reduce their chances of success in their upcoming election. The second, the in-state differentiation hypothesis, built off of insights from Schiller (2000b) to assert that senators with a same-state counterpart who already has a reputation as a disadvantaged-group advocate are less likely to themselves have a reputation for advocacy of the same group. Finally, the collective amplification hypothesis asserted that the larger the number of senators with reputations as group advocates present in a given Congress, the more likely that others would elect to incorporate such advocacy into their reputation. After performing the analysis, only the collective amplification hypothesis was supported, implying that the presence of other advocates within the institution will encourage additional senators to include advocacy for disadvantaged groups in their own legislative reputation as well, at least at a superficial level.

In the next and penultimate chapter, I flip on its head the analysis as it has been performed up to this point, and instead consider member reputation as a pivotal explanatory variable. In doing so, I am able to specifically evaluate several of the potential drawbacks inherent to prior research in which specific legislative actions are assumed to be the preferred means of representing disadvantaged groups, and thereby carve out a new potential direction for legislative scholars to follow. Specifically, I analyze the extent to which members with reputations for disadvantaged-group advocacy tend to use bill sponsorship and cosponsorship as tools for building or maintaining their legislative reputations, and discuss the role that the committee structure and the perceived deservingness of a particular group can play in shaping sponsorship and cosponsorship decisions. This provides further evidence of the value of using legislative reputation as a primary measure of representation with the inherent flexibility required to apply across the range of disadvantaged groups.

6

Reputation-Building Tactics in the Senate and House of Representatives

During the 113th Congress, Diana DeGette, Democrat from Colorado's 1st District, was known for giving "women's health Wednesday" speeches, to bring attention to the gendered inequities in the healthcare that women receive, and was one of the primary forces pushing for the creation of the Violence Against Women Office in the Department of Justice. Rick Renzi, Republican representing Arizona's 1st District in the 2000s, used his perch on the Resources Committee to provide increased government funds for the Native American tribes in his district. Kathy Castor, former representative of Florida's 11th District, fought to prevent changes to Medicare that she saw as harmful to seniors. Each of these members had the same goal – to represent a particular disadvantaged group – but each pursued a different method of achieving this goal. What explains these tactical differences?

A consciously cultivated legislative reputation is one of the main ways that representatives communicate their priorities to constituent groups and demonstrate that they are working on their constituents' behalf. When it comes to building these reputations, members of Congress have an enormous amount of discretion when it comes to the means by which they choose to signal that they are working to serve as a particular group advocate.[1] As discussed in Chapter 2, this broad range of potential actions generally necessitates that representation scholars make a priori assumptions about the types of representative acts that members will seek to engage in, and then use measures of those activities to draw conclusions about the quality of representation

[1] A full accounting of all of the different legislative actions a member can engage in to form their reputations can be found in Table 3.1.

members provide. But because this project introduces a measure of representation that does not rely on these specific assumptions, I am able to work backwards to investigate what actions members of Congress with reputations for advocacy actually chose to utilize to represent a particular group.

In Chapter 3, member reputation and its key characteristics are described at great length. One of the primary advantages to utilizing member reputation as a way of conceptualizing and measuring the representation that members of Congress offer to disadvantaged groups is that it does not depend upon these a priori assumptions about which legislative actions a member will choose to engage in to provide that representation. Instead, this measure captures the considerable latitude members of Congress have in their tactical decision-making. To highlight the importance of these myriad representational methods, in Table 3.2, I presented preliminary evidence of the strategic differences among advocates of disadvantaged groups in the extent to which they employ common tools like bill sponsorship and cosponsorship as a means of building their legislative reputations. This initial analysis demonstrated that member reputations are not synonymous with bill introduction and cosponsorship behaviors, and there is great variation in when and to what extent these specific tools are utilized.

In this chapter, I specifically address the reasons behind this tactical variation. I examine *when* and *why* members of Congress who build their reputation as an advocate for disadvantaged groups make the decision to exercise that advocacy through the common representational tools of bill sponsorship and cosponsorship. To begin, I will discuss the reasons why bill sponsorship and cosponsorship are important and worthwhile legislative actions to consider. Next, I will introduce a theory for how the type of reputation a member is seeking to build, and for whom, as well as their place within Congress' institutional structures, impacts which type of legislative tools members of Congress choose to lean on to build their legislative reputations. Finally, I analyze the effects of advocacy reputations and institutional position on sponsorship and cosponsorship activity using a series of ordinary least squares regression models.

6.1 REPUTATION AND THE USE OF REPRESENTATIONAL TOOLS: BILL SPONSORSHIP AND COSPONSORSHIP

There is a broad consensus among legislative scholars that sponsorship and cosponsorship can be important opportunities for members to engage in individual agenda setting (Baumgartner and Jones, 1993; Kingdon, 2005). Though it is true that any given act of sponsoring or cosponsoring a bill is highly unlikely to result in actual changes in the law, these actions are seen as offering an important signal for a member's representational priorities and preferences. Sponsorship and cosponsorship are legislative actions that are relatively low-cost when it comes to a member's time and energy (particularly cosponsorship, which does not require any new policy ideas or staff energy to prepare legislative text). This makes these actions very different from activities like roll-call votes or calling a committee hearing, which require institutional power and collective action from a number of different members working together.

As discussed in greater detail in Chapter 2, the symbolic role for bill sponsorship and cosponsorship has been a particular point of emphasis for scholars evaluating the impact of having descriptive representatives in the legislature (i.e., Canon, 1999; Swers, 2002, 2013; Bratton, 2006; Dodson, 2006; Carnes, 2013). Research in this vein essentially uses sponsorship, cosponsorship, or other actions as a proxy for representation, and then seeks to determine what sorts of characteristics (for instance, being a woman, a person of color, or someone from a working class background) are associated with increased sponsorship, cosponsorship, and so on. These associations are then used as a broader argument for why members with these characteristics offer better representation for the groups in question. This research has been extremely valuable for representation scholars, and has offered great insight into the quality of representation different members can provide. That said, this methodological formulation has meant that some interesting avenues of inquiry have been previously unavailable. As a result of the necessary a priori assumption that individuals seeking to engage in representation will sponsor or cosponsor bills, any nuanced differences in who chooses to engage in these particular behaviors and when have largely remained hidden.

Analyzing representation through the lens of a member's legislative reputation bypasses the need for a starting assumption about which legislative actions are most likely to be chosen as a means of signaling representation, and allows for an exploration of those nuances in the choice of representative actions different group advocates may undertake. Members must make strategic decisions about which actions they will engage in to get their intended message to be picked up by the Congress-watchers in the media, and then hopefully transmitted back to their constituents.

In an ideal world, a legislator might want to equally represent all groups present in their district, and to do so in as many ways as possible. In reality, though, members must make choices about which groups they are going to focus on, and the best ways to engage in that representation given the very real constraints on their time and resources. Member decision-making becomes particularly interesting when considering members who choose to advocate for different disadvantaged groups. These members are faced with the task of selecting representative actions that are most likely to draw attention and approval from the members of a targeted disadvantaged group (or those who view the group with sympathy), while not also alienating those who view potential government action to help a particular group with more skepticism.

Any member who has developed a reputation for disadvantaged-group advocacy has only gotten to that point by answering two specific questions: first, do they wish to be known by their constituents as an advocate for a particular disadvantaged group (or groups), and second, how are they going to build that reputation as a disadvantaged-group advocate? In answering the first question, members consider a variety of factors, including the size of the group in their district, feelings toward that group, and their own personal experiences. As shown in the previous two chapters, members of Congress are generally more likely to form a reputation as a disadvantaged-group advocate when the group has a relatively large presence in their district, when that group is held in positive regard by other constituents, and when they themselves are a member of that disadvantaged group.

The second question, regarding the choice in the tactics a member selects when seeking to build or maintain their legislative reputation, particularly in service to disadvantaged groups, has not been directly addressed in prior research. The final component of this book sheds light on this question in two ways. First, given the centrality of symbolic bill sponsorship and cosponsorship as representational actions, this chapter investigates the circumstances under which members *do* choose to cultivate their reputations as advocates by devoting a considerable portion of their bill sponsorship and cosponsorship activities to bills relevant to a particular disadvantaged group, as is commonly assumed in the congressional representation literature. Second, this chapter highlights the groups for which members elect *not* to use bill sponsorship or cosponsorship as an important component of their advocacy, *despite* their commitment to representing a particular disadvantaged group.

6.2 WHEN DO MEMBERS OF CONGRESS USE BILL SPONSORSHIP AND COSPONSORSHIP AS REPUTATION-BUILDING TACTICS?

Broadly speaking, I expect that members of Congress with reputations for disadvantaged-group advocacy are indeed going to be more likely to devote a large proportion of their bill sponsorship and cosponsorship activity to bills that can impact their group. This expectation is in line with the assumption in the prior research that sponsorship and cosponsorship are important for representation. Within those broad strokes, however, lies important nuance. Recognizing this, I argue that there are two primary conditions driving when a member of Congress may choose bill sponsorship or cosponsorship as their primary means of representing a disadvantaged group. The first of these conditions is the extent to which a particular disadvantaged group is considered to be deserving of government action on their behalf. Second, a member's representational choices are impacted by how well a group's issues fit in line with the breakdown of standing committees and subcommittees.

Not all disadvantaged groups are held in the same regard by non-group members. Instead, there are three broad categories of groups that can largely be delineated by the degree to which the group is considered to be deserving of government assistance, as discussed in greater detail in Chapter 2. To review, those general categories are as follows: those generally considered to be highly deserving of government programming (such as veterans and seniors), those toward whom the public is neutral or has mixed feelings (such as women, immigrants,[2] Native Americans, and the poor), and those largely considered to be undeserving of government assistance (such as racial/ethnic minorities and the LGBTQ community.)

I expect that members of Congress will condition their decisions about which representational tactics to deploy as a group advocate as a result of these differences in the perceptions of group deservingness of government assistance. This conditioning, however, looks slightly different for cosponsorship decisions than it does for sponsorship decisions.

---

[2] As discussed in greater detail in Chapter 2, these categories are subject to change over time. For example, in the period examined here, veterans are held in much higher regard than was the case in the Vietnam era, where perceptions of how much assistance returning veterans deserved was more mixed. In a similar way, one could argue that perceptions of immigrants as deserving of government assistance have declined over the past decade, particularly in the run-up to and aftermath of the 2016 election. That said, for the bulk of the period studied here, perceptions of the deservingness of immigrants were more mixed, with repeated and bipartisan attempts to reform the immigration system in a way that would take into account at least some of the needs of even those immigrants who were undocumented. For this reason, legislative actions on behalf of immigrants are again included here in the intermediate category of mixed perceived deservingness.

6.2.1 Bill Cosponsorship

Cosponsorship is an important but extremely low cost means by which members can take a position and engage in agenda setting (Arnold, 1990; Kessler and Krehbiel, 1996; Wawro, 2001; Koger, 2003). As a result, I argue that members primarily consider two main factors when deciding whether or not to cosponsor a bill on behalf of a disadvantaged group, assuming they generally agree with the bill's premise. First, they consider the potential visibility of their action. In other words, how likely is it that important media observers will notice their action, and incorporate it into the reputation that is transmitted to their constituents? Second, they consider any potential risk involved in associating themselves with a particular piece of legislation. In short, is this action likely to result in the alienation or aggravation of other groups, so that any increased visibility has a negative effect?

Visibility takes into account the environment a member is in, and the likelihood that a particular action will be noticed. Actions that are less common are going to be more visible than actions that are more common. Figures 6.1 and 6.2 show the frequency of cosponsorships across a variety of group-specific areas for five Congresses in the House and the Senate. Generally speaking, the rarity of cosponsorship activity is inversely related to the perceived deservingness of a disadvantaged group. Vastly more cosponsorships of bills related to the needs of veterans occur in a given

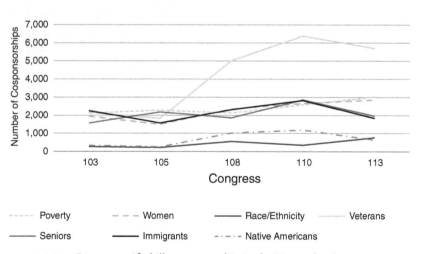

FIGURE 6.1 Group-specific bill cosponsorship in the House, by Congress
Note: Figure displays total cosponsorships pertaining to each group in a given Congress.

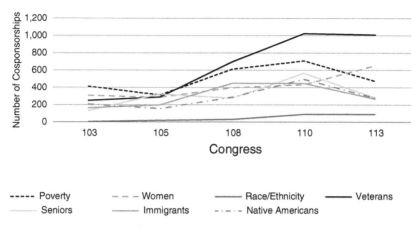

FIGURE 6.2 Group-specific bill cosponsorship in the Senate, by Congress
Note: Figure displays total cosponsorships pertaining to each group in a given
Congress.

Congress (particularly for the post-9/11 108th, 110th, and 113th
Congresses) than those of bills pertaining to any other group. On the
opposite end, on average, there are considerably fewer cosponsorships
of bills that could potentially benefit racial and ethnic minorities.

Cosponsoring a bill that could benefit a group considered to be highly
deserving of government assistance holds little to no risk to a member of
Congress. Signing on to legislation to benefit groups with an intermediate
level of perceived deservingness carries a corresponding low to medium
amount of risk. Bills intended to assist groups that are considered to be less
deserving are markedly riskier. For example, more potential backlash
might be expected in cosponsoring a bill advocating for a committee to
study reparations for descendants of enslaved African Americans than
a bill aiming to prevent older Americans being scammed by robocallers.

For groups with a high level of perceived deservingness of government
action, visibility may be fairly low, but so is the risk. As cosponsorship
requires little of a member in the way of time, effort, and resources,
I would expect that any member who wants to be seen as dedicating
some portion of their legislative reputation to one of these groups would
find cosponsorship to be a worthwhile activity. Similarly, while there may
be slightly higher risk for a group that has a mixed level of perceived
deservingness of assistance, it is balanced by marginally higher visibility.
Members seeking to be known as representing these groups are thus likely
to choose cosponsorship as a valid representational tactic. Yet, for groups

with low levels of perceived deservingness of government assistance – namely racial and ethnic minorities – even a low-energy activity like cosponsorship results in potentially high visibility and increased risk of negative repercussions. Thus, I expect that only members who are particularly committed to devoting a considerable portion of their legislative reputation to advocating for racial and ethnic minorities will engage in related cosponsorship.

6.2.2 Bill Sponsorship

Bill sponsorship, while still of great use as a symbolic representational tool, is different from cosponsorship in important ways. Bill sponsorship requires a greater outlay of effort from a member of Congress than cosponsorship, which simply expresses support for someone else's legislation. To sponsor a bill, a member must either have their own original policy idea or spend time in contact with interest groups or other individuals who have a specific policy idea in mind. Further, the member and their staff must devote time and resources to transforming that idea into appropriately formatted legislative language. As sponsored bills have a member's name most directly attached, members also bear greater responsibility for the ideas contained within, which can be beneficial or problematic, depending on the circumstances. This makes bill sponsorship generally more risky as a symbolic action than cosponsorship.

While risk may be higher for sponsorship relative to cosponsorship, the general patterns of visibility are similar, as seen in Figures 6.3 and 6.4. But given these important characteristics of bill sponsorship, members' sponsorship decisions are conditioned by an additional factor that members may not take into account for bill cosponsorship. While members of Congress still consider the visibility and risk involved in sponsorship activities, because of the additional effort required, they also factor in the likelihood that a bill could actually gain the support it would require to pass. This is not to say that passage is a purely necessary or sufficient condition; other factors may lead a member not to sponsor a bill that could potentially be popular, or to sponsor a bill that is highly unlikely to ever go anywhere. However, members still consider the possibility before deciding whether or not the time and resources required to sponsor a bill are worth it.

Sponsoring bills with the potential to benefit groups that are considered to be less deserving of government assistance may be visible and risky, as discussed earlier, but those bills also are much less likely to gain the

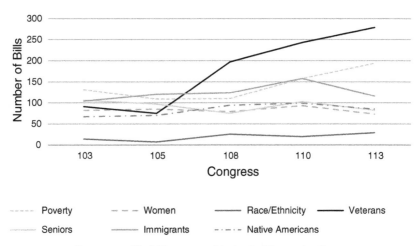

FIGURE 6.3 Group-specific bill sponsorship in the House, by Congress
Note: Figure displays total sponsorships pertaining to each group in a given Congress.

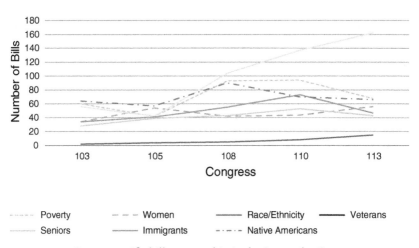

FIGURE 6.4 Group-specific bill sponsorship in the Senate, by Congress
Note: Figure displays total sponsorships pertaining to each group in a given Congress.

support they would need to eventually pass. For a member who devotes a smaller portion of their reputation to serving one of these disadvantaged groups, these circumstances are likely to make bill sponsorship a less appealing means of representing the group than other potential representational actions. A member seeking to devote a high level of their sponsorship activity to benefit a group that is generally thought to be deserving of government assistance must consider a rather different set of factors. The risk of backlash is low, but so is potential visibility. This lends a high level of uncertainty to the possibility of a sponsored bill actually passing. Because sponsoring a non-controversial bill on behalf of a well-regarded group can be a popular idea, eventual passage is likely dependent upon other institutional factors (particularly the committee system, the effects of which are discussed in greater detail below). I expect that bill sponsorship will be most common among members seeking to build any level of reputation as an advocate for a disadvantaged group that is generally held with more mixed perceptions of deservingness, because all three factors – risk, visibility, and potential for passage – tend to be at more moderate levels.

6.2.3 Differences in Expectations between the House and the Senate

There are 435 members of the House of Representatives, compared to only 100 in the Senate. This means that in the Senate, every action that is taken has a higher level of visibility relative to the House. There are two expected side-effects of this greater visibility. First, senators are likely to be able to build their reputations more easily, because they are not fighting for media attention with as many other members. I anticipate that the magnitude of the effects of member reputation in the Senate will be lower than in the House, because senators may have to take fewer individual actions to build or maintain their reputations. Second, because of this higher level of visibility, senators are likely to be more cautious in their risk assessment, particularly for groups with lower levels of perceived deservingness of government assistance, and may prefer to engage in representative actions that are less likely to create a backlash from other groups in their districts.

6.3 EVALUATING BILL SPONSORSHIP AND COSPONSORSHIP ACTIVITY

I test these hypotheses using an extension of the original dataset of members of the US Senate and House of Representatives introduced in Chapter 3, and utilized in Chapters 4 and 5. This analysis again makes use of the *reputation* variable already described, but transforms it from an ordinal variable into a series of discrete indicators, which serve as the pivotal explanatory variables in the models to follow. To evaluate the extent to which members of Congress make the choice to engage in group-related bill sponsorship and cosponsorship as the specific means of building their legislative reputations, the subsequent models will employ two different dependent variables. These dependent variables of interest are the percentage of a member's cosponsorship activity that is relevant to a particular disadvantaged group, and the percentage of a member's bill sponsorship activity that is relevant to a particular disadvantaged group. I perform a series of ordinary least squares regressions to investigate the impact of member reputation and other relevant variables on sponsorship and cosponsorship activity on behalf of disadvantaged groups.[3] Each of these variables is discussed in greater detail below.

6.3.1 Reputation

As stated above, in this analysis, the reputation variable is employed not as an ordinal dependent variable, but rather as individual explanatory variables. Dichotomous variables indicating whether someone is a *primary advocate*, *secondary advocate*, or *superficial advocate* are included in the model as potential predictors of a member's proclivity to sponsor or cosponsor legislation relevant to a particular disadvantaged group. For those groups with extremely limited numbers of primary advocates, those with reputations for primary and secondary advocacy are combined into a single category. This is discussed in greater detail below, in association with the relevant models.

6.3.2 Bill Sponsorship and Cosponsorship

The dependent variables for these analyses are the percentage of a member's *sponsorship* or *cosponsorship* activities that involve bills relevant to a particular disadvantaged group. Relevant bills are determined using Adler and Wilkerson's *Congressional Bills Project* dataset, which includes the Baumgartner and Jones *Policy Agendas Project* topic codes. These codes are used to classify every bill proposed in a given Congress into a specific issue area. Any bill with topics that are directly related to one of the disadvantaged groups examined here are included in the analysis as being a relevant potential sponsorship or cosponsorship.[4]

---

[3] The dependent variables used (percentages of bill cosponsorship and cosponsorship activity) approximate the characteristics of an interval variable.

[4] The selected sub-topic codes for each group interest areas are as follows: poverty (unemployment, employment training, fair labor standards, social welfare low-income assistance, housing low-income assistance, homeless, underprivileged education), women (gender discrimination, family issues, child care), race (minority discrimination, voting rights), veterans (veterans' housing, military personnel issues), seniors (age discrimination, long-term care, elderly social welfare assistance, elderly housing), and Native Americans (indigenous affairs).

There are fourteen total dependent variables that are utilized in the analysis to follow. These are the percentage of a member's bill sponsorship activity that is devoted to legislation related to the poor, women, immigrants, racial/ethnic minorities, veterans, seniors, or Native Americans, as well as the percentage of a member's cosponsorship activity on bills relevant to the same groups.[5] The choice to evaluate sponsorship and cosponsorship on behalf of particular disadvantaged groups as a percentage rather than as a count is an intentional, theory-driven decision.

Members are widely varied in their approach to bill sponsorship and cosponsorship. Some choose to sponsor or cosponsor as many bills as possible, potentially diluting their signal, even if there are a relatively large number of them. Others may only sponsor or cosponsor a few bills, but if they are consistent in their targets, they can send a clearer message than someone with more bills in terms of sheer numbers. Expressing group-specific bill sponsorship or cosponsorship as a percentage of total activity, rather than as a count of individual bills, takes into account this diversity of opportunity for member decision-making. Two members that each choose to devote 40 percent of the bills they cosponsor to those that could benefit seniors are much more similar in the representational message that they send than would otherwise be apparent by just knowing that one of these members cosponsored seventy bills to benefit older Americans, and the other just seven.

Considering group-bill sponsorship and cosponsorship as a percentage is also important because it accounts for the fact that members do not just have different preferences for the use of sponsorship and cosponsorship overall, but that these preferences can change across groups. To demonstrate this, we can consider two more hypothetical members, each with a relatively high overall tendency toward bill sponsorship, and a reputation for secondary advocacy of different disadvantaged groups. One of these members may include within their otherwise high bill sponsorship totals bills that are intended to benefit their group, while the other member may have high overall totals, but bills for their group play only a small part within that. For this first member, bill sponsorship is considered to be an important tool in maintaining their reputation, but for the second, sponsorship is clearly considered to be a less effective tool in advocating for their particular

---

[5] Because PAP subtopic codes do not include specific designations for LGBTQ issues, the legislative activities of those with reputations as LGBTQ advocates are not analyzed here. This does not imply that these actions would not be interesting or relevant, but simply that such an analysis is beyond the bounds of the methodology employed in this chapter.

disadvantaged group, despite deploying bill sponsorship to achieve other goals within the legislature.

6.3.3 Other Variables

I include several other relevant controls in my models. First, I account for the member's *party affiliation*. Given that Democrats have a reputation for being a party based more heavily on group coalitions, while Republicans are considered to be the more ideological party (Grossman and Hopkins, 2016), I expect that Democrats, on average, are more likely to engage in bill sponsorship and cosponsorship activity pertaining to specific disadvantaged groups. I also account for other individual factors such as whether or not a member is a part of party *leadership*, coded as a dichotomous variable, where leadership includes the positions of Speaker of the House, Majority or Minority Leader, Assistant Majority or Minority Leader, and Majority or Minority Whip. Binary variables indicating if a member is a part of the congressional *majority* or is in their *first term* are included as well. The two final individual-level variables included in the models, *sponsorship quartile* and *cosponsorship quartile*, account for the overall sponsorship and cosponsorship activity of a member. Specifically, I control for whether a member is in the first, second, third, or fourth quartile among all members in a given Congress when it comes to the total number of bills sponsored or cosponsored.[6] Lastly, all models also control for congress-specific fixed effects, and display standard errors clustered by member.[7]

6.4 UPHOLDING REPUTATIONS FOR GROUP ADVOCACY USING BILL SPONSORSHIP AND COSPONSORSHIP

The coefficients of the models evaluating the impact of reputation and other variables indicating a member's position within the institution (excluding committee membership, which is covered separately in the next section) on cosponsorship and sponsorship in the House of Representatives and the Senate are found in Tables 6.1–6.4. These data

[6] This measure is used in lieu of a raw count to avoid the endogeneity concerns derived from including an independent variable that also serves as the denominator for the dependent variable.

[7] Also noteworthy is what is *not* included in this model. Constituency level variables are the driving force behind members' decisions to build legislative reputations as disadvantaged group advocates, discussed in great detail in the previous chapters. Thus, as these variables are essentially already incorporated into the reputation variables, they are not included here to prevent overspecification of the models.

show that, fairly consistently, whether or not a member has a reputation for disadvantaged-group advocacy is one of the best predictors for sponsoring or cosponsoring bills related to that group. This is in line with the first broad hypothesis, that members seeking to build a reputation as a disadvantaged-group advocate will be more likely to take advantage of bill sponsorship and cosponsorship as representational tools. Within this broader trend, however, there is evidence of important distinctions between the representational strategies for different disadvantaged groups. These are considered in turn below, according to the group's perceived level of deservingness of government assistance, and the chamber in which a member operates.

6.4.1 Sponsorship and Cosponsorship Activity in the House of Representatives

6.4.1.1 *Groups with High Perceived Deservingness*

As seen in the first two columns of Table 6.1, members with a reputation for advocacy on behalf of groups generally seen as deserving of government assistance are significantly more likely to devote a higher proportion of their cosponsorships to bills relevant to those groups. This is true for members with reputations for advocating on behalf of both veterans and seniors, the two groups that are in this category. Because these actions are low risk and low effort, even with potentially limited visibility, it was expected that cosponsorship in the House would be popular for members with any level of reputation for advocacy.

Members that are in the highest quartiles for bill cosponsorship more generally are also more likely to cosponsor bills related to the needs of these groups. This further speaks to the low-risk nature of cosponsoring bills relevant to veterans and seniors. Because working on behalf of these groups that are broadly considered to be deserving of government assistance is non-controversial, it is reasonable that members who tend to cosponsor more bills across the board would not hesitate to also cosponsor bills related to these groups.

As expected, party affiliation plays only a limited role in determining which members will devote a larger share of their cosponsorship activity to bills targeting veterans and seniors. Party is not a significant factor in determining which members will engage in cosponsorship for seniors. Democrats are more likely to cosponsor veterans' bills, but the magnitude of this effect is only a quarter of the effect from having a reputation as a primary advocate for veterans. Given the increasing levels of

TABLE 6.1 *Committee membership and the percentage of bills cosponsored across disadvantaged groups in the House*

	(1) Veterans	(2) Seniors	(3) Native Americans	(4) Women	(5) Poor	(6) Immigrants	(7) Race/Ethnicity
Primary Advocates	2.738	0.341	5.361	2.159	1.991	2.922	0.655
	1.048	0.156	0.236	1.157	0.187	0.360	0.072
Secondary Advocates	–	–	–	1.157	1.259	1.882	0.423
				0.179	0.123	0.332	0.056
Superficial Advocates	2.279	0.238	1.515	0.421	0.453	1.092	0.287
	0.217	0.102	0.182	0.134	0.087	0.231	0.048
Cosponsorship Quartile	0.221	0.208	-0.006	0.267	0.129	0.149	0.003
	0.056	0.030	0.020	0.031	0.032	0.042	0.012
Sponsorship Quartile	0.005	-0.020	0.050	-0.016	-0.035	-0.027	-0.001
	0.053	0.028	0.019	0.029	0.030	0.039	0.011
Republican	-0.688	-0.109	-0.245	-1.437	-0.839	1.212	-0.182
	0.113	0.059	0.041	0.062	0.066	0.084	0.025
Leadership	-1.055	-0.783	0.149	1.404	0.830	0.756	0.435
	0.531	0.279	0.192	0.291	0.299	0.394	0.112
Majority	-0.531	-0.439	0.018	0.040	0.402	-0.942	-0.277
	0.108	0.057	0.039	0.059	0.061	0.080	0.023
First Term	1.074	-0.007	0.127	0.166	0.100	-0.092	0.015
	0.143	0.075	0.052	0.079	0.082	0.107	0.031

(continued)

Constant	**4.931**	**1.549**	**0.510**	**2.632**	**2.813**	**1.355**	**0.899**
	0.228	0.120	0.082	0.125	0.130	0.170	0.048
N	2,032	2,032	2,032	2,032	2,032	2,032	2,032
Adjusted R^2	0.332	0.126	0.300	0.391	0.300	0.192	0.274

Note: Coefficients calculated using OLS regression, with Congress fixed effects (not shown) and standard errors clustered by member (in gray). All coefficients with *p*-values greater than or equal to 0.05 are in bold.

partisanship from the 1990s up through to the current decade, this min-imal role of party affiliation is striking.

Columns (1) and (2) of Table 6.2 demonstrate that the decision by a member of the House of Representatives to sponsor a bill related to a group that is broadly considered to be deserving of government assist-ance is a bit more complex than that of the decision to cosponsor, as the theory would suggest. Here, those with a reputation for superficial vet-erans' advocacy are more likely to sponsor a larger share of bills, while members with a reputation for primary or secondary advocacy on behalf of veterans are not significantly more likely to sponsor veterans' bills. This pattern is reversed for those with a reputation for advocacy for seniors. Primary and secondary seniors' advocates are more likely to devote a large portion of their sponsorship activities to legislation relevant to seniors, while superficial advocates are not.

There are noteworthy differences when considering some of the other control variables as well. Unlike the pattern seen with cosponsorship, someone who is in the higher quartiles of bill sponsorship is not signifi-cantly more likely to sponsor bills benefiting seniors or veterans. And once again, though party affiliation is not the strongest factor in determining the percentage of sponsorship activity expended on groups that are con-sidered to be highly deserving of government assistance, the pattern of significance has flipped for sponsorship relative to cosponsorship. In this instance, it is Republicans that are more likely to sponsor bills related to seniors. This continues to demonstrate that these trends are certainly not an exclusively partisan phenomenon. In the post-1990s polarized world, the surprising lack of clear partisan direction in sponsorship decisions stands out as important evidence that both Republicans and Democrats are still making similar evaluations about their representational choices for at least some disadvantaged groups.

6.4.1.2 *Groups with Mixed Perceived Deservingness*
When it comes to cosponsorship, the results of representational decision-making pertaining to groups with mixed perceived levels of deservingness look quite similar to those of high deservingness groups, as seen in columns (3)–(6) of Table 6.1. Regardless of the level of advocacy a member has a reputation for providing, cosponsorships related to women, Native Americans, immigrants, and the poor are likely to make up a broader share of a member's overall cosponsorship activity than those members with no reputation for advocacy at all. This fits with

TABLE 6.2 *Committee membership and the percentage of bills sponsored across disadvantaged groups in the House*

	(1) Veterans	(2) Seniors	(3) Native Americans	(4) Women	(5) Poor	(6) Immigrants	(7) Race/Ethnicity
Primary Advocates	6.906	1.787	17.735	8.988	4.746	7.450	2.926
	3.980	0.558	1.298	0.843	0.858	1.472	0.272
Secondary Advocates	—	—	—	2.738	3.487	9.682	0.838
				0.588	0.568	1.332	0.212
Superficial Advocates	6.931	0.598	8.950	1.020	0.790	2.261	0.216
	0.828	0.365	1.001	0.443	0.401	0.925	0.184
Cosponsorship Quartile	-0.031	0.214	0.085	0.265	0.346	0.095	-0.075
	0.215	0.106	0.113	0.102	0.147	0.168	0.045
Sponsorship Quartile	-0.247	0.183	-0.017	-0.038	0.031	0.147	0.054
	0.201	0.100	0.106	0.096	0.137	0.158	0.042
Republican	-0.491	0.515	-0.044	-0.498	-0.324	0.827	-0.024
	0.429	0.213	0.225	0.205	0.303	0.339	0.093
Leadership	-1.812	-0.388	-1.040	-0.354	6.511	-1.097	-0.304
	2.016	0.998	1.057	0.957	1.375	1.580	0.425
Majority	-0.457	-0.152	-0.046	0.391	0.304	-0.332	-0.078
	0.413	0.204	0.216	0.196	0.282	0.324	0.087
First Term	2.294	0.364	-0.086	0.216	0.046	0.343	0.170
	0.547	0.271	0.287	0.260	0.376	0.430	0.116

(continued)

TABLE 6.2 (*continued*)

	(1) Veterans	(2) Seniors	(3) Native Americans	(4) Women	(5) Poor	(6) Immigrants	(7) Race/Ethnicity
Constant	**5.795**	−0.052	0.823	0.472	**2.311**	0.901	**0.449**
	0.874	0.431	0.457	0.413	0.599	0.687	0.184
N	2,032	2,032	2,032	2,032	2,032	2,032	2,032
Adjusted R^2	0.066	0.012	0.115	0.075	0.057	0.036	0.062

Note: Coefficients calculated using OLS regression, with Congress fixed effects (not shown) and standard errors clustered by member. Standard errors are in presented in gray, and all coefficients with *p*-values greater than or equal to 0.05 are in bold.

theoretical expectations laid out for the evaluation of this relatively low risk and low effort activity.

The effects of partisanship on cosponsorship related to these groups of mixed perceived deservingness of assistance are also of note here. Cosponsorship of bills pertaining to women, Native Americans, and the poor is more likely to be carried out by Democrats, while Republicans are significantly more likely to cosponsor bills relevant to immigrants. These marginally stronger ties with Democrats are not particularly surprising, given the embrace of these groups (particularly women and the poor) among the general Democratic coalition, but the tendency of Republicans to devote a higher percentage of their cosponsorship activity to bills related to immigrants is less expected, at least from a modern perspective. This effect is likely due to two main factors. First, Republicans during this time frame were much more likely to engage in legislative advocacy on behalf of policies such as a pathway to citizenship or legal residency than is currently the case. Second, immigrants are a diverse group, and members may respond differently to the various cohorts within that group. For example, Republicans may choose to cosponsor legislation benefiting high-skilled immigrants, even if they would not cosponsor a bill seeking to limit deportations of undocumented immigrants.

When it comes to bill sponsorship decisions, as expected, the choice seems to be more straightforward for members seeking to advocate for these groups with mixed perceptions of deservingness than for those advocating for seniors or veterans. Members with reputations for any level of advocacy on behalf of Native Americans, women, the poor, or immigrants, are significantly more likely to devote a higher percentage of their sponsorship activity to legislation benefiting these groups, as can be seen in columns (3)–(6) of Table 6.2. Because there are not consistently negative perceptions of government assistance to these groups, bill sponsorship is not considered to be highly risky, and there is at least moderate potential for being able to gather the needed coalition for a bill's eventual passage. For members deciding what proportion of their sponsored bills to devote to Native Americans or the poor, party is not a significant determining factor. For women, however, as with immigrants, party does play a significant role – this time, with Democrats more likely to sponsor a higher proportion of bills related to women's interests, and Republicans more likely to have a higher portion of their sponsorship activity on bills related to immigrants.

6.4.1.3 *Groups with Low Perceived Deservingness*

The final column of Table 6.1 provides the results of the analysis of the cosponsorship decisions related to racial and ethnic minorities, which are broadly considered in the United States to be less deserving of government assistance than the other groups evaluated. As with all other group related cosponsorships in the House of Representatives that have been considered here, members with reputations for the advocacy of racial and ethnic minorities at any level are more likely to engage in a higher percentage of cosponsorship pertaining to this group. That said, the magnitude of this effect is considerably smaller for those with reputations as minority advocates than for advocates of any other group besides seniors. This implies that while those with reputations for advocacy of racial/ethnicity minorities may choose to cosponsor slightly more bills relevant to their interests, this is not the primary means by which they distinguish themselves.

As predicted, a slightly different pattern appears when considering the percentage of a member's cosponsorship activity that is devoted to racial and ethnic minorities, as can be seen in column (7) of Table 6.3. Higher risk, higher visibility, and a diminished chance of eventual passage make the introduction of bills relevant to racial/ethnic minorities less appealing than other representational tactics for members with a reputation for only superficial forms of advocacy. Again, this does not mean that there are no members who have a reputation for superficial advocacy on behalf of racial and ethnic minorities – Figure 3.7 shows that this is clearly not the case. These other members may have built superficial reputations, but they decided that increased levels of bill sponsorship were not the right way to do it.

There is an additional variable that is notable for *not* being statistically significant. After controlling for the effects of a member's reputation as an advocate for racial/ethnic minorities on sponsorship decisions, a member's party affiliation does not have a significant impact. This emphasizes the unique treatment of the needs of racial/ethnic minorities, relative even to the other disadvantaged groups considered. This distinction is not one that is purely rooted in partisanship, but rather the specific choices of members to build reputations as advocates of racial/ethnic minorities.

6.4.2 Sponsorship and Cosponsorship Activity in the Senate

6.4.2.1 *Groups with High Perceived Deservingness*

As can be seen in Tables 6.3 and 6.4, the patterns of which members are more prone to sponsoring or cosponsoring bills related to veterans and seniors – both groups with a generally high perceived deservingness of

TABLE 6.3 *Committee membership and the percentage of bills cosponsored across disadvantaged groups in the Senate*

	(1) Veterans	(2) Seniors	(3) Native American	(4) Women	(5) Poor	(6) Immigrant	(7) Race/ Ethnicity
Primary Advocates	**2.080**	**0.681**	**6.222**	**1.401**	**1.082**	**2.189**	-0.049
	0.571	0.222	0.580	0.289	0.247	0.623	0.163
Superficial Advocates	**2.115**	**0.374**	**5.323**	**0.767**	**0.795**	**0.809**	0.073
	0.391	0.151	0.652	0.227	0.180	0.348	0.118
Cosponsorship Quartile	0.143	**0.371**	-0.144	-0.071	0.151	-0.166	-0.030
	0.113	0.056	0.119	0.079	0.080	0.091	0.025
Sponsorship Quartile	0.117	-0.163	0.305	-0.061	0.065	0.080	0.017
	0.108	0.054	0.114	0.076	0.076	0.087	0.024
Republican	-0.747	-0.456	0.295	-1.636	-1.343	0.483	-0.015
	0.192	0.096	0.201	0.134	0.136	0.154	0.042
Leadership	0.061	-0.219	0.067	-0.427	0.025	-0.383	**0.274**
	0.456	0.225	0.478	0.317	0.319	0.363	0.101
Majority	0.023	0.111	0.161	0.232	-0.360	-0.305	-0.019
	0.195	0.096	0.203	0.136	0.137	0.156	0.043
First Term	0.252	-0.127	-0.231	0.269	0.483	0.151	-0.009
	0.278	0.137	0.289	0.193	0.194	0.221	0.061
Constant	**4.117**	**0.654**	0.311	**4.108**	**2.303**	**1.504**	**0.479**
	0.397	0.195	0.411	0.273	0.276	0.314	0.086

(continued)

TABLE 6.3 (continued)

	(1) Veterans	(2) Seniors	(3) Native American	(4) Women	(5) Poor	(6) Immigrant	(7) Race/ Ethnicity
N	494	494	494	494	494	494	494
Adjusted R^2	0.325	0.329	0.293	0.373	0.304	0.120	0.128

Note: Coefficients calculated using OLS regression, with Congress fixed effects (not shown) and standard errors clustered by member (in gray). All coefficients with *p*-values greater than or equal to 0.05 are in bold.

government assistance – are quite similar to those that were seen in the House, with only a few distinctions. As in the House, members with a reputation for any kind of advocacy on behalf of seniors or veterans are more likely to devote a higher percentage of their cosponsorship activity to bills relevant to those groups. In the Senate, however, Democrats are significantly more likely than Republicans to cosponsor bills pertaining to veterans and seniors, rather than exclusively veterans.

Sponsorship activity for bills related to the needs of veterans is also higher for senators with a reputation for any level of veterans' advocacy, unlike in the House, where primary advocates are more prone to other types of activities. Bills relevant to seniors, however, compose a higher percentage of sponsorships for members with primary or secondary reputations for advocacy, but not for those with superficial reputations. As was the case in the House, this indicates that superficial advocacy can be sufficiently communicated through cosponsorship or other activities, and sponsorship is much more commonly used as a reputation-building tool only by those that wish to be known for devoting a considerable portion of their reputation to serving seniors.

6.4.2.2 Groups with Mixed Perceived Deservingness

Members with reputations for advocacy on behalf of disadvantaged groups perceived to have a mixed level of deservingness can be seen to behave slightly differently in the Senate compared to the House, depending upon the specific group in question. Once again, choosing to engage in a higher percentage of cosponsorship activity relevant to Native Americans, women, the poor, and immigrants is significantly more common among those members with a reputation for any level of group advocacy, as seen in columns (3)–(6) of Table 6.3. The impact of partisanship on cosponsorship activity pertaining to these groups, however, is not exactly the same in the Senate as it is in the House.

Most notably, unlike in the House, cosponsorship of bills relevant to Native Americans does not have a significant partisan dimension after members' reputations for advocacy are taken into account. This indicates that Republican senators are just as likely as Democratic senators to make the decision to cosponsor bills benefiting Native Americans, even if they are not specifically seeking to build or maintain a reputation as an advocate on their behalf. Higher cosponsorship activity related to women and the poor is still more common among Democrats, but Republicans again are more likely to utilize more of their cosponsorship agenda on

TABLE 6.4 *Committee membership and the percentage of bills sponsored across disadvantaged groups in the Senate*

	(1) Veterans	(2) Seniors	(3) Native Americans	(4) Women	(5) Poor	(6) Immigrants	(7) Race/Ethnicity
Prim/Sec Advocates	**4.994**	**1.250**	**8.620**	**3.143**	**2.438**	**9.033**	−0.141
	1.739	0.626	1.275	0.687	0.725	1.590	0.315
Superficial Advocates	**5.710**	0.705	**12.507**	0.776	**1.137**	1.666	**0.505**
	1.192	0.425	1.433	0.539	0.529	0.887	0.229
Cosponsorship Quartile	−0.118	**0.431**	−0.177	−0.239	−0.185	0.215	−0.067
	0.346	0.159	0.261	0.189	0.234	0.232	0.048
Sponsorship Quartile	0.105	−0.265	0.269	−0.132	0.089	−0.263	**0.104**
	0.330	0.152	0.251	0.180	0.224	0.222	0.047
Republican	**−1.341**	0.238	0.865	**−0.939**	−0.459	0.501	−0.013
	0.587	0.270	0.443	0.319	0.400	0.392	0.082
Leadership	−0.322	−0.661	−0.757	−0.868	−0.496	1.777	−0.271
	1.390	0.635	1.051	0.752	0.936	0.939	0.196
Majority	−0.358	0.465	0.021	0.382	−0.438	−0.430	−0.034
	0.594	0.272	0.447	0.323	0.402	0.397	0.083
First Term	**1.684**	**−0.986**	−0.334	0.266	0.011	0.673	−0.061
	0.850	0.387	0.638	0.460	0.572	0.566	0.119
Constant	**5.419**	0.120	1.278	**2.995**	**2.851**	1.119	0.319
	1.217	0.552	0.909	0.653	0.816	0.806	0.169
N	494	494	494	494	494	494	494
Adjusted R^2	0.098	0.027	0.187	0.065	0.032	0.077	0.014

Note: Coefficients calculated using OLS regression, with Congress fixed effects (not shown) and standard errors clustered by member (in gray). All coefficients with p-values greater than or equal to 0.05 are in bold.

legislation related to immigrants (though the magnitude of that difference is less than half the size of that in the House).

Differences between the Senate and the House are even more apparent when considering sponsorship decisions, displayed in columns (3)–(6) of Table 6.4. Senators with reputations as primary or secondary advocates are still more likely to assign a higher proportion of their sponsorship activity to bills related to Native Americans, women, the poor, or immigrants, but the same is not true for all senators with reputations as superficial advocates for one of these groups. For superficial advocates of Native Americans and the poor, sponsoring one's own bills on issues directly relevant to these groups is used as a significant component of reputation building, while this is not the case for superficial advocates of women or immigrants.

Senators' party affiliation also has less of a significant role to play in the sponsorship decisions pertaining to most of the groups that generally have mixed perceptions of their deservingness of government assistance. Democrats are significantly more likely to choose to devote a higher percentage of their overall bill sponsorship activity to women's issue bills, even for senators that are not seeking to build reputations as women's advocates. When it comes to bills relevant to Native Americans, immigrants, and the poor, on the other hand, Democratic and Republican members without reputations for advocacy are equally likely to sponsor bills related to these groups. This is especially interesting when considering bills pertaining to the poor, as economic concerns have long been a central point of differentiation between the Republican and Democratic parties.

6.4.2.3 Groups with Low Perceived Deservingness

Racial/ethnic minorities are the only group for which senators seeking to be known as an advocate do not consistently engage in a high percentage of bill cosponsorship relevant to the group. Even when bill sponsorship is considered, only senators with a reputation for superficial advocacy of racial/ethnic minorities devote a significantly higher portion of those actions to bills related to minorities. Coefficients for each of these models are found in the last columns of Tables 6.3 and 6.4. This means that regardless of the type of reputation a senator is seeking to build as an advocate of racial/ethnic minorities, cosponsorship is not considered to be an important reputation-building strategy, and additional bill sponsorship is a strategy mostly deployed by those seeking to build a reputation for the lowest level of advocacy.

Partisanship is also not a significant determining factor of the percentage of sponsorship and cosponsorship activity on bills directly related to racial/ethnic minorities in which a senator will engage. This is surprising, given the strength of the link between racial/ethnic minorities, particularly Black Americans, and the Democratic Party coalition during this time period. Because neither partisanship nor a senator's reputation for advocacy are strong determinants of sponsorship or cosponsorship activity in most cases, this implies that advocates for racial/ethnic minorities in the Senate have a strong preference for taking other representative actions outside of sponsorship and cosponsorship.

6.5 BILL SPONSORSHIP AND COSPONSORSHIP AND THE COMMITTEE STRUCTURE

How deserving of government assistance a group is generally perceived to be explains a considerable amount of the variation in the sponsorship and cosponsorship choices among the members of Congress that choose to build reputations as disadvantaged groups advocates, but certainly not all. There remain some important differences in these sponsorship and cosponsorship decisions pertaining to disadvantaged groups within each category, particularly for those groups that have the highest and the lowest perceived levels of deservingness of government assistance. I argue that a considerable amount of this variation across groups that would otherwise be considered to be fairly similar in how they are regarded by the American people can be explained by taking a closer look at the ways in which different disadvantaged groups are integrated into the committee structure within the Congress.

6.5.1 Committee Structure and the Choice of Representative Actions

Congressional committees benefit members of Congress in two ways that are particularly relevant for sponsorship and cosponsorship decisions. Committee membership lends a member the presumption of expertise about the topic area, which in turn increases their visibility on related issues. Committees also provide members with access to institutional mechanisms that can increase the likelihood that a member's preferred policies actually make it into law. These potential benefits of committee membership have differential levels of impact on the decision of how to represent different disadvantaged groups, relative to how a group's interests map onto the purview of a particular committee.

This possible committee-group interest agreement can fall into three general categories. First, there is an obvious match between group interests and a single committee's jurisdiction. Second, there may be a readily apparent match between group interests and committee jurisdiction, but it is split between a few specific committees. Or, finally, a group's interests may not fall clearly under the jurisdiction of any particular committee (or committees). Because the placement of group interests within the committee system can take on such very different forms, it is expected to condition a member's evaluations of the risk, visibility, and potential passage of any group-specific piece of legislation.

In the first scenario, where group interests clearly map onto the jurisdiction of a single committee, it is expected that committee membership will be quite important in a member's decisions about the proportion of their bill sponsorship or cosponsorship activity that they are going to devote to that particular disadvantaged group. If a group's interests clearly match up with a single committee's jurisdiction, there will be a higher level of competition for attention for legislative actions like bill sponsorship and cosponsorship between members on the committee going about their work, and those outside of the committee who are seeking to advocate on behalf of the group.[8] This increase in the number of potential group experts (those on the committee as well as those with advocacy reputations) is likely to further drive down the visibility of potential bill sponsorship actions, and decrease the chances that non-committee members would be able to advance bills through the legislature (due to the institutional benefits committee membership provides for advancing bills through the legislative process). Though

---

[8] Obviously, there is expected to be some overlap between these two groups, as individuals who know they want to form reputations as group advocates may well seek out the committee from which they can most readily do so. But there is far from perfect overlap between these two groups. While there is a positive correlation between having a reputation as a group advocate and being a member of one of the committees identified, the correlations are fairly low, as can be seen in the table below. This is no group for which the correlation exceeds 0.3, and most are below 0.1. It is clear that members seeking to build a reputation as a group advocate do not automatically gain membership on one of these committees, nor does committee membership automatically lead one to being an advocate.

Pearson Correlations Between Committee Membership and Reputation of Advocacy in the House of Representatives

Veterans	Seniors	Native Americans	Women	Poor	Immigrants	Race/Ethnicity
0.21	0.16	0.13	0.09	0.06	0.12	0.04

Pearson Correlations Between Committee Membership and Reputation of Advocacy in the Senate

Veterans	Seniors	Native Americans	Women	Poor	Immigrants	Race/Ethnicity
0.25	0.10	0.08	0.07	0.20	0.19	0.08

cosponsorship remains a low effort activity, non-committee members seeking to devote a large portion of their reputation to serving this group may forgo engaging in a high level of cosponsorship of related legislation, as it is perceived to have limited payoff. This is especially likely to be true if the group is broadly considered to be highly deserving of government assistance, because the low levels of risk makes cosponsorship of legislation benefiting such groups appealing to a wider range of members.

For bill sponsorship, the calculus may change further. Sponsoring a single bill, particularly for someone outside the committee, may be sufficient to boost a superficial reputation as a group advocate, but someone wanting to devote a large portion of their reputation to serving this group may prefer other legislative actions with greater potential to draw attention or affect policy outcomes. However, for members seeking to represent groups with mixed or low levels of perceived deservingness who are not already fighting against limited potential visibility, bill sponsorship and cosponsorship may remain attractive tools for reputation building, because the higher levels of potential risk may make such actions less common, and raise visibility.

Considerations are similar for members facing the second scenario, where they are interested in representing groups whose interests fit in well with the jurisdictions of several different committees. Here, again, it is expected that members serving on a committee whose jurisdiction clearly includes specific group interests will devote a larger portion of their sponsorship and cosponsorship activities to legislative action related to that group. That said, because these group interests are spread across multiple committee jurisdictions, the impact on visibility and potential passage is expected to be less severe, though still present. I expect that these diminished impacts will maintain the attractiveness of cosponsorship for all members wishing to be known for representing the group, regardless of their perceived level of deservingness. Because cosponsorship is still considered a viable option for those only wanting to devote a small portion of their reputation to serving a group, bill sponsorship is likely to remain within the purview of those with the strongest reputations for group advocacy.

For members finding themselves in the third scenario, wherein group interests do not clearly map onto the jurisdiction of any specific committee more so than any other, committee membership should not play a significant role in the decision to incorporate disadvantaged-group advocacy into bill sponsorship and cosponsorship decisions. Because visibility, risk, and potential for passage are not likely to be impacted by the committee structure, member decisions are expected to remain in line with the expectations set out by the characteristics of the group, and the actions themselves, rather than jurisdictional factors. As committee membership is not a significant element of the decision-making regarding these groups, other conditions, such as partisanship, may play an increased role.

6.6 IMPACT OF COMMITTEE-GROUP ALIGNMENT ON SPONSORSHIP AND COSPONSORSHIP DECISIONS

In this final component of the analysis, I reconsider the differences in the choice of legislative actions that members building reputations as advocates of various disadvantaged groups make, after taking into account the particular disadvantaged group's position within the structure of committee jurisdiction. To do this, I re-evaluate the models introduced above, this time controlling for membership on a committee relevant to a given disadvantaged group. In the remaining sections of the chapter, I explain the formation of the committee membership variable in greater detail, and then analyze the impact of committee membership on the decision to sponsor or cosponsor legislation related to particular disadvantaged groups, first in the House of Representatives, and then in the Senate.

6.6.1 Measuring Committee Membership

Membership on a relevant *committee* is coded as a dichotomous variable for each group of interest, where a member is either on a potentially related committee or they are not. I also include an indicator variable for members who are the *committee chair* for a relevant committee.[9] Committee assignments were obtained from Charles Stewart and

---

[9] As an additional robustness check, I also evaluated an alternate form of these models for the US Senate that considered the potential interaction between group advocacy and the presence of a same state, same party senator with membership on a relevant committee. This is relevant because one-party state delegations are generally not assigned to the same committees, potentially impacting the sponsorship and cosponsorship decisions a senator may make. I find that having a same-state, same-party colleague assigned to a relevant committee has no substantive effect on a senator's cosponsorship decisions, and only substantively impacts the sponsorship activity of senators with a reputation for immigrant advocacy. This outlier is likely due to the coding scheme for relevant committees (listed in full in the next paragraph), as immigrants are the only group for which issues pursuant to them are explicitly categorized as under the jurisdiction of a single committee. All other groups have at least two committees for potential advocacy, which would be expected to dilute or eliminate the impact of the committee assignment of a senator's same-state, same-party colleague. The nature of the substantive impact on sponsorship behavior for immigrant advocates is discussed in an additional footnote later in the chapter, as part of the broader consideration of substantive significance.

Jonathan Woon's dataset on modern congressional standing committees. Relevant committees were determined by comparing the relevancy of committee and subcommittee jurisdictions to particular groups and group interests.

A member of the House of Representatives is considered to be on a committee with greater potential to handle issues relevant to people in poverty if they are on the Agriculture, Education and Labor, Public Works, or Ways and Means Committees. Committees with jurisdictions potentially the most relevant to women's concerns are Education and Labor, Commerce, and Judiciary, while concerns of racial and ethnic minorities are likely to be addressed on the Education and Labor and Judiciary Committees. Veterans' issues are more likely to come before the Armed Services and Veterans' Affairs Committees, seniors' issues before Judiciary, Commerce, and Ways and Means, immigrants' issues before the Judiciary, and issues relevant to Native Americans before Education and Labor and the Natural Resources Committee.[10] The relevant committee designations are largely similar for members of the Senate, but with Finance Committee members being treated as the equivalent of members of the Ways and Means Committee.

6.6.2 Committee-Group Alignment and Sponsorship and Cosponsorship Activity in the House of Representatives

6.6.2.1 High Committee-Group Alignment
Issues pertaining to veterans, Native Americans, and immigrants are almost entirely dealt with by a single committee – Veterans' Affairs for veterans, Natural Resources for Native Americans, and Judiciary for immigrants. As a consequence of this, committee membership is expected play a significant role in the percentage of sponsored or cosponsored bills that relate to these groups. The results of the committee analysis for issues pertaining to veterans, Native Americans, and immigrants are found in the first, second, and third columns, respectively, of Tables 6.5 and 6.6.

The cosponsorship of bills relevant to all three of these groups is impacted by partisanship. For bills related to veterans and Native Americans, Democrats are more likely to have a high percentage of cosponsored bills, while sponsorship decisions are made on a non-partisan basis. The

---

[10] The names of committees have changed over the life-time of this dataset depending upon whether the House was in the hands of Democrats or Republicans, but the jurisdictions have remained largely the same.

TABLE 6.5 *Committee membership and the percentage of bills cosponsored across disadvantaged groups in the House*

	(1) Veterans	(2) Native Americans	(3) Immigrants	(4) Poor	(5) Race/ Ethnicity	(6) Seniors	(7) Women
Primary Advocates	1.260	5.259	2.804	1.978	0.644	0.365	2.157
	0.981	0.236	0.354	0.185	0.072	0.157	0.256
Secondary Advocates	–	–	1.598	1.250	0.419	–	1.166
			0.328	0.121	0.056		0.179
Superficial Advocates	1.513	1.414	0.925	0.452	0.287	0.252	0.427
	0.207	0.182	0.228	0.086	0.048	0.102	0.134
Committee Member	2.318	0.233	1.175	0.196	0.071	-0.083	-0.047
	0.133	0.049	0.135	0.060	0.029	0.062	0.063
Committee Chair	-0.666	0.365	-0.161	1.788	-0.274	0.042	0.499
	1.100	0.285	0.775	0.313	0.159	0.335	0.348
Cosponsorship Quartile	0.217	-0.010	0.148	0.135	0.000	0.207	0.270
	0.053	0.020	0.041	0.032	0.012	0.030	0.031
Sponsorship Quartile	0.025	0.041	-0.047	-0.049	-0.002	-0.014	-0.016
	0.049	0.019	0.039	0.030	0.011	0.028	0.029
Republican	-0.694	-0.254	1.188	-0.836	-0.185	-0.107	-1.434
	0.105	0.041	0.083	0.065	0.025	0.059	0.062
Leadership	-0.745	0.178	0.829	0.919	0.442	-0.800	1.401
	0.495	0.191	0.387	0.297	0.112	0.279	0.291

(continued)

TABLE 6.5 *(continued)*

	(1) Veterans	(2) Native Americans	(3) Immigrants	(4) Poor	(5) Race/ Ethnicity	(6) Seniors	(7) Women
Majority	−0.537	0.014	−0.944	0.373	−0.276	−0.439	0.035
	0.101	0.039	0.079	0.061	0.023	0.057	0.060
First Term	**0.715**	**0.104**	−0.123	0.089	0.008	−0.018	**0.168**
	0.135	0.052	0.105	0.081	0.031	0.076	0.079
Constant	**4.642**	**0.511**	**1.314**	**2.754**	**0.898**	**1.565**	**2.636**
	0.214	0.082	0.167	0.129	0.048	0.120	0.125
N	2,032	2,032	2,032	2,032	2,032	2,032	2,032
Adjusted R^2	0.419	0.308	0.221	0.316	0.276	0.126	0.391

Note: Coefficients calculated using OLS regression, with Congress fixed effects (not shown) and standard errors clustered by member (in gray). All coefficients with *p*-values greater than or equal to 0.05 are in bold.

sponsorship and cosponsorship of bills impacting immigrants, however, is more common among Republicans. The impact of reputation is also slightly different for bills related to each of these groups. For veterans' bills, after the significant impact of committee membership is taken into account, only those members with reputations for superficial advocacy are markedly more likely to have higher percentages of sponsorship and cosponsorship.

This lack of a significant effect of reputations for primary advocacy on the sponsorship and cosponsorship of bills related to veterans is not entirely unexpected under the theoretical framework laid out. If the Veterans' Affairs Committee did not exist, members seeking to advocate for veterans would already be facing a busy representational space with low risk, but low visibility. The presence of committee experts depresses both visibility and the likelihood of the passage of any one bill, meaning that even someone who sponsors a higher percentage of bills related to veterans may not actually stand out. In this circumstance, individuals with a reputation for primary advocacy for veterans may very well prefer to engage in a different representational tactic that has the potential to be higher profile.

For bills pertaining to Native Americans and immigrants, groups with generally mixed levels of perceived deservingness, committee members are significantly more likely to have a higher percentage of bill sponsorship and cosponsorship, but this does not supplant the effects of members having developed a reputation for advocacy. As was seen in Figures 6.1–6.4, though there is some variation, there are generally fewer bill sponsorships or cosponsorships relevant to Native Americans or immigrants than for those groups that are generally considered to have a high level of perceived deservingness of government assistance. This means that any legislative action related to these groups already has a high level of visibility. Thus, even with the competition with specific committee experts for attention when it comes to introducing and cosponsoring bills relevant to Native Americans or immigrants, members with reputations for advocacy still consider both of these actions to be worthwhile.

6.6.2.2 Moderate Committee-Group Alignment

Full results of the committee analysis of the interests of racial/ethnic minorities and the poor are seen in columns (4) and (5) of Tables 6.5 and 6.6. Unlike the interests of veterans, Native Americans, and immigrants, bills pertaining to the issues of racial/ethnic minorities and the poor are likely to be addressed by several different specific committees. As an example, the Supplemental Nutrition Assistance Program (SNAP)

TABLE 6.6 *Committee membership and the percentage of bills sponsored across disadvantaged groups in the House*

	(1) Veterans	(2) Native Americans	(3) Immigrants	(4) Poor	(5) Race/Ethnicity	(6) Seniors	(7) Women
Primary Advocates	3.436	17.475	7.198	4.618	2.866	1.737	8.977
	3.896	1.303	1.453	0.857	0.272	0.562	0.843
Secondary Advocates	–	–	8.706	3.457	0.829	–	2.763
			1.321	0.566	0.212		0.589
Superficial Advocates	5.146	8.700	1.686	0.741	0.209	0.570	1.043
	0.826	1.006	0.917	0.400	0.184	0.368	0.444
Committee Member	5.433	0.594	4.048	0.919	0.273	0.178	-0.153
	0.529	0.270	0.548	0.278	0.109	0.224	0.209
Committee Chair	-5.436	0.814	0.035	1.490	0.040	-0.153	0.778
	4.368	1.576	3.124	1.450	0.600	1.197	1.145
Cosponsorship Quartile	-0.048	0.076	0.094	0.341	-0.082	0.216	0.271
	0.210	0.113	0.166	0.147	0.046	0.107	0.102
Sponsorship Quartile	-0.199	-0.041	0.075	0.006	0.047	0.171	-0.034
	0.196	0.106	0.156	0.137	0.042	0.101	0.097
Republican	-0.505	-0.068	0.740	-0.331	-0.038	0.509	-0.491
	0.419	0.225	0.334	0.302	0.093	0.213	0.205
Leadership	-1.102	-0.967	-0.846	6.855	-0.272	-0.354	-0.371
	1.967	1.056	1.560	1.375	0.424	0.999	0.958
Majority	-0.472	-0.054	-0.339	0.265	-0.081	-0.151	0.384
	0.403	0.217	0.320	0.282	0.087	0.205	0.197

(continued)

	(1)	(2)	(3)	(4)	(5)	(6)	(7)
First Term	**1.464**	−0.147	0.244	−0.064	0.149	0.389	0.218
	0.540	0.288	0.425	0.378	0.116	0.273	0.260
Constant	**5.140**	0.824	0.764	**2.081**	**0.446**	−0.084	0.488
	0.855	0.456	0.678	0.601	0.184	0.433	0.414
N	2,015	2,015	2,015	2,015	2,015	2,015	2,015
Adjusted R^2	0.112	0.116	0.061	0.062	0.064	0.011	0.074

Note: Coefficients calculated using OLS regression, with Congress fixed effects (not shown) and standard errors clustered by member (in gray). All coefficients with p-values greater than or equal to 0.05 are in bold.

benefits (formerly food stamps) are handled on the Agriculture Committee, while Pell Grants are the purview of the Education and Labor Committee. Thus, while committee membership does still have a significant impact upon the percentage of bills that a member sponsors or cosponsors that are relevant to their group, it is not as strong an effect as that seen in the previous section. As was the case for members representing most groups with a high level of overlap between committee and group interests, however, partisanship generally plays a significant role only in a member's cosponsorship decisions, but not sponsorship.

Members with reputations as advocates for each of these groups still consider cosponsorship as a viable way to boost their reputations, even after committee membership is taken into account. This indicates that a member's risk/reward analysis for this action is still on the side of cosponsorship, despite having some additional competition for attention coming from committee experts. This calculus becomes slightly different for these groups when considering the effects of committee membership and reputation on sponsorship decisions.

In both instances, members with reputations for superficial group advocacy do not have elevated bill sponsorship percentages, though primary and secondary advocates do. Though these results appear to be the same across groups, I expect that there is slightly different reasoning behind it. Potential advocates for racial/ethnic minorities are already facing a higher risk, higher visibility environment. While the presence of other committee experts may alleviate some of that potential visibility, the risk is likely to still be considered too high for those with reputations for only superficial advocacy, and they are content to engage in actions like cosponsorship instead. For those seeking to advocate on behalf the poor, this logic may be inverted. As seen in Figures 6.1 and 6.3, sponsorship and cosponsorship related to the poor is more common than for any of the other groups with mixed levels of perceived deservingness, meaning that the visibility from sponsorship is lower. When paired with the further reduction of visibility and likelihood of passage that comes from competing with committee experts, superficial advocates likely evaluate the bill sponsorship to be not worth the increased efforts, while secondary and primary advocates remain willing to try.

6.6.2.3 Low Committee-Group Alignment

The interests pertaining to the final two groups, women and seniors, do not have as clear a home within the committee system. As a result of this, membership on particular committees is not a driving force behind sponsorship and cosponsorship decisions, as seen in columns (6) and (7) of Tables 6.5 and 6.6. Rather, the choice to sponsor or cosponsor bills related to these groups stand out for a different reason – the persistent effects of partisanship. The lack of a clear committee match increases the partisan considerations for bill sponsorship, but not in the same direction. Republicans remain more likely to sponsor a higher percentage of bills related to seniors, while bills pertaining to women's interests make up a higher proportion of sponsorship activity for Democrats. These results follow in line with the theoretical expectations, whereby representational decisions for these groups are conditioned by group perceptions, but not by committee membership.

6.6.3 Committee-Group Alignment and Sponsorship and Cosponsorship Activity in the Senate

6.6.3.1 *High Committee-Group Alignment*
The dynamics of sponsorship and cosponsorship in the Senate differ in important ways from those of the House, as seen in Tables 6.7 and 6.8. In the House, membership on one of the committees with clear jurisdiction over the issues pertaining to veterans, immigrants, and Native Americans is significantly related to relevant sponsorship and cosponsorship activity. But while this is true for immigrants' and veterans' bills in the Senate, the same cannot be said for legislation addressing concerns of Native Americans. This implies that even with clear committee jurisdiction, senators still have a wide range of latitude over the issues they cover. Particularly in the modern Senate, in which the former Indian Affairs Committee has been eliminated and its jurisdiction rolled into the Resources Committee, senators have a great deal of leeway when deciding which of the issues fitting under the umbrella of Resources they want to work on. Thus, given the status of Native Americans as a group about which the broader American public tends to have more mixed perceptions, senators who are not intentionally seeking to form a reputation as a Native American advocate are unlikely to pursue legislation on their behalf, even if they sit on the committee that would most readily facilitate such actions.

In the House, members with reputations for superficial advocacy of veterans were significantly more likely to cosponsor or sponsor bills related to veterans' issues, but those with primary/secondary reputations were not. This was not unexpected, as the size of the House makes it much less likely that any singular action on behalf of a well-regarded group would be highly visible, particularly when there is a clear alignment between committee jurisdiction and group interests. In the Senate, the inherently

TABLE 6.7 *Committee membership and the percentage of bills cosponsored across disadvantaged groups in the Senate*

	(1) Veterans	(2) Native Americans	(3) Immigrants	(4) Poor	(5) Race/ Ethnicity	(6) Seniors	(7) Women
Prim/Sec Advocates	**1.260**	**6.188**	**1.804**	**0.906**	−0.069	**0.675**	**1.375**
	0.549	0.580	0.610	0.246	0.163	0.223	0.290
Superficial Advocates	**1.447**	**5.214**	0.561	**0.697**	0.055	**0.366**	**0.773**
	0.380	0.653	0.341	0.179	0.119	0.152	0.227
Committee Member	**1.365**	0.389	**1.026**	**0.407**	0.069	0.067	0.136
	0.192	0.199	0.191	0.133	0.043	0.094	0.131
Committee Chair	1.223	0.223	0.050	**1.083**	0.072	0.013	0.521
	0.637	0.735	0.726	0.387	0.147	0.290	0.382
Cosponsorship Quartile	0.178	−0.155	−0.166	**0.155**	−0.032	**0.373**	−0.072
	0.107	0.119	0.088	0.078	0.025	0.056	0.079
Sponsorship Quartile	0.127	**0.307**	0.021	0.043	0.014	**−0.171**	−0.081
	0.103	0.115	0.085	0.075	0.024	0.055	0.077
Republican	**−0.786**	0.280	**0.463**	**−1.407**	−0.017	**−0.458**	**−1.643**
	0.182	0.201	0.149	0.135	0.042	0.096	0.134
Leadership	0.496	0.156	−0.439	0.026	**0.280**	−0.228	−0.405
	0.434	0.479	0.358	0.313	0.101	0.226	0.316
Majority	−0.029	0.143	−0.274	**−0.447**	−0.022	0.114	0.213
	0.185	0.204	0.152	0.136	0.043	0.098	0.137

(continued)

First Term	0.213	−0.216	0.070	**0.535**	−0.014	−1.127	0.270
	0.263	0.289	0.216	0.191	0.061	0.137	0.194
Constant	**3.556**	0.194	**1.494**	**2.150**	**0.468**	**0.632**	**4.080**
	0.384	0.416	0.305	0.277	0.087	0.198	0.277
N	494	494	494	494	494	494	494
Adjusted R^2	0.399	0.296	0.169	0.331	0.130	0.327	0.375

Note: Coefficients calculated using OLS regression, with Congress fixed effects (not shown) and standard errors clustered by member (in gray). All coefficients with *p*-values greater than or equal to 0.05 are in bold.

TABLE 6.8 *Committee membership and the percentage of bills sponsored across disadvantaged groups in the Senate*

	(1) Veterans	(2) Native Americans	(3) Immigrants	(4) Poor	(5) Race/ Ethnicity	(6) Seniors	(7) Women
Prim/Sec Advocates	2.913	8.585	8.061	1.853	-0.153	1.240	3.034
	1.689	1.279	1.560	0.720	0.317	0.627	0.687
Superficial Advocates	3.766	12.402	1.049	0.790	0.482	0.685	0.781
	1.169	1.440	0.872	0.524	0.230	0.427	0.537
Committee Member	2.882	0.377	2.567	1.518	0.131	0.189	0.568
	0.593	0.440	0.492	0.392	0.084	0.265	0.311
Committee Chair	8.300	0.144	-0.178	2.497	-0.083	-0.439	1.306
	1.959	1.621	1.857	1.046	0.286	0.818	0.905
Cosponsorship Quartile	0.018	-0.189	0.211	-0.190	-0.072	0.431	-0.250
	0.331	0.263	0.226	0.230	0.049	0.159	0.189
Sponsorship Quartile	0.030	0.273	-0.412	0.049	0.101	-0.276	-0.195
	0.317	0.254	0.218	0.221	0.047	0.156	0.181
Republican	-1.433	0.850	0.457	-0.673	-0.017	0.240	-0.963
	0.560	0.444	0.382	0.394	0.082	0.271	0.317
Leadership	0.775	-0.672	1.623	-0.552	-0.267	-0.703	-0.807
	1.336	1.057	0.915	0.918	0.196	0.637	0.750

(continued)

	(1)	(2)	(3)	(4)	(5)	(6)	(7)
Majority	−0.660	0.007	−0.355	−0.667	−0.031	0.493	0.341
	0.569	0.450	0.389	0.398	0.084	0.275	0.325
First Term	**1.676**	−0.318	0.456	0.149	−0.077	**−0.997**	0.238
	0.812	0.639	0.554	0.561	0.119	0.388	0.461
Constant	**4.349**	1.160	1.141	**2.218**	0.296	0.041	**2.849**
	1.187	0.925	0.785	0.819	0.170	0.561	0.661
N	492	492	492	492	492	492	492
Adjusted R^2	0.180	0.185	0.125	0.074	0.015	0.024	0.073

Note: Coefficients calculated using OLS regression, with Congress fixed effects (not shown) and standard errors clustered by member (in gray). All coefficients with *p*-values greater than or equal to 0.05 are in bold.

increased visibility makes cosponsorship appealing for senators with reputations for any level of veterans' advocacy, but sponsorship is only used as a tool to maintain reputations for superficial advocacy, as the smaller number of actors within the chamber only goes so far to mitigate the effects of having to compete with committee experts as well. Conversely, senators maintaining reputations as primary or secondary advocates of immigrants are significantly more likely to use sponsorship and cosponsorship to bolster their reputations, likely reflecting the smaller pool of competitors for immigrant advocates compared to a highly regarded group like veterans. Senators with reputations at all levels of advocacy for Native Americans are markedly more likely to dedicate higher percentages of their sponsorship and cosponsorship activity to the group. The magnitude of these effects can be seen in Figures 6.5 and 6.6.

Evident in Figure 6.5 is the generally limited impact of party affiliation on cosponsorship decisions, especially when compared to the effects of reputation and committee membership. For legislation related to veterans, a group that is broadly perceived as being highly deserving of government assistance, committee membership has the largest effect on cosponsorship decisions, particularly in the House. Over the time period studied, in the

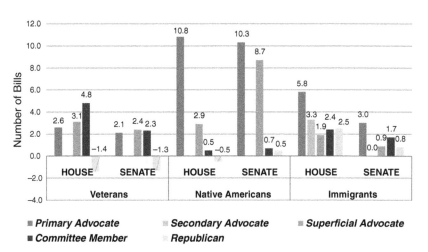

FIGURE 6.5 Number of additional bills cosponsored benefiting disadvantaged groups with high committee-group alignment
Note: Figure shows estimated additional bills that would be cosponsored by the median member, based on the sample median member with 206 cosponsorships in the House, and 167 cosponsorships in the Senate. Substantive significance is calculated for member reputation, committee membership, and party affiliation.

House, the median member cosponsored 206 bills. Thus, if that same median member served on the Veterans' Affairs Committee in the House, it would be expected that they would cosponsor approximately five additional bills related to veterans' issues than a member not on the committee. In the Senate, the substantive effect is smaller, with committee members expected to cosponsor roughly two additional bills (based on a median of 167 cosponsorships).

When it comes to Native Americans and immigrants, groups for whom general perceptions of deservingness have tended to be more mixed, committee membership has a more limited substantive effect, with members cosponsoring an average of one to two additional bills in the House or the Senate. The effects of being a member with a reputation for advocacy, however, are considerably larger in both chambers. A median member in the House and the Senate with a reputation for primary or secondary advocacy is expected to cosponsor over ten additional Native American issue bills and three to six additional immigrant issue bills relative to a member without such a reputation.

Patterns are similar for bill sponsorship, as seen in Figure 6.6. Members with reputations for primary or secondary advocacy for veterans are not significantly more likely to sponsor legislation relevant to veterans. At the

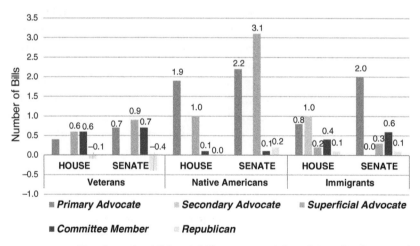

FIGURE 6.6 Number of additional bills sponsored benefiting disadvantaged groups with high committee-group alignment
Note: Figure shows estimated additional bills that would be sponsored by the median member, based on the sample median member with 11 sponsorships in the House, and 25 sponsorships in the Senate. Substantive significance is calculated for member reputation, committee membership, and party affiliation.

same time, there are significant and comparable effects for superficial advocates and committee members, with the median member likely to sponsor just under one additional bill in both the House and the Senate. For members with reputations as Native American advocates, though, the median member can be expected to sponsor an average of two to three additional Native American issue bills, with committee membership holding little substantive significance. These effects are similar for members with reputations as immigrant advocates, where the median member sponsors one to two additional bills.

These differences are expected, given the variation in the generally perceived levels of deservingness between these two groups. Given the broadly perceived high status of veterans, most members would be happy to be linked with veterans' legislation, even if they are not seeking to build a clear reputation as a veteran's advocate. This is easiest to accomplish if one is a member of the Veteran's Affairs Committee. However, because of the additional activity on issues pertaining to this group, risk may not be high but visibility is fairly low. Thus, those who seek to build a reputation as a primary advocate choose other, more visible forms of legislative activities to solidify that reputation. When it comes to Native American issues, on the other hand, the relatively higher risk that comes from the mixed perceptions of how deserving this group is of government assistance makes sponsorship and cosponsorship less broadly appealing, and members on the Resources Committee tend to focus their attention on other issues. But because of the lower amount of legislative action on behalf of Native Americans, as seen in Figures 6.1–6.4, visibility is high, making bill sponsorship and cosponsorship appealing ways to build a reputation. The behavior of immigrant advocates falls somewhere in between these two groups, where primary and secondary reputations for advocacy has the strongest effect on bill sponsorship and cosponsorship decisions, but membership on the Judiciary Committee also plays a significant role.[11]

---

[11] As was discussed in section 6.6.1, alternative versions of these models evaluating the impact of having a same-state, same-party senator assigned to a relevant committee were also considered. Immigrants were the only group for which the committee assignment of the same-state, same-party senator had substantively significant effect on the sponsorship behavior of members with reputations for advocacy. This is likely a result of the coding of committee jurisdiction, as immigrant issue bills are only explicitly mentioned as falling under the jurisdiction of a single committee (Judiciary), whereas all other group issue bills are coded in the Policy Agendas Project to at least a marginal degree under the jurisdiction of no less than two committees (for example, veterans' issues are occasionally addressed on the Armed Services Committee, even if the bulk of such work takes place on the Veterans' Affairs Committee). The median senator with a primary or secondary

6.6.3.2 *Moderate Committee-Group Alignment*

In the House, there was a clear pattern of sponsorship and cosponsorship pertaining to the poor and racial/ethnic minorities. Members with a reputation for any level of advocacy on behalf of these groups were more likely to dedicate a higher percentage of their cosponsorship activity to bills related to these groups, while members with reputations for primary or secondary advocacy were more likely to engage in relevant sponsorship. Additionally, in the House, committee membership played a significant role in sponsorship and cosponsorship for each of these groups. In the Senate, however, there is much more variation among each of these groups, despite each having a moderate level of alignment between committee jurisdiction and group interests.

Sponsorship and cosponsorship on behalf of the poor are driven by the same factors in the Senate as they are in the House. For legislation pertaining to racial/ethnic minorities, however, the pattern of significant influences change. In the Senate, committee membership does not have a significant impact on sponsorship or cosponsorship activity benefiting racial/ethnic minorities, and neither does party affiliation. Even more distinctive is the impact (or lack thereof) of a senator's reputation as an advocate on these legislative activities. Senators with reputations for any level of advocacy are not significantly more likely to cosponsor a larger amount of legislation pertaining to racial/ethnic minorities. Similarly, sponsorship related to racial/ethnic minorities is significantly boosted for members with a reputation for superficial group advocacy, but not for those with higher levels of advocacy. These patterns are entirely unique among the different groups studied, and are further evidence that the representation of racial/ethnic minorities takes a very different form in the Senate than that of even the other disadvantaged groups.

The substantive effects of these results are seen in Figures 6.7 and 6.8. For these groups, committee membership and member reputation has a consistent and significant effect on cosponsorship and sponsorship decisions pertaining to nearly all groups evaluated. Advocacy reputations have a more substantive impact than committee membership, with advocates generally sponsoring between zero and one additional bill, and

reputation for advocacy without a same-state, same-party colleague sponsored an average of three additional immigrant-related bills compared to a senator with a similar reputation but with a same-state, same-party senator on the Judiciary committee.

cosponsoring between one and four additional bills, depending upon the group. The important deviation from these patterns is the percentage of a member's bills sponsored or cosponsored related to racial/ethnic minorities. Member reputation and committee membership have substantively small (when compared to other groups) but significant impacts on the percentage of bills cosponsored by members in the House, but not in the Senate. Additionally, these variables have almost no significant effects on sponsorship activity in the House or the Senate.

When evaluating these results, it is worth keeping in mind that the greatest difference between the number of members with reputations for advocacy in the House and the Senate lies in the advocates for racial/ethnic minorities. In the House, more than 12 percent of members have built a reputation for some level of advocacy on behalf of minorities, while the same is true for less than 5 percent of all senators studied. So within this limited group, none of these senators look to cosponsorship as a helpful or desired means of building their reputations, and only those with reputations for the lowest level of advocacy look to sponsorship for the same purpose.

In all likelihood, the strategic avoidance of cosponsorship and sponsorship as reputation-building tactics is directly attributable to the high levels of perceived risk and visibility in the Senate, combined with an

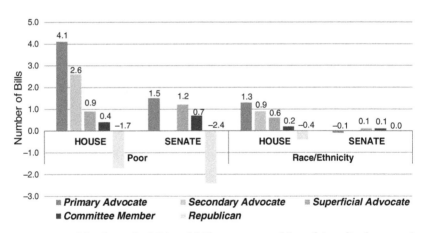

FIGURE 6.7 Number of additional bills cosponsored benefiting disadvantaged groups with moderate committee-group alignment
Note: Figure shows estimated additional bills that would be cosponsored by the median member, based on the sample median member with 206 cosponsorships in the House, and 167 cosponsorships in the Senate. Substantive significance is calculated for member reputation, committee membership, and party affiliation.

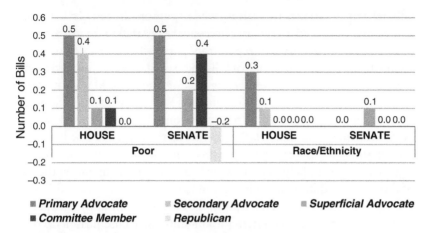

FIGURE 6.8 Number of additional bills sponsored benefiting disadvantaged groups with moderate perceived deservingness

Note: Figure shows estimated additional bills that would be sponsored by the median member, based on the sample median member with 11 sponsorships in the House, and 25 sponsorships in the Senate. Substantive significance is calculated for member reputation, committee membership, and party affiliation.

abysmally low chance that the legislation will be successful. The Senate has long been the chamber wherein bills seeking to benefit racial/ethnic minorities reach an ignominious end, if they are even considered at all. These results deliver two key implications. First, the Senate seemingly remains a place where the representation of racial/ethnic minorities is rarely achieved through traditional legislative means. Second, researchers should look to actions within the chamber outside of sponsorship and cosponsorship to better understand how the representation of racial/ ethnic minorities in the Senate, to the extent that it exists, actually takes place.

6.6.3.3 *Low Committee-Group Alignment*

For groups with a low level of alignment between their interests and committee jurisdiction, the factors with a significant impact on sponsorship and cosponsorship decisions look quite similar between the House and the Senate. In the Senate, as expected, sponsorship and cosponsorship related to women and seniors is not dependent upon membership on a specific standing committee. Additionally, as in the House, senators with reputations for any level of advocacy are significantly more likely to cosponsor bills related to women or seniors, while sponsorship activity is boosted among members with a primary or secondary reputation for advocacy.

The substantive effects of reputation, party affiliation, and committee membership on the percentage of bills sponsored and cosponsored related to women and seniors are seen in Figures 6.9 and 6.10. Median members with primary or secondary reputations as women's advocates are expected to cosponsor two to four additional bills, and to sponsor one more women's issue bill relative to members who have not built such a reputation. Members with reputations for seniors' advocacy are also significantly more likely to sponsor or cosponsor bills, but only at the level of zero to one additional bill in a given Congress.

This difference in the magnitude of the effects is not wholly unexpected. There is no standing committee (or committees) whose jurisdictions are particularly well aligned with the interests of seniors or women, so membership on a committee is not a determinative factor. The other variation between the two groups can be explained by their perceived deservingness of government assistance. Seniors are another group that is broadly considered to be highly deserving of government assistance, while perceptions

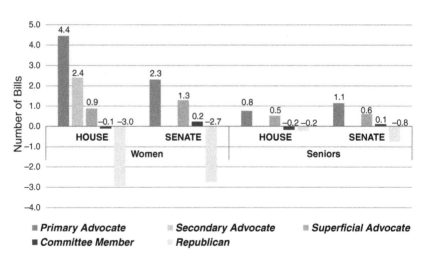

■ *Primary Advocate*   ▦ *Secondary Advocate*   ▦ *Superficial Advocate*
■ *Committee Member*   *Republican*

FIGURE 6.9 Number of additional bills cosponsored benefiting disadvantaged groups with low committee-group alignment
Note: Figure shows estimated additional bills that would be cosponsored by the median member, based on the sample median member with 206 cosponsorships in the House, and 167 cosponsorships in the Senate. Substantive significance is calculated for member reputation, committee membership, and party affiliation.

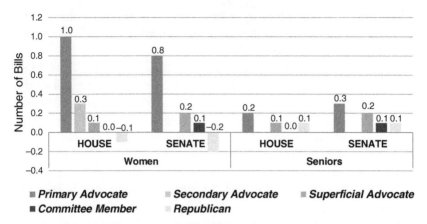

FIGURE 6.10 Number of additional bills sponsored benefiting disadvantaged groups with low committee-group alignment
Note: Figure shows estimated additional bills that would be sponsored by the median member, based on the sample median member with 11 sponsorships in the House, and 25 sponsorships in the Senate. Substantive significance is calculated for member reputation, committee membership, and party affiliation.

of women as a group are more mixed. While the potential risk of sponsoring or cosponsoring bills on behalf of seniors is low, so too is visibility. Because more members are likely to take these actions, even if they are not seeking to specifically build a reputation as an advocate, the effects of reputation are smaller. As women's advocacy is more likely to come from those who are seeking to have a reputation and be known as such, reputations for women's advocacy have a more substantive impact on sponsorship and cosponsorship activities.

6.7 CONCLUSION

Specific legislative actions within the Congress have frequently been regarded as tools that can deployed in the same way, for the same reasons, for all potential issues. Members who want to inject a new idea onto the congressional agenda, for instance, may choose to sponsor a bill, while those seeking to signal their support for a constituent group may elect to cosponsor a piece of related legislation offered by a colleague. In this chapter, I investigated the bill sponsorship and cosponsorship decisions of members who are already known to have a reputation for representing a given disadvantaged group. This moves beyond the one-size-fits-all framework of legislative actions, and has allowed for a determination of what sorts of group advocacy is best suited to expression through bill sponsorship and cosponsorship, and when members may choose to pursue other representational avenues.

I theorized that members of Congress will evaluate the risk, visibility, and potential for passage of a bill while they are making their sponsorship and cosponsorship decisions, and that these evaluations are conditioned by the broad perceptions of how deserving a group is of government assistance and the match between a group's issues and the existing division of jurisdiction within the committee structure. In line with these theoretical expectations, I found that, while members with a reputation for group advocacy are more likely to engage in group-specific bill sponsorship and cosponsorship than members without a similar reputation, these decisions do vary in important ways based upon the groups that a member is seeking to represent.

Members with more superficial reputations for advocacy of groups with a lower level of perceived deservingness are unlikely to engage in bill sponsorship or cosponsorship as a representational tool, while those advocating for groups with more mixed levels of deservingness are likely to pursue sponsorship and cosponsorship as appealing options. When a member's aim is representing a group generally considered to be highly deserving of government assistance, the fit between group issues and committee jurisdiction changes the decisions a member makes about sponsorship and cosponsorship. A member building a reputation for strong advocacy of a group perceived as being highly worthy of help from the government whose issues are largely addressed by a single committee, for instance, may choose to pursue higher profile means of maintaining that reputation than what is offered by bill sponsorship or cosponsorship. A member who is not competing with other members with clear jurisdictional expertise for attention, however, may still find value in engaging in sponsorship of their own bills. These patterns are exacerbated in the Senate, where increased visibility results in a higher-risk environment when considering sponsoring or cosponsoring bills to benefit groups with low or mixed levels of perceived deservingness.

These differences in sponsorship and cosponsorship across group issues matter for two main reasons. First, it demonstrates that by focusing solely on particular legislative actions, rather than legislative reputations more broadly, other forms of representation can be missed. Second, this shows that members choose to advocate for different groups in a variety of ways, and not all of these methods are equivalently tied into the nuts-and-bolts lawmaking process. There are important differences between group advocates who focus on drafting new legislation to positively impact their group, because they think there is a high likelihood that it could eventually make it through the process, and those group advocates who, cognizant that many people view assistance to their group with skepticism, instead center their energies on calling out injustice in less traditional ways, and thereby try to shift those group perceptions. Each are doing important representative work, but only one is likely to result in legislative change in the short term.

In Chapter 7, I offer concluding remarks on the principal contributions of this project, and emphasize the important insights to be gained by viewing representation through the lens of the legislative reputations that members of Congress choose to cultivate. Additionally, I reflect on the normative implications of this project, especially for the representation of racial/ethnic minorities. Finally, I will discuss the next steps for this research agenda.

7

Conclusions

In every state and district, there are a number of groups jostling for the attention of their member of Congress. Not all of these groups, however, are on an equal playing field. Disadvantaged groups, from the poor to racial/ethnic minorities to veterans, are uniquely positioned in that they face additional challenges and have been recognized across levels of government as requiring additional protections to ensure their equal treatment. Given this recognition, it is particularly important to determine how well Congress is actually doing at providing adequate representation and group advocacy.

This research offers a new approach to the topic, and reconfigures the way that the representational relationship between members of Congress and their constituents has previously been conceived. It has explored which legislators are the most likely to prioritize representing disadvantaged groups and why, by investigating the formation of legislative reputations as disadvantaged-group advocates. Taken together, this project suggests three major conclusions.

First, members of Congress cultivate specific group-centered legislative reputations as one of the primary means of fulfilling their representational responsibilities and of communicating their legislative activities to constituents. Second, the framework of the advocacy window makes an important theoretical contribution to understanding the constituency-specific constraints a member faces when making decisions about whether or not to include a group in their legislative reputation, as well as the circumstances under which those constraints can be overcome. Third, the representation of racial/ethnic minorities consistently takes a different form than that of other disadvantaged groups, with members, particularly in the Senate, demonstrating a marked wariness to forming a reputation as a minority advocate. In the sections to follow, I explore these conclusions in greater detail, and discuss the normative implications of each.

7.1 LEGISLATIVE REPUTATIONS AS AN ESSENTIAL CONDUIT FOR REPRESENTATION

This project presents legislative reputations as a critically important, but frequently overlooked, means of understanding how representation happens on a realistic, practical level. The overwhelming majority of the constituents of a member of Congress will be almost entirely in the dark about the specific actions that a member engages in while in the legislature. Instead, what they know about their representative is filtered through the media, and commonly comes in the form of a distilled picture of which groups a member tends to focus their attentions on. Recognizing this, most members seek to create a pattern of behavior that can trickle down to their constituents in a way that will effectively signal which groups on whose behalf they are working. This requires that members make specific choices about which groups they wish to try to center their reputations around. The central focus of this book has been to determine when and why members of Congress choose to cultivate legislative reputations as advocates for disadvantaged groups, in particular.

Chapter 3 demonstrates the frequency with which members include disadvantaged-group advocacy in their legislative reputations, and finds that a significant percentage of legislators do make the choice to include this advocacy in their reputations. Within that group of legislators, though, there is a considerable degree of variation in terms of the level of advocacy being offered, and the particular group that is the focus of those advocacy efforts. A higher percentage of Democrats hold these reputations for group advocacy than Republicans, with reputations for primary advocacy being more common in the House, and superficial advocacy being more common in the Senate.

Legislative reputations are both universal and adaptable. All members of Congress, whether they serve in the House or the Senate, have a reputation surrounding their work within the institution. But at the same time, the focal point of these reputations and the means by which they are built can be vastly different. Every member may have a consciously cultivated reputation, but they were able to craft that reputation in a variety of different ways based upon the particular groups they are seeking to represent, their positions within the leadership or committee structure, or even just based upon their own strengths and preferences. Focusing on reputation, rather than on particular discrete legislative actions paints a broader and more realistic portrait of the means by which representation takes place, as seen in Chapter 6.

While it is true that some members will use common tactics like sponsorship or cosponsorship to uphold their reputations as group advocates, these actions are not one-size-fits-all for all groups. Bill sponsorship and cosponsorship may be appealing for building a reputation as an advocate of groups with mixed perceptions of how deserving they are of assistance from the government, such as Native Americans or the poor, but less appealing for groups with especially high or low levels of perceived deservingness, such as veterans or racial/ethnic minorities. By utilizing member reputation as a big-picture conception of how representation occurs, scholars can also avoid overlooking disadvantaged-group advocacy that exists, but may take a less traditional form than is most commonly the point of focus in the literature.

7.1.1 Normative Implications

To truly understand the quality of representation being offered to disadvantaged groups, it is necessary to take a big-picture view of what representation looks like. If representation is about forming these group-based legislative reputations that can serve as a place of shared understanding for representatives and their constituents, it becomes necessary to survey the entire landscape of reputation building within the House and the Senate to comprehend how equitable our congressional politics really are. Under this framework, constituency characteristics do play an important role in shaping which disadvantaged groups members of Congress will choose to include in their reputations. But at the same time, no member can possibly represent all of the groups within their state or district at once – there is a finite limit to the number of groups that can be included in a single member's legislative reputation. Given this, the likelihood is that any particular group included will also be the most important.

This group-centered view of politics, wherein legislators must make choices about which groups they choose to advocate for, reflects many of the norms of a pluralist system. Each group cannot expect to find an advocate in every member, but they should be able to expect a similar chance that a member will choose to represent them, relative to the size of their group. But, as the preceding chapters have clearly shown, this pluralistic norm breaks down, even among already disadvantaged groups. Groups that are considered less deserving of government assistance generally do not receive the same level of advocacy as those groups that are broadly considered to be highly deserving of government assistance. This discrepancy matters and can make a real difference in people's lives.

On a purely substantive level, group advocacy on the part of members of Congress is necessary to ensure that the needs of a group are addressed, and to push for their inclusion within important legislation. But this advocacy can have more symbolic effects as well. Individuals who feel that their needs are getting a fair hearing in the legislature are more likely to have confidence in the political system, and to be active and engaged in the political process (Uslaner and Brown, 2005). Groups that do not feel that they are being adequately represented, however, can be disincentivized from participating in the political system, exacerbating the inequality that already exists.

7.2 MEMBER REPUTATION AND THE ADVOCACY WINDOW

Chapter 2 of this book introduced the concept of the advocacy window to explain some of the primary drivers of a member's choice about whether or not to include disadvantaged-group advocacy in their legislative reputation. The advocacy window demonstrates the level of discretion that a member has in their choice to include advocating for a disadvantaged group as a component of their reputation, once the size of a group and the ambient temperature toward a group are taken into account. The advocacy window, as depicted in Figure 2.2, is essentially the range in the amount of group representation that a member could engage in without unduly risking the ire of the constituency at large and damaging their electoral prospects. The floor of the advocacy window, the level of representation that would be expected as a starting point, represents the size of the disadvantaged group within the district, while the ceiling, the high point of representation that a member could reasonably engage in, reflects the level of negative feelings toward a group in a district.

As demonstrated in Chapters 4 and 5, the advocacy window is a useful means of conceptualizing which members will choose to focus their advocacy on disadvantaged groups, and why. In the House, group size is seen to be an important baseline factor in determining the level of representation that a group will receive for nearly all groups under evaluation (with women being the sole exception). Consistently, members with a higher percentage of group members in their district are more likely to form a reputation as a group advocate. Similarly, for all but the most highly regarded group (seniors), the ambient temperature does serve as a high water mark on the representation offered, with members being significantly less likely to form a reputation as a group advocate the lower the ambient temperature toward the group in their district.

While there is a good deal to be learned from these instances in which disadvantaged group representation follows the expectations of the advocacy window, there are also important insights to be gained by examining the conditions under which group representation occurs in ways that are not predicted by the advocacy window. When considering representation in the House of Representatives, for instance, the representation of women essentially serves as the exception that proves the rule. Women are unique, in that they not only have very little variation in their size from district to district, but that size – around 50 percent of a constituency – always has the capacity to make a considerable electoral impact.[1] Thus, for women, the floor of the advocacy window would be almost entirely stationary from district to district. Instead, other factors, such as the district ambient temperature, partisanship, and most especially, having a representative who is a woman, have an outsized influence on the reputations as women's advocates that are formed.

Over in the Senate, representation of disadvantaged groups – particularly those who are not generally considered to be highly deserving of government assistance – defy some of the expectations for the advocacy window in extremely important ways. Chief among them is the placement of the floor of the advocacy window. For groups such as seniors and veterans, the larger the group presence within a state, the more likely it is that a senator will include advocacy on their behalf as a component of their legislative reputation, as the advocacy window would predict. But for nearly all of the groups that are not consistently seen as being deserving of government assistance, increasing a group's size within a state does not actually make their senator more likely to form a reputation as a group advocate. This means, in practice, that for groups that are not generally seen as deserving of government assistance, the floor for an acceptable level of representation in the Senate is doing nothing at all. This is strikingly different from the advocacy window in the House, where, regardless of the disadvantaged group under consideration, group size in

---

[1] Obviously, women do not vote anywhere near a monolithic block, but all the same, there is no district in which it could be argued that women did not at least have the potential to be an electorally important constituency.

a district does have a significant effect on the minimum level of representation that a group receives.

Finally, Chapters 4 and 5 have also provided insight into which members of Congress are most likely to take advantage of the existence of a wider advocacy window. Generally speaking, descriptive representatives in the House are more likely to take advantage of having a wider advocacy window to boost the level of representation that they offer a group than non-descriptive representatives. This tends to be true for each group, at each level of advocacy, but with two important exceptions. The first exception is, once again, the representation of women. Female representatives are significantly more likely to have a reputation as a women's advocate than men, regardless of the size of the advocacy window. The second exception is narrower, and refers exclusively to those descriptive representatives who form a reputation for primary or secondary advocacy of racial/ethnic minorities. Unlike in other instances, in which descriptive representatives are more likely to take advantage of the larger advocacy window, minority representatives are more likely to form a reputation as a primary or secondary advocate when the advocacy window is *small*. As discussed in Chapter 4, this is important, as it implies that a minority representative acts to maximize their representation of racial/ethnic minorities in conditions where the threat level is higher, and their margin of error is lower.

In the Senate, the role of descriptive representatives more closely resembles the behavior of racial/ethnic minority representatives with reputations for primary or secondary advocacy in the House. Though female representatives are once again more likely to have a reputation as women's advocates regardless of the size of the advocacy window, for other descriptive representatives in the Senate, they too receive a stronger push to action relative to non-descriptive representatives when facing a narrower advocacy window. In the Senate, then, descriptive representatives are not seeking to maximize the representation they offer to a group when the advocacy window is at its widest, but rather are more likely to include at least some level of group advocacy into their legislative reputation when the advocacy window is at risk of closing.

7.2.1 Normative Implications

There are a number of normative consequences that stem from these findings about how members of Congress alter their representational decision-making based upon the advocacy window that they face. First and foremost, the differences in the location of the floor of the advocacy window between the House and the Senate have some troubling implications in terms of the representation that different groups receive. One of the most basic theories of how representative democracy should work contends that representation must be rooted in the needs of the constituency itself. In the House, this holds up reasonably well. But in the Senate, the choice to form a reputation as a disadvantaged-group advocate is, in many cases, untethered from the size of the group within the constituency. This means that, especially for groups that are considered to be less deserving of government assistance, simply being present in a state, even in large numbers, does not guarantee the level of representation that would otherwise be expected.

Generally speaking, the representational scheme through which seats are allocated in the Senate tends to work to the detriment of disadvantaged groups, as they are unlikely to ever represent a majority of a state (women being the exception to this). But these results show that this handicap may in fact be even worse for those disadvantaged groups who are not considered to be broadly deserving of government assistance, as the degree of representation they receive is not even significantly related to what they could expect given their size within a state. Given the bicameral nature of the lawmaking process in the United States, this asymmetric representation of groups that are less well regarded by the population at large could have outsized effects. Even if disadvantaged groups tend to receive more appropriate levels of representation in the House than in the Senate, it is not enough to guarantee that their needs actually make it into law, as all legislation must pass through both chambers.

There are also normative implications to the reluctance of members to utilize the openings that their advocacy windows present to provide a higher level of representation for the disadvantaged. This hesitancy is evident in both the House and the Senate, where, even for groups whose size within a district provides a stable floor for the level of representation that can be expected, few members seek to move above that floor. This tendency of most members to avoid shooting for the ceiling can make the disconnect between group size and representation in the Senate even more problematic. If the floor for the majority of groups who are not considered to be the most deserving of government assistance is actually doing nothing at all, and members are hesitant to utilize the additional representational space that their advocacy window provides, that means that less well-regarded disadvantaged groups can end up having few or no advocates in the Senate (as is largely the case over the time period studied for racial/ethnic minorities and the LGBTQ community).

Even in the House, where group size does generally represent a solid floor that can be relied upon when members are making their representational decisions, most members are unwilling to take risks and take advantage of the level of disadvantaged-group advocacy that could be permitted, given the size of the advocacy window. The overt caution of most lawmakers when it comes to the advocacy window available to them makes the placement of the floor within a district especially crucial. Because most members tend not to budge from the floor of their advocacy window, the intentional creation of things like majority-minority districts can bolster the representation that a disadvantaged group receives. Steve Cohen (D), for example, is one of the few white members of Congress representing a majority non-white district, the 9th District of Tennessee. To meet the level of representation that would be expected given his advocacy window, he assiduously cultivates his reputation as an advocate for racial/ethnic minorities, once even petitioning to join the Congressional Black Caucus.

Finally, these results do clearly show the importance of having descriptive representatives of the disadvantaged present within Congress. While it is far from a new argument to say that descriptive representatives lead to better representation, this project is able to demonstrate this in a comprehensive way, across a number of different groups, including those that have been less subject to scholarly scrutiny. The advocacy window, in an ideal world, should work in the same way for all representatives – with each being equally likely to utilize their discretion and boost their advocacy on behalf of any given group. The clear separation between descriptive and non-descriptive representatives when it comes to making the decision to incorporate disadvantaged-group advocacy – especially for groups that aren't broadly considered to be highly deserving of government assistance – demonstrates the extent to which it cannot simply be assumed that any representative for a state or district will represent that group in the same way. Instead, for most groups (with the primary exception receiving further discussion below), boosting the number of descriptive representatives in Congress is an effective means of increasing the likelihood that a member of Congress will prioritize their representation.

7.3 THE REPRESENTATION OF RACIAL/ETHNIC MINORITIES

One of the last big takeaways from this project is that, quite simply, the representation of racial/ethnic minorities is different than that of other disadvantaged groups in a number of key ways. Most crucially, these differences tend to only run in a single direction – that of receiving less representation than would otherwise be expected. The previous two sections have alluded to several of these distinctions, but it is worth examining them at greater length. To begin, as seen in Chapter 3, the partisan and chamber-specific differences in who chooses to cultivate a reputation as an advocate for racial/ethnic minorities are markedly unlike those seen for any other disadvantaged group.

Chapter 3 demonstrated that, though Democrats are more likely to have a reputation as a disadvantaged-group advocate overall, the breakdown of which groups a member is an advocate for are rather similar, with one particular exception. Namely, there are very few Republicans with reputations for advocacy of racial/ethnic minorities. Even among Democrats, however, the bulk of these advocates are found in the House and not in the Senate. In fact, there is only one senator sampled with a reputation as a primary advocate of racial/ethnic minorities, compared to fifty-five in the House. There is no other disadvantaged group studied for which these discrepancies by party and by chamber are this stark.

As discussed in the previous section, descriptive representation can be a means through which disadvantaged groups that are generally considered to be less deserving of government assistance can bolster the level of representation that they receive. But is this also true for racial/ethnic minorities? The unsatisfying answer to this question is: it depends. As highlighted above, in the House, representation generally tends to nicely follow along with the broad precepts of the advocacy window. As expected, members who are themselves racial/ethnic minorities are more likely to form reputations as disadvantaged-group advocates, even after the percentage of non-white individuals in a district is taken into account.

Racial/ethnic minorities serving in the Senate, however, are not significantly more likely to form reputations as minority advocates. This is quite different from what is seen for the descriptive representatives of most other disadvantaged groups perceived as being less than highly deserving of government assistance in the Senate, and a departure from the effect of minority representation in the House. It is likely, however, that this outcome for minority representation in the Senate is a direct result of the small sample of racial/ethnic minorities that ever make it to the Senate in the first place. As an example, there are only two Black senators out of all of the Congresses sampled. One of these, Carol Moseley-Braun (D), former senator from Illinois, is the only senator included in the sample with a primary reputation as an advocate for racial/ethnic minorities. So, while suggestive of the potential benefits of electing more descriptive representatives to the Senate, the limited numbers make it difficult to estimate what the predicted effects of having a greater number of racial/ethnic minorities might be, and what conclusions should be drawn.

It is also possible that there are systematic differences between the racial/ethnic minorities that get elected to the House, and those that get elected to the Senate. Much of the previous research into effects of descriptive representation of racial/ethnic minorities has looked at the House (for the obvious reason that minority representatives are so scarce in the Senate). But if the electoral environment of running for statewide office makes it less likely that racial/ethnic minorities will be elected to serve in the Senate, and those who are elected are less likely to serve as advocates than those elected to the House, it makes it much more difficult to resolve the representational inequalities that exist.

7.3.1 Normative Implications

The consequences of this unequal access to representation for racial/ethnic minorities, even relative to other disadvantaged groups, may be straightforward and easy to diagnose, but exceedingly difficult to solve. For most of the groups evaluated over the course of this project, the best ways to increase the likelihood that a member will form a reputation as a group advocate is to boost the percentage of group members within a state, or to elect more descriptive representatives. But in the case of the representation of racial/ethnic minorities in the Senate, neither of these are a sure-fire solution.

Ultimately, this representation deficit has real and consequential effects on the amount of effort Congress as a whole puts into addressing the problems facing racial/ethnic minorities in the United States. The reluctance of most members of Congress to incorporate minority advocacy into their legislative reputation, even when their advocacy window would allow for it, speaks to the uniquely precarious position of racial/ethnic minorities, even among other disadvantaged groups. This tendency, particularly in the Senate, for members of Congress to shirk the representational responsibilities that would be expected for nearly any other group serves to exacerbate the challenges that racial/ethnic minorities already face, and makes it markedly less likely that their needs will be addressed.

It is also noteworthy that even those members who do choose to build a reputation as an advocate of racial/ethnic minorities are much less likely, particularly in the Senate, to uphold that reputation through bill sponsorship or cosponsorship, which are the tools that are most closely tied to actual legislation. This implies that two potentially troubling forces could be at work. First, these trends may demonstrate that advocates themselves may frequently be pessimistic about the prospect of positive change and/or community assistance through the most common legislative means. Or, secondly, the risk of committing to a specific bill to address racial inequalities is seen as posing too high of a risk of backlash to be worth it, especially for those holding state-wide office, even for members who are seeking to build some form of reputation for advocacy. If one or both of these forces are at work, it suggests that advocates of racial/ethnic minorities face an even steeper climb to producing tangible results than advocates of other disadvantaged groups.

7.4 NEXT STEPS FOR THIS RESEARCH AGENDA

This project has provided a deeper understanding of which members of Congress will choose to build a reputation as a disadvantaged-group advocate, and why. In doing so, it also opens the door to new questions that are worthy of further research. The three most interesting of these paths for future research involve evaluating further links between member reputation and specific legislative actions, exploring the extent to which members of Congress actively campaign on their legislative reputations, and investigating the frequency with which disadvantaged-group advocates in the House move to the Senate.

Utilizing legislative reputation as a means of understanding the groups that members of Congress choose to represent has an important advantage over other ways of conceptualizing representation by not placing a priori requirements on the types of issues or actions that a member may choose to undertake on behalf of a group. However, once those reputations are established, there is value to understanding any specific patterns in the ways that members tend to form their reputations as advocates for specific groups compared to others, or if there are consistencies in how superficial advocates act relative to primary or secondary advocates. Considering the connections between bill sponsorship and cosponsorship and member reputation has started this process, but there are many more steps in the legislative process that should be investigated. Pursuing further understanding of the patterns of which actions members choose to engage in to cultivate their reputations as advocates for disadvantaged groups could provide important information about the stage of the process in which advocates tend to put their efforts. It could also be used to demonstrate the effectiveness of these efforts at advancing bills in the legislative process or expanding the size of legislative coalitions within the institution.

Throughout this project, the focus has been directed solely at a member's actions within the legislature. But a member's actions within Congress itself and on the campaign trail are not wholly separate, and there a good deal that could be learned be evaluating the extent to which members of Congress advertise their reputations as disadvantaged-group advocates. Or, in the case of non-incumbents running for office, how clearly they foreshadow their future disadvantaged-group advocacy. Additionally, examining any variation in how selectively members with reputations as advocates for different groups tout those reputations during their campaigns could provide valuable information about how wary members are about deterring other voters who are not themselves group members. This could be particularly important for members of the House who are choosing to run for the Senate, which ties in directly to the last of the most promising next steps for this research agenda.

Since some of the earliest Congresses, between roughly 30–50 percent of individuals serving in the Senate had previously been elected to the House of Representatives (Glassman and Wilhelm, 2017). In recent years, the percentage of senators with prior service in the House on their resume has stayed near the top end of that range, with fifty out of 100 senators in the 115th Congress having previous House experience. Thus, to better understand the differences in the type and degree of disadvantaged-group advocacy that exist between the House and the Senate, an important place to look would be among members of the House who attempt to move to the Senate. This is a particularly interesting extension of the research agenda, and would have the potential to answer three questions. Specifically, are members of the House with reputations as advocates for a given disadvantaged group more or less likely to: make the decision to run for the Senate, win those races for a Senate seat, or change their legislative reputation upon arrival in the Senate? Providing answers to these questions could provide valuable insight into why the House and the Senate provide such different levels of representation across disadvantaged groups, and also point toward some potential solutions.

7.5 CONCLUDING THOUGHTS

Questions about who gets represented in the United States Congress, and when, and why, and how, make up the very bedrock of our system of representative democracy. This project has contributed to these perennial questions by investigating which members of Congress make the choice to represent some of the most vulnerable groups in our society, and by providing a theoretical framework for understanding what drives those decisions. The research has demonstrated that not all disadvantaged groups receive equivalent levels of representation. Members of Congress are highly cognizant of how their representational choices could affect their reelection prospects, and are particularly wary when it comes to representing those disadvantaged groups that are not widely seen as being deserving of government assistance.

Group-based legislative reputations are a conduit through which members can express their representational priorities in ways that match up with how their constituents understand the political world. By centering this investigation on the critical but underappreciated role that legislative reputations play in the representational relationship, this project offers a fresh perspective and a new step toward a better understanding of congressional representation as a whole, while also offering insight into the specific representation that disadvantaged groups receive. This research provides an opportunity to fill in some of the gaps in our knowledge about why representational inequality exists, and in doing so, sheds light on a potential path to more equal representation within the US Congress.

Appendices

APPENDIX A
Issue Coding for Disadvantaged Group Advocacy for Reputation Measure

Table A-1 presents the list of issues that are included as instances of advocacy for a disadvantaged group, in addition to all actions that are specifically attributed to being done to serve a particular group.

TABLE A-I *Issue coding by disadvantaged group*

Veterans

- Employment assistance (workforce training/increased licensures and certifications from military experience/employer tax credits for hiring/employment protections for returning guard members)
- Creation of veteran job corps
- Educational assistance (tuition assistance/GI Bill)
- Healthcare (head trauma/PTSD/benefits expansion/telemedicine for rural vets/ veteran suicide prevention/access to mental health care/counseling on deployment and return)
- Assistance for disabled vets (housing/benefits/employment)
- Housing benefits (homelessness prevention/special assistant at HUD)
- VA improvements (fixing backlog/higher reimbursements for longer travels/ automatic enrollment and training in using the system)
- Resources for survivors of military sexual assault
- Improvement of reintegration programs (counseling/financial planning)
- Veterans History Project

Seniors
- Protecting against financial scams
- Medicare protection/expansion
- Social Security protection/expansion (COLA increases/eliminating income cap)
- Opposition to voter registration/ID laws (because of effects on elderly)
- Expanding prescription drug coverage for seniors

(continued)

TABLE A-I *(continued)*

- Senior nutrition and other services
- Older Americans Act
- Expanding access to hospice and long-term care

LGBTQ
- Repeal DADT
- Repeal DOMA
- Legalizing same-sex marriage
- Employment protections
- Government employee benefits for same-sex partners
- Anti-bullying and nondiscrimination policies
- Domestic violence/sexual assault protections (VAWA)
- HIV/AIDS

Racial/Ethnic Minorities
- Confinement/racial profiling/marijuana and other drug offenses/former inmate reintegration/police brutality
- Reparations (slavery/Japanese internment)
- Treatment HIV/AIDS (including in prison)
- Voting rights (opposition to attempts to end early voting and require additional voter registration or ID/simplify voter registration of Voting Rights Act)
- Civil Rights Act
- Housing assistance
- Employment (increase federal grants and contracts to minority-owned business/assistance to Black farmers)
- African American History Museum
- MLK birthday as federal holiday
- Education (minorities in STEM, government and private partnerships with minority colleges/funding)

Immigrants
- Immigration reform (path to citizenship/legal status/worker status/asylum seekers)
- Shorten citizenship waiting period (members of military/family reunification)
- DREAM act
- Domestic violence protections (VAWA)
- Citizenship education programs (English language assistance/naturalization workshops)
- Legal status for military/college
- Elimination of country caps

Women
- Reproductive rights (abortion coverage/contraception coverage and availability)

(continued)

- Employment (equal pay/pregnancy discrimination/breast pump space)
- Healthcare (mammograms/breast cancer/nopays for preventative care)
- Sexual assault and domestic violence (VAWA/military programs/expansion of definition of rape/homelessness prevention for domestic violence victims)
- Military (expansion of roles for women/equipment like body armor to fit women)

Poor
- Employment assistance (worker training/new WPA or other job corps/tax credits for employers hiring someone unemployed or on public assistance/ create "empowerment zones" providing tax credits for companies going into impoverished areas)
- Unemployment benefits
- Housing assistance (renters/homelessness/heating assistance/Home Energy Assistance Program/Affordable Housing Trust Fund/foreclosure assistance/ tax credit for the creation of low-income housing)
- Nutrition (expansion of SNAP benefits/SNAP at farmer's markets/free and reduced lunch benefits)
- Education (Head Start/access to art, economics, civics, and foreign language classes/TRIO programs and outreach to disadvantaged students)
- Healthcare (Children's Health Insurance Program/Medicaid expansion/dental coverage/support for community health centers/continuous open enrollment for Medicaid and CHIP)
- Expanded access to child care
- Broadband access for low-income communities
- Minimum wage increase
- Free tax prep for low-income individuals and families and financial literacy programs
- TANF benefit extensions

APPENDIX B
Reputations for Primary and Secondary Disadvantaged-Group Advocacy in the House and the Senate

The following tables present a list of members who are coded in the 103rd, 105th, 108th, 110th, or 113th Congresses as having a reputation for primary or secondary advocacy of disadvantaged groups. Table B-1 shows the members with these reputations in the House of Representatives, while Table B-2 does the same for those in the Senate.

TABLE B-I *Reputations for primary and secondary advocacy by disadvantaged group in the House of Representatives (103rd, 105th, 108th, 110th, 113th Congresses)*

Veterans

Jeff Miller (R-FL1)	Rich Nugent (R-FL11)	Dave Weldon (R-FL15)
Gus Bilirakis (R-FL12)	Bruce Braley (D-IA1)	Bill Pascrell (D-NJ8)
Dan Benishek (R-MI01)	Niki Tsongas (D-MA3)	Marcy Kaptur (D-OH9)
Joe Runyan (R-NJ3)	Tim Walz (D-MN1)	Mike Doyle (D-PA14)
Joe Wilson (R-SC2)	Carol Shea-Porter (D-NH1)	Silvestre Reyes (D-TX14)
Vic Snyder (D-AR02)	Christopher Smith (R-NJ1)	Bob Stump (R-AZ3)
Bob Filner (D-CA51)	Terry Everett (R-AL02)	Luis Gutierrez (D-IL4)
Susan Davis (D-CA53)	Cliff Stearns (R-FL6)	Steve Buyer (R-IN5)
Ginny Brown-Waite (R-FL5)	John Tierney (D-MA6)	Maxine Waters (D-CA35)
Tom Latham (R-IA04)	Stephen Lynch (D-MA9)	George Sangmeister (D-IL11)
Henry Brown (R-SC1)	Michael Michaud (D-ME2)	Jill Long (D-IN4)
Solomon Ortiz (D-TX27)	Chet Edwards (D-TX17)	David Bonior (D-MI10)
Lane Evans (D-IL17)	Ciro Rodriguez (D-TX23)	Jack Fields (R-TX8)
Sonny Montgomery (D-MS3)	Jo Ann Davis (R-VA1)	Frank Tejeda (D-TX28)
Douglas Applegate (D-OH18)	Ron Kind (D-WI3)	Mike Rogers (R-AL3)
Corrine Brown (D-FL5)	Michael Bilirakis (R-FL9)	Elton Gallegly (R-CA24)

Seniors

Mike Rogers (R-AL3)	Henry Waxman (D-CA30)	Richard Burr (R-NC5)
Pete Stark (D-CA13)	John Larson (D-CT1)	Steve Israel (D-NY2)
Tom Allen (D-ME1)	Robert Wexler (D-FL19)	Rob Portman (R-OH2)
Jo Ann Emerson (R-MO8)	David Loebsack (D-IA2)	Jim Turner (D-TX2)
Lloyd Doggett (D-TX25)	Richard Neal (D-MA2)	Sam Johnson (R-TX3)

(continued)

Earl Pomeroy (D-ND1)
Gerald Kleczka (D-WI4)
William Clay (D-MO1)
Jill Long (D-IN4)
Jeff Miller (R-FL1)
Gus Bilirakis (R-FL12)
Joe Wilson (R-SC2)
Terry Everett (R-AL2)
Dennis Moore (D-KS3)
Carolyn Maloney (D-NY14)
Pat Tiberi (R-OH12)
Ted Strickland (D-OH6)
Kent Bentson (D-TX25)
Ted Deutch (D_FL21)
Peter DeFazio (D-OR4)
David McKinley (R-WV4)
Marion Berry (D-AR1)

LGBTQ

Jerrold Nadler (D-NY10)
Henry Waxman (D-CA29)
Lynn Woolsey (D-CA6)
Lois Capps (D-CA24)

Racial/Ethnic Minorities

Barbara Lee (D-CA13)
John Lewis (D-GA5)
Keith Ellison (D-MN5)
William Clay (D-MO1)
Earl Hilliard (D-AL7)

Dave Camp (R-MI4)
John Dingell (D-MI15)
Jim Ramstad (R-MN3)
Bill Pascrell (D-NJ8)
Joseph Crowley (D-NY7)
John Peterson (R-PA5)
Shelley Moore Capito (R-WV2)
Robert Matsui (D-CA5)
Nancy Johnson (R-CT5)
Peter Deutch (D-FL20)
E. Clay Shaw (R-FL22)
Jan Schakowski (D-IL9)
Jim McCrery (R-IA4)
John Tierney (D-MA6)
Benjamin Cardin (D-MD3)
Michael Michaud (D-ME1)
Gil Gutknecht (R-MN1)

Jared Polis (D-CO2)
Barney Frank (D-MA4)
Jim Kolbe (R-AZ8)
Nancy Pelosi (D-CA8)

Gregory Meeks (D-NY6)
Sheila Jackson-Lee (D-TX18)
Cynthia McKinney (D-GA4)
Donald Payne (D-NJ10)
Norman Mineta (D-CA15)

Bernard Sanders (I-VT1)
Earl Hilliard (D-AL7)
Matthew Martinez (D-CA31)
Greg Ganske (R-IA4)
Dennis Hastert (R-IL14)
Dale Kildee (D-MI9)
Richard Gephardt (D-MO3)
Charles Rangel (D-NY15)
Sherrod Brown (D-OH13)
Chaka Fattah (D-PA2)
Tim Holden (D-PA6)
Patrick Kennedy (D-RI1)
Al McCandless (R-CA44)
C.W. Bill Young (R-FL10)
Andrew Jacobs (D-IN10)
Sander Levin (D-MI12)
J.J. Pickle (D-TX10)

Patricia Schroeder (D-CO1)
Jim McDermott (D-WA7)

Bob Clement (D-TN5)
Ben Ray Lujan (D-NM3)
Artur Davis (D-AL7)
Ed Pastor (D-AZ4)
Hilda Solis (D-CA32)

(continued)

TABLE B-I (continued)

Tom Latham (R-IA04)	Don Edwards (D-CA16)	Grace Napolitano (D-CA38)
Xavier Becerra (D-CA31)	Ileana Ros-Lehtinen (R-FL18)	Joe Baca (D-CA43)
Gene Green (D-TX29)	Cardiss Collins (D-IL7)	Kendrick Meek (D-FL17)
Bennie Thompson (D-MS2)	Kwesi Mfume (D-MD7)	William Jefferson (D-LA2)
Ciro Rodriguez (D-TX23)	Barbara-Rose Collins (D-MI15)	Albert Wynn (D-MD4)
Yvette Clark (D-NY9)	Craig Washington (D-TX18)	Emanual Cleaver (D-MO5)
Ruben Hinojosa (D-TX15)	Edolphus Towns (D-NY10)	G.K. Butterfield (D-NC1)
Solomon Ortiz (D-TX27)	Pete Stark (D-CA13)	Jose Serrano (D-NY16)
Juanita Millender-McDonald (D-CA37)	Chaka Fattah (D-PA2)	Silvestre Reyes (D-TX16)
Maxine Waters (D-CA43)	Cliff Stearns (R-FL6)	Charlie Gonzalez (D-TX20)
Bobby Rush (D-IL1)	Raul Grijalva (D-AZ7)	Robert Menendez (D-NJ13)
John Conyers (D-MI13)	Linda Sanchez (D-CA39)	Amo Houghton (R-NY29)
Marcia Fudge (D-OH11)	Alcee Hastings (D-FL23)	Robert Matsui (D-CA5)
Steve Cohen (D-TN9)	Charles Rangel (D-NY15)	Lincoln Diaz-Balart (R-FL21)
Robert Scott (D-VA3)	Lacy Clay (D-MO1)	Floyd Flake (D-NY6)
Michael Honda (D-CA15)	Jesse Jackson (D-IL2)	Henry Bonilla (R-TX23)
Diane Watson (D-CA33)	Joseph Kennedy (D-MA8)	Alan Wheat (D-MO5)
Danny Davis (D-IL7)	Nydia Velazquez (D-NY12)	Major Owens (D-NY11)
Carolyn Cheeks Kirkpatrick (D-MI13)	Lane Evans (D-IL-17)	Hamilton Fish (R-NY19)
Melvin Watt (D-SC12)	Terry Everett (R-AL2)	Louis Stokes (D-OH11)
Eddie Bernice Johnson (D-TX30)	Henry Brown (R-SC1)	Tom Sawyer (D-OH14)
Ed Pastor (D-AZ4)	Jack Fields (R-TX8)	Thomas Foglietta (D-PA1)
Lucille Roybal-Allard (D-CA34)	Luis Gutierrez (D-IL4)	
Elijah Cummings (D-MD7)	James Clyburn (D-SC6)	

Immigrants

Xavier Becerra (D-CA31)	Hilda Solis (D-CA32)	Bob Filner (D-CA50)
Yvette Clark (D-NY9)	Zoe Lofgren (D-CA19)	Barney Frank (D-MA4)
Lucille Roybal-Allard (D-CA34)	Linda Sanchez (D-CA39)	Loretta Sanchez (D-CA46)
Ed Pastor (D-AZ4)	Mario Diaz-Balart (R-FL25)	Raul Labrador (R-ID1)

(continued)

Raul Grijalva (D-AZ7)
Nydia Velazquez (D-NY21)
Terry Everett (R-AL2)
Jose Serrano (D-NY16)
Ileana Ros-Lehtinen (R-FL18)
Lincoln Diaz-Balart (R-FL21)

Women

Linda Sanchez (D-CA38)
Lucille Roybal-Allard (D-CA34)
Don Edwards (D-CA16)
Cardiss Collins (D-IL7)
Carolyn Maloney (D-NY14)
Nita Lowey (D-NY18)
Gwen Moore (D-WI4)
Loretta Sanchez (D-CA47)
Juanita Millender-McDonald (D-CA37)
Patricia Schroeder (D-CO1)
Jackie Speier (D-CA14)
Rosa DeLauro (D-CT3)
Diana DeGette (D-CO1)
Louise Slaughter (D-NY28)
Barbara Kennelly (D-CT1)
Patsy Mink (D-HI2)
Constance Morella (R-MD8)
Susan Molinari (R-NY13)
Sheila Jackson-Lee (D-TX18)

Poor

Gwen Moore (D-WI4)
Juanita Millender-McDonald (D-CA37)

Howard Berman (D-CA26)
Ruben Hinojosa (D-TX15)
Sheila Jackson-Lee (D-TX18)
Kendrick Meek (D-FL17)
Judy Chu (D-CA27)
Major Owens (D-NY11)
Zoe Lofgren (D-CA19)
Hilda Solis (D-CA32)
Lois Capps (D-CA24)
Sam Farr (D-CA17)
Barbara Lee (D-CA13)
Edolphus Towns (D-NY10)
Chaka Fattah (D-PA2)
Eddie Bernice Johnson (D-TX30)
Lynn Woolsey (D-CA6)
Ed Royce (R-CA40)
Jerrold Nadler (D-NY10)
Henry Waxman (D-CA30)
Corrine Brown (D-FL3)
Susan Davis (D-CA53)
Tom Allen (D-ME1)
Douglas Applegate (D-OH18)
Tammy Baldwin (D-WI2)
Sue Kelly (R-NY19)
Elizabeth Furse (D-OR1)
Barbara Kennelly (D-CT1)
Linda Sanchsz (D-CA39)

Mary Bono (R-CA45)
Tom Campbell (R-CA15)
Romano Mazzoli (D-KY3)
Luis Gutierrez (D-IL4)
Grace Napolitano (D-CA38)
Olympia Snowe (R-ME2)
Barbara Vucanovich (R-NV2)
Ron Wyden (D-OR3)
Steve Buyer (R-IN5)
John Shimkus (R-IL19)
Tim Ryan (D-OH17)
Anna Eshoo (D-CA14)
Melissa Hart (R-PA4)
Nancy Johnson (R-CT6)
Steny Hoyer (D-MD5)
Ike Skelton (D-MO4)
Jennifer Dunn (R-WA8)
Vic Fazio (D-CA3)
John Edward Porter (R-IL10)
Tony Hall (D-OH3)
Ronald Machtley (R-RI1)
Marilyn Lloyd (D- TN 3)

Jill Long (D-IN4)
Jeff Miller (R-FL1)

(continued)

Patsy Mink (D-HI2)	Sheila Jackson-Lee (D-TX18)	Ted Strickland (D-OH6)
Hilda Solis (D-CA32)	Edolphus Towns (D-NY10)	John Tierney (D-MA6)
Barbara Lee (D-CA13)	Diana DeGette (D-CO1)	Bernard Sanders (I-VT1)
Lynn Woolsey (D-CA6)	Tom Allen (D-ME1)	Matthew Martinez (D-CA31)
Henry Waxman (D-CA29)	Tammy Baldwin (D-WI2)	Earl Pomeroy (D-ND1)
Tony Hall (D-OH3)	Ron Wyden (D-OR3)	Anthony Weiner (D-NY9)
Nydia Velazquez (D-NY21)	Louise Slaughter (D-NY28)	John Peterson (R-PA5)
Maxine Waters (D-CA43)	Gene Green (D-TX29)	Max Sandlin (D-TX1)
Carolyn Cheeks Kirkpatrick (D-MI13)	John Conyers (D-MI13)	Walter Capps (D-CA22)
Charles Rangel (D-NY15)	Michael Bilirakis (R-FL9)	Jim Maloney (D-CT5)
Chaka Fattah (D-PA2)	Jesse Jackson (D-IL2)	Carrie Meek (D-FL17)
Xavier Becerra (D-CA31)	William Clay (D-MO1)	Jerry Costello (D-IL12)
Raul Grijalva (D-AZ7)	Dale Kildee (D-MI9)	Karen McCarthy (D-MO5)
Ruben Hinojosa (D-TX15)	Stephanie Tubbs Jones (D-OH11)	William Coyne (D-PA14)
Major Owens (D-NY11)	Phil English (R-PA3)	Bob Stump (R-AZ3)
Jose Serrano (D-NY16)	George Miller (D-CA11)	David Loebsack (D-IA2)
Al Green (R-TX9)	Chellie Pingree (D-ME1)	Brett Guthrie (D-KY2)
John Lewis (D-GA5)	Judy Biggert (R-IL13)	Michael Turner (R-0H10)
Keith Ellison (D-MN5)	Luis Gutierrez (D-IL4)	Spencer Bachus (R-AL6)
Tom Latham (R-IA04)	Mary Bono (R-CA45)	David Obey (D-WI7)
Marcia Fudge (D-OH11)	Tom Sawyer (D-OH14)	Terri Sewell (D-AL7)
Robert Scott (D-VA3)	Jan Schakowski (D-IL9)	John Larson (D-CT1)
Diane Watson (D-CA33)	Sam Farr (D-CA17)	David Scott (D-GA13)
Danny Davis (D-IL7)	Jim McGovern (D-MA3)	Carol Shea-Porter (D-NH1)
Barbara-Rose Collins (D-MI15)	Sander Levin (D-MI12)	Timothy Bishop (D-NY1)
Joseph Kennedy (D-MA8)	Earl Hilliard (D-AL7)	Mark Souder (R-IN3)
Henry Brown (R-SC1)	Bennie Thompson (D-MS2)	Martin Olav Sabo (D-MN5)

(continued)

Artur Davis (D-AL7)	Donald Payne (D-NJ10)	Mike McIntyre (D-NC7)
Bobby Rush (D-IL1)	Kwesi Mfiime (D-MD7)	Virgil Goode (R-VA5)
Floyd Flake (D-NY6)	Pete Stark (D-CA13)	Tom Petri (R-WI6)
Andre Carson (D-IN7)	Cliff Stearns (R-FL6)	Scott Baesler (D-KY6)
Julia Carson (D-IN7)	G.K. Butterfield (D-NC1)	John Olver (D-MA1)
Eva Clayton (D-NC1)	Gregory Meeks (D-NY6)	Jim Ramstad (R-MN3)
Barney Frank (D-MA4)	Henry Bonilla (R-TX23)	Bruce Vento (D-MN4)
Jim McDermott (D-WA7)	Thomas Foglietta (D-PA1)	Louis Stokes (D-OH11)
Frederica Wilson (D-FL24)	Frank Pallone (D-NJ6)	Ron Klink (D-PA4)
Lloyd Doggett (D-TX25)	Albert Wynn (D-MD4)	Jon Fox (R-PA13)
Ric Keller (R-FL8)	Lacy Clay (D-MO1)	Thomas Barrett (D-WV1)
Jack Quinn (R-NY27)	Loretta Sanchez (D-CA47)	Neil Abercrombie (D-HI1)
Benjamin Cardin (D-MD3)	Harold Ford (D-TN9)	James Oberstar (D-MN8)
Nita Lowey (D-NY18)	Julian Dixon (D-CA32)	Ronald Dellums (D-CA9)
Rosa DeLauro (D-CT3)	Christopher Shays (R-CT4)	Lucille Roybal-Allard (D-CA34)

TABLE B-2 *Reputations for primary and secondary advocacy by disadvantaged group in the Senate (103rd, 105th, 108th, 110th, 113th Congresses)*

Veterans

Tom Daschle (D-SD)	John Rockefeller (D-WV)	Patty Murrary (D-WA)
John Glenn (D-OH)	Arlen Specter (R-PA)	John Boozman (R-AR)
Frank Murkowski (R-AK)	Tim Johnson (D-SD)	Bill Nelson (D-FL)
Barbara Mikulski (D-MD)	Larry Craig (R-ID)	

Seniors

John Rockefeller (D-WV)	David Pryor (D-AR)	Jon Corzine (D-NJ)
Bill Nelson (D-FL)	John McCain (R-AZ)	Mark Dayton (D-MN)
Debbie Stabenow (D-MI)	Daniel Patrick Moynihan (D-NY)	Ron Wyden (D-OR)
Marco Rubio (R-FL)	Harry Reid (D-NV)	Herb Kohl (D-WI)
Tim Johnson (D-SD)	William Roth (R-DE)	Benjamin Cardin (D-MD)
Bernard Sanders (I-VT)	John Breaux (D-LA)	Tom Harkin (D-IA)

LGBTQ

Tammy Baldwin (D-WI)	Gordon Smith (R-OR)	Charles Robb (D-VA)

Racial/Ethnic Minorities

Carol Moseley-Braun (D-IL)	Bob Dole (R-KS)	Bill Bradley (D-NJ)
Edward Kennedy (D-MA)	John Danforth (R-MO)	
Howard Metzenbaum (D-OH)	James Jeffords (R-VT)	

Immigrants

Spencer Abraham (R-MI)	Larry Craig (R-ID)	Robert Menendez (D-NJ)
Richard Durbin (D-IL)	Alan Simpson (R-WY)	
Edward Kennedy (D-MA)	John McCain (R-AZ)	

Women

Carol Moseley-Braun (D-IL)	Bill Bradley (D-NJ)	Harry Reid (D-NV)
Barbara Mikulski (D-MD)	Charles Schumer (D-NY)	Bob Packwood (R-OR)
Patty Murray (D-WA)	Kay Bailey Hutchison (R-TX)	Joseph Biden (D-DE)
Olympia Snowe (R-ME)	Tammy Baldwin (D-WI)	John Chafee (R-RI)
Barbara Boxer (D-CA)	Kirsten Gillibrand (D-NY)	

Poor

John Rockefeller (D-WV)	Gordon Smith (R-OR)	Richard Durbin (D-IL)

(continued)

TABLE B-2 *(continued)*

Bernard Sanders (I-VT)	Claiborne Pell (D-RI)	Christopher Dodd (D-CT)
Olympia Snowe (R-ME)	Daniel Patrick Moynihan (D-NY)	Blanche Lincoln (D-AR)
Tom Harkin (D-IA)	Jon Corzine (D-NJ)	Peter Fitzgerald (R-IL)
Paul Wellstone (D-MN)	Orrin Hatch (R-UT)	Maria Cantwell (D-WA)
Edward Kennedy (D-MA)	Charles Grassley (R-IA)	Paul Sarbanes (D-OR)
Robert Menendez (D-NJ)	Daniel Coats (R-IN)	Jeff Merkley (R-OR)
Paul Simon (D-IL)	Jeff Bingaman (D-NM)	Jack Reed (D-RI)
Bob Dole (R-KS)	Pete Domenici (R-NM)	

APPENDIX C
Multilevel Regression with Poststratification and Estimating State and District Ambient Temperature

Multilevel regression with poststratification (MRP) is a technique that uses multilevel modeling and Bayesian statistics to generate estimates that are a function of both demographic and geographic characteristics (Park, Gelman, and Bafumi, 2004; Lax and Phillips, 2009; Warshaw and Rodden, 2012). This method combines demographic and public opinion data to create predictions for small subsets of the population, which are then weighted by subgroup population within a geographic area and summed for all subgroups within that area (in this case, a congressional district.) For data with an inherently hierarchical structure (as is the case for individuals within districts that are within states), multilevel models have an advantage over classical regression models. Classical regression models use either complete pooling data to generate effects (as when no district or state effects are taken into account) or no pooling (as when models include fixed effects for a respondent's state or district). Multilevel regression models allow for data to be partially pooled to a degree dictated by the data, based upon group sample size and variation. These models thus allow for the effects of demographics to vary by geography, while also pulling the estimates for states or districts with limited numbers of observations or high variance toward the mean, and allowing estimates for states and districts with more robust samples and tighter variances to be more influenced by district-specific effects.

MRP generated estimates of public opinion outperform both disaggregated means and presidential vote share measures at the state-, congressional district-, and state senate district-levels, producing estimates that are more correlated with population means, have smaller errors, and are more reliable (Lax and Phillips, 2009; Warshaw and Rodden, 2012). These differences are even more apparent with the smaller sample sizes (2,500 for congressional districts) common to most national surveys. MRP estimates are also far less subject to bias than disaggregated means. Disaggregating from nationally (rather than district or state) representative samples can result in biased predictions. MRP avoids this pitfall because all estimates are weighted according to the percentage of a state or district that any particular subgroup makes up. Additionally, nonresponse bias is less likely to influence within-group estimates for MRP relative to disaggregation because of the effects of partial pooling (Lax and Phillips, 2009).

Buttice and Highton (2013) find that MRP is most effective as an estimator when higher-level variables (in this case, state or district) are strongly predictive of the concept of interest, and when there is a high level of geographic variation in the quantity being estimated.[1] To ensure the greatest level of validity and reliability in my estimates, I include a number of state- and district-level predictors with a clear theoretical tie to expected levels of warmth or hostility toward the selected disadvantaged groups. I also have a clear expectation that due to geographically driven district heterogeneity and distinct state and district cultures, inter-district variability should be high.

DATA

To model individual responses, I use the ANES aggregated time-series data from 1992 to 2016. This data set is intended to be nationally representative, and has a total of 24,122 observations. Given the sampling technique and relatively small sample size (relative to the CCES or the NAES), MRP is the best estimator for generating unbiased and reliable measures of district opinion. To account for over-time changes in district lines and public opinion, I model each decade separately, with 9,085 observations for the 1990s; 5,006 observations for the 2000s; and 10,031 observations for the 2010s. Feeling thermometer estimates are generated for each group in each of the three decades.

In each of these models, the dependent variable is the group feeling thermometer score. The individual-level predictor variables in each of these

---

[1] This greater importance of constituency level variables over individual variables is also confirmed in research by Hanretty, Lauderdale, and Vivyan, (2016) investigating British opinion regarding the EU.

models includes a respondent's gender (two categories: male, female),[2] race/ethnicity (four categories: white, Black, Hispanic, other), education (five categories: less than high school completion, completed high school, some college, college graduate, graduate school), state, and congressional district. Additionally, district-level predictors (average income, percent urban, percent military, same-sex couples, percent Hispanic, and percent African American) and state-level predictors (region, percent union, and percent Evangelical or Mormon) were obtained using decennial US Census data, as well as data from the US Religion Census. Survey year is also included to account for any variation in context or questions.

MODEL

I generate estimates of district hostility by modeling individual responses as a function of individual-level demographic characteristics as well as district- and state-level predictors. I model this as a multilevel linear regression equation, using the lmer package in R.[3] The structure of the model estimating individual feelings toward the poor is given by the following:

$$
\begin{aligned}
y_i^{ft\ poor} &= \gamma_0 + \alpha_{r[i]}^{race} + \alpha_{f[i]}^{female} + \alpha_{e[i]}^{educ} + \alpha_{y[i]}^{year} + \alpha_{d[i]}^{district} \\
\alpha_r^{race} &\sim N(0,\ \sigma_r^2),\ \text{for } r = 1,\ 2,\ 3,\ 4 \\
\alpha_f^{female} &\sim N(0,\ \sigma_f^2) \\
\alpha_e^{educ} &\sim N(0,\ \sigma_e^2),\ \text{for } e = 1,\ 2,\ 3,\ 4,\ 5 \\
\alpha_p^{year} &\sim N(0,\ \sigma_y^2),\ \text{for } p = 1,\ 2
\end{aligned}
\tag{1}
$$

The random effects across each level of these individual predictors (e.g., all five categories of education) are modeled.[4] These effects are expected to be normally distributed with a mean of 0, and a variance determined by the data. Both the district- and state-levels model random effects for each district and state (respectively) in the dataset as well as fixed effects for the other relevant predictors, while random effects are modeled for each of the four region categories:[5]

---

[2] While gender is not a strictly binary concept, data constrictions require it to be treated as such for the purposes of this project.

[3] The framework for the code sequences used comes from the study replication file for Warshaw and Rodden (2012).

[4] Because gender is coded as a dichotomous dummy variable for whether or not a respondent identifies as female, only fixed effects are modeled.

[5] District-level effects are modeled for all district ambient temperature estimates, but are not included for state ambient temperature estimates.

$$\alpha_d^{district} \sim N(k_{s[d]}^{state} + \gamma^{inc} * income_d + \gamma^{urban} * urban_d + \gamma^{mil} * military_d$$
$$+ \gamma^{hisp} * hispanic_d + \gamma^{black} * black_d, \sigma_{district}^2), \text{ for } d = 1, ..., 435$$

$$\alpha_s^{state} \sim N(\alpha_{z[s]}^{region} + \beta^{union} * union_s + \beta^{relig} * religion_s, \sigma_{state}^2), \text{ for } s = 1, ..., 50$$

$$\alpha_z^{region} \sim N(0, \sigma_{region}^2), \text{ for } z = 1, 2, 3, 4$$

POSTSTRATIFICATION

This model is then used to generate district hostility estimates for the average member of each of 17,400 subgroups. Each of these subgroups represents a unique combination of demographic categories by which the sample is weighted: race (4), gender (2),[6] education (5), and congressional district (435).[7] Once predictions for average feeling thermometer scores are generated for each of these subgroups (from white men with less than a high school education in the first district of Alabama to non-white, Black, or Hispanic women with a graduate education in the large district of Wyoming), these estimates are then weighted according to the proportion of a district that is composed of members of these subgroups, and summed across districts.

Formally, weighted district opinion estimates are obtained using this method:

$$y_{district} = \frac{\sum_{c \in d} N_c \theta_c}{\sum_{c \in d} N_c} \tag{2}$$

where c represents each of the forty demographic subcategories (race, gender, and education) within d, a given congressional district, θ_c is the prediction associated with each subcategory, and N_c is the frequency of individuals within a district that belong to a demographic subcategory. To weight my estimates, I use the calculated frequency proportions for each demographic category in each state or district. A summary of the estimates generated is given in Table 4.1, and graphical illustrations of each of the estimates produced are given in Figure 4.1.

---

[6] For the 1990 Census, data are not available for gender by race by education by district categories, but only for race by education by district categories, so this poststratification scheme is used for this decade instead. This reduces the total number of poststratification categories to 8,700.

[7] For the state ambient temperature estimates, the demographic categories used are gender by race by education by state, resulting in a total of 2,000 categories.

APPENDIX D

Generalized Ordered Logit Model Showing Effects of Constituency and Descriptive Representation on Reputations for Women's Advocacy

Table D-1 displays the models of the effects of group size and ambient temperature on women's advocacy that were presented in Table 5.6, but with descriptive representation included. These models show that the relationship between the percentage of women in a state and reputation formation seen in Table 5.6 is in fact a spurious correlation that is better explained by whether or not a state's senator is a woman.

TABLE D-1 *Group size, ambient temperature, descriptive representation, and member reputation for advocacy for women*

	Women					
	0	1	0	1	0	1
Group Size	0.256	-0.173			0.261	-0.191
	0.34	0.74			0.33	0.76
Ambient Temperature			-0.069	-0.095	-0.074	-0.063
			0.17	0.37	0.14	0.65
Descriptive Representative	3.551	3.938	3.523	4.196	3.642	3.983
	0.00	0.00	0.00	0.00	0.00	0.00
Republican	0.038	0.124	0.066	0.274	0.088	0.176
	0.92	0.87	0.87	0.72	0.82	0.84
Dem Pres Vote	0.032	0.108	0.044	0.102	0.034	0.112
	0.26	0.01	0.10	0.04	0.23	0.01
South	-0.847	0.738	-0.591	0.637	-0.812	0.806
	0.05	0.36	0.13	0.44	0.06	0.32
1990s	2.045	1.494	2.100	1.264	1.978	1.451
	0.00	0.06	0.00	0.06	0.00	0.09
2000s	0.450	-0.098	0.755	0.046	0.676	0.136
	0.28	0.87	0.09	0.93	0.13	0.80
First Term	-1.531		-1.501		-1.524	
	0.00		0.00		0.00	
Constant	-18.131	-2.186	-2.177	-5.471	-14.549	1.940
	0.18	0.93	0.49	0.24	0.30	0.94

(continued)

TABLE D-I *(continued)*

	Women					
	0	1	0	1	0	1
N		500		500		500
Wald's Chi^2		80.0		64.7		84.0
Pseudo-R^2		0.2875		0.2857		0.2908

Note: Coefficients calculated using generalized ordered logit, with First Term modeled as a parallel proportional term and all others as partial proportional terms. Standard errors are clustered by member, and p-values are in gray. Model 0 represents the likelihood of a shift from no advocacy to superficial or primary/ secondary advocacy, and Model 1 is no advocacy or superficial advocacy to primary/secondary advocacy.

APPENDIX E
Effects of the Advocacy Environment and Electoral Insecurity on Reputation Formation in the House

Tables E-1 and E-2 display the results for the analysis of the electoral insecurity hypothesis and the collective amplification hypothesis. The effects of the total number of advocates within the House resemble those of the Senate — for nearly all groups, having a greater number of advocates in the House makes it more likely that a member will also make the decision to form a reputation as a group advocate. The effects of electoral insecurity, however, are different in the House than they are in the Senate. While a senator's most recent vote share does not have a significant impact on their representational decision-making, it does have a significant effect in the House, under some circumstances. For groups that are generally considered to be highly deserving of government assistance, like seniors and veterans, a member's electoral security does not change the likelihood that they will choose to serve as a group advocate. But for most groups that are considered to be less deserving of assistance, members with more marginal prior election vote totals are less likely to risk forming a reputation as a group advocate. This demonstrates that while in the Senate, there is no margin at which senators feel comfortable as a disadvantaged group advocate, members of the House of Representatives who hold safer seats are significantly more likely to serve as a group advocate, even for groups that are not considered highly deserving of government assistance.

TABLE E-1 *Institutional and electoral effects on member reputation for advocacy for veterans, seniors, racial/ethnic minorities, and the LGBTQ community in the House of Representatives (1993–2014)*

	Veterans			Seniors			LGBTQ	Race/Ethnicity		
	0	1	2	0	1	2	logit	0	1	2
Total Advocates	0.027	0.077	0.264	0.025	0.008	-0.009	0.217	0.025	-0.027	0.073
	0.45	0.20	0.36	0.00	0.36	0.67	0.06	0.29	0.37	0.13
Previous Vote Share	-0.005	0.013	-0.010	0.005	-0.010	0.008	0.020	0.024	0.035	0.018
	0.52	0.17	0.80	0.45	0.24	0.82	0.18	0.00	0.00	0.24
Group Size	0.197	0.265	0.417	0.097	0.119	0.091	1.937	0.049	0.061	0.054
	0.00	0.00	0.00	0.00	0.00	0.48	0.00	0.00	0.00	0.00
Ambient Temperature	0.049	0.096	0.013	-0.016	0.086	-0.094	0.040	-0.010	-0.058	-0.044
	0.10	0.12	0.89	0.66	0.33	0.61	0.20	0.77	0.17	0.56
Republican	-0.468	-0.901	-1.237	-0.814	-1.073	-1.570	-1.308	-1.854	-2.218	-2.890
	0.02	0.02	0.12	0.00	0.00	0.10	0.04	0.00	0.00	0.01
Dem Pres Vote	0.002	0.023	0.034	0.016	-0.005	-0.096	0.054	-0.033	-0.055	-0.034
	0.86	0.27	0.63	0.20	0.79	0.22	0.18	0.07	0.02	0.24
South	0.050	0.306	0.383	0.029	-0.281	-1.667	0.221	-0.073	-0.050	0.340
	0.83	0.52	0.59	0.89	0.47	0.20	0.70	0.79	0.88	0.44
1990s	-0.240	1.540	5.640	0.097	-0.607	-1.752	2.471	0.641	1.382	-1.453
	0.83	0.38	0.44	0.63	0.11	0.03	0.00	0.21	0.03	0.18

(continued)

TABLE E-1 (continued)

	Veterans			Seniors			LGBTQ	Race/Ethnicity		
	0	1	2	0	1	2	logit	0	1	2
2000s	-0.612	-0.265	-0.800				1.159	0.283	1.628	-2.667
	0.03	0.61	0.38				0.11	0.73	0.13	0.14
First Term		-1.091			-0.805		-1.201		-1.788	
		0.00			0.00		0.14		0.00	
Constant	-8.441	-19.010	-24.111	-4.130	-10.120	7.896	-14.208	-4.201	-0.423	-4.834
	0.01	0.00	0.11	0.17	0.15	0.61	0.00	0.14	0.89	0.33
N	2,175			1,740			2,175	2,175		
Wald's Chi²	123.4			163.2			68.7	434.1		
Pseudo-R²	0.0742			0.0708			0.1977	0.3185		

Note: Coefficients for LGBTQ are estimated using logistic regression, as necessitated by the bivariate coding of the LGBTQ advocacy reputation variable. Coefficients calculated using generalized ordered logistic regression, with First Term modeled as a parallel proportional term and the rest of the independent variables modeled as partial proportional terms. Standard errors are clustered by member, and p-values are in gray. Model 0 represents the likelihood of a shift from no advocacy to superficial, secondary, or primary advocacy; Model 1 is no advocacy or superficial advocacy to primary or secondary advocacy; and Model 2 is any of the lower categories of advocacy to primary advocacy. Feeling thermometer questions for seniors were not included in the ANES of the 2010s, so the decade base category for seniors is the 2000s.

TABLE E-2 *Institutional and electoral effects on member reputation for advocacy for immigrants, women, and the poor in the House of Representatives (1993–2014)*

	Immigrants			Poor			Women		
	0	1	2	0	1	2	0	1	2
Total Advocates	0.067	0.066	-0.158	0.016	0.014	-0.004	0.076	0.096	0.476
	0.03	0.16	0.37	0.00	0.00	0.64	0.02	0.06	0.01
Previous Vote Share	0.021	0.006	0.071	0.013	0.020	0.027	0.005	-0.006	0.018
	0.06	0.69	0.01	0.03	0.01	0.07	0.43	0.56	0.28
Group Size	0.119	0.149	0.301	0.060	0.075	0.072	-0.008	-0.103	0.017
	0.00	0.00	0.00	0.00	0.00	0.00	0.86	0.29	0.95
Ambient Temperature	-0.046	-0.008	-0.045	-0.007	0.025	-0.073	0.042	0.040	-0.102
	0.04	0.83	0.49	0.81	0.58	0.35	0.07	0.13	0.33
Republican	-0.618	-0.394	-4.552	-1.179	-1.830	-2.081	-0.713	-1.291	-2.823
	0.04	0.50	0.01	0.00	0.00	0.00	0.00	0.00	0.00
Dem Pres Vote	-0.079	-0.065	-0.404	0.015	0.003	-0.013	0.057	0.075	0.228
	0.00	0.09	0.03	0.14	0.84	0.74	0.01	0.02	0.01
South	-0.442	-0.522	-4.298	-0.391	-0.966	-0.638	-0.490	-0.964	-0.939
	0.26	0.41	0.01	0.03	0.00	0.37	0.11	0.05	0.48
1990s	0.426	0.460	-0.603	0.079	0.197	-0.595	-0.907	-1.815	-9.635
	0.41	0.54	0.72	0.70	0.48	0.22	0.21	0.10	0.01

(continued)

TABLE E-2 *(continued)*

	Immigrants			Poor			Women		
	0	1	2	0	1	2	0	1	2
2000s	−0.159	0.049	−1.930	0.037	0.121	−0.112	−0.822	−1.751	−8.018
	0.52	0.89	0.10	0.87	0.70	0.82	0.19	0.06	0.00
First Term		−1.691			−1.065			−1.196	
		0.00			0.00			0.00	
Constant	−1.346	−4.928	13.261	−4.088	−7.324	0.150	−9.563	−5.600	−24.731
	0.48	0.05	0.28	0.06	0.02	0.98	0.00	0.33	0.08
N		2,175			2,175			2,175	
Wald's Chi^2		370.2			302.6			176.4	
Pseudo-R^2		0.3121			0.1344			0.1036	

Note: Coefficients calculated using generalized ordered logistic regression, with First Term modeled as a parallel proportional term and the rest of the independent variables modeled as partial proportional terms. Standard errors are clustered by member, and p-values are in gray. Model 0 represents the likelihood of a shift from no advocacy to superficial, secondary, or primary advocacy; Model 1 is no advocacy or superficial advocacy to primary or secondary advocacy; and Model 2 is any of the lower categories of advocacy to primary advocacy.

References

Adler, E. Scott and John Wilkerson. 2019. *Congressional Bills Project: (1993–2014). NSF 00880066 and 00880061.* The views expressed are those of the authors and not the National Science Foundation. Accessed January, 2019. www.congressionalbills.org/.

Alba, Richard, Ruben Rumbaut, and Karen Marotz. 2005. "A Distorted Nation: Perceptions of Racial/Ethnic Group Sizes and Attitudes toward Immigrants and Other Minorites." *Social Forces*, 84(2): 901–919.

Allen, Amanda and Chris White, eds. 2014. *Politics in America (the 113th Congress).* Washington, DC: CQ-RollCall, Inc. http://library.cqpress.com/pia/document.php?id=OEpia113_0.1

Alvarez, R. M. and P. Gronke. 1996. "Constituents and Legislators: Learning about the Persian Gulf Way Resolution." *Legislative Studies Quarterly*, 21(1): 105–127.

Ansolabehere, Stephen and Phillip Edward Jones. 2010. "Constituents' Responses to Congressional Roll-Call Voting." *American Journal of Political Science*, 54 (3): 583–597.

Arnold, Douglas. 1990. *The Logic of Congressional Action.* New Haven: Yale University Press.

Bartels, Larry M. 1991. "Constituency Opinion and Congressional Policy Making: The Reagan Defense Buildup." *American Political Science Review*, 85: 457–474.

Bartels, Larry M. 2008. *Unequal Democracy: The Political Economy of the Guilded Age.* Princeton: Princeton University Press.

Baumgartner, Frank R. and Bryan D. Jones. 1993. *Agendas and Instability in American Politics.* Chicago: University of Chicago Press.

Bernard, William and Tracy Sulkin. 2018. *Legislative Style.* Chicago: University of Chicago Press.

Bishin, Benjamin G. 2009. *Tyranny of the Minority: The Subconstituency Politics Theory of Representation.* Philadelphia: Temple University Press.

Blumer, Herbert. 1958. "Race Prejudice as a Sense of Group Position." *Sociological Perspectives*, 1(1): 3–7.

Brady, David W., Hahrie Han, and Jeremy C. Pope. 2007. "Primary Elections and Candidate Ideology: Out of Step with the Primary Electorate?" *Legislative Studies Quarterly*, 32(1): 79–105.

Brant, Rollin. 1990. "Assessing Proportionality in the Proportional Odds Model for Ordinal Logistic Regression." *Biometrics*, 46(4): 1171–1178.

Bratton, Kathleen A. 2006. "The Behavior and Success of Latino Legislators: Evidence from the States." *Social Science Quarterly*, 87: 1136–1157.

Bratton, Kathleen A. and Kerry L. Haynie. 1999. "Agenda Setting and Legislative Success in State Legislatures: The Effects of Gender and Race." *The Journal of Politics*, 61(3): 658–679.

Bratton, Kathleen A., Kerry L. Haynie, and Beth Reingold. 2006. "Agenda Setting and African American Women in State Legislatures." *Journal of Women, Politics & Policy*, 28: 71–96.

Breitman, Kendall. 2015. "Poll: Majority of Millennials Can't Name a Senator from Their Home State." *Politico.com.* www.politico.com/story/2015/02/poll-millennials-state-senators-114867. Accessed March 3, 2018.

Burden, Barry C. 2007. *Personal Roots of Representation.* Princeton: Princeton University Press.

Burnes, David, Christine Sheppard, Charles R. Henderson, Monica Wassel, Richenda Cope, Chantal Barber, and Karl Pillemer. 2019. "Interventions to Reduce Ageism Against Older Adults: A Systematic Review and Meta-Analysis." *American Journal of Public Health*, 109(8): e1–e9.

Buttice, Matthew K. and Benjamin Highton. 2013. "How Does Multilevel Regression and Poststratification Perform with Conventional National Surveys?" *Political Analysis*, 21(4): 449–467.

Campbell, A., P. E. Converse, W. E. Miller, and D. E. Stokes. 1960. *The American Voter.* Chicago: University of Chicago Press.

Canes-Wrone, Brandice, David Brady, and John F. Cogan. 2002. "Out of Step, Out of Office: Electoral Accountability and House Members' Voting." *American Political Science Review*, 96(1): 127–140.

Canon, D. T. 1999. *Race, Redistricting, and Representation: The Unintended Consequences of Black Majority Districts.* Chicago: University of Chicago Press.

Carnes, N. 2013. *White-collar Government: The Hidden Role of Class in Economic Policy Making.* Chicago: University of Chicago Press.

Chisholm, Shirley. 1970. *Unbought and Unbossed.* Boston: Houghton Mifflin.

Clinton, J., S. Jackman, and D. Rivers. 2004. "The Statistical Analysis of Roll Call Data." *American Political Science Review*, 98(2): 355–370.

Clinton, J. D. and J. Tessin. 2007. "Broken Fire Alarms: Exploring Constituency Knowledge of Roll Calls." Unpublished Manuscript. Princeton: Princeton University.

Cnudde, Charles F. and Donald J. McCrone. 1966. "The Linkage between Constituency Attitudes and Congressional Voting Behavior: A Causal Model." *American Political Science Review*, 60(1): 66–72.

Cohen, Robin A. and Whitney K. Kirzinger. 2014. Financial Burden of Medical Care: A Family Perspective. NCHS Data Brief (142). Centers for Disease Control and Prevention. www.cdc.gov/nchs/data/databriefs/db142.pdf

Conover, Pamela J. 1984. "The Influence of Group Identifications on Political Perception and Evaluation." *Journal of Politics*, 46(3): 760–785.

Converse, P. E. 1964. "The Nature of Belief Systems in Mass Publics." In *Ideology and Discontent*, edited by D. Apter, pp. 206–261. New York: Free Press.

Cox, G. W. and M. D. McCubbins. 2007. *Legislative Leviathan: Party Government in the House*, 2nd ed. Cambridge: Cambridge University Press.

Craig, Maureen A. and Jennifer A. Richeson. 2014. "More Diverse Yet Less Tolerant? How the Increasingly Diverse Racial Landscape Affects White Americans' Racial Attitudes." *Personality and Social Psychology Bulletin*, 40 (6): 750–761.

Crenshaw, K. 1995. "Mapping the Margins: Intersectionality, Identity Politics, and Violence against Women of Color." In *Critical Race Theory: The Key Writings That Formed the Movement*, edited by K. Crenshaw, N. Gotanda, G. Peller, and K. Thomas, pp. 1241–1299. New York: New Press.

Curry, James M. 2015. *Legislating in the Dark: Information and Power in the House of Representatives*. Chicago: University of Chicago Press.

Dahl, Robert A. 1956. *A Preface to Democratic Theory*. Chicago: University of Chicago Press.

Delli Carpini, M. X. and S. Keeter. 1996. *What Americans Know about Politics and Why It Matters*. New Haven: Yale University Press.

Dodson, Debra L. 2006. *The Impact of Women in Congress*. New York: Oxford University Press.

Dolan, J. 1997. "Support for Women's Interests in the 106th Congress: The Distinct Impact of Congressional Women." *Women & Politics*, 18: 81–94.

Dovi, Suzanne. 2002. "Preferable Descriptive Representatives: Will Just Any Woman, Black, or Latino Do?" *American Political Science Review*, 96(4): 729–743.

Duncan, Phil, ed. 1994. *Politics in America (the 103rd Congress)*. Washington, DC: CQ Press.

Duncan, Phillip and Christine Lawrence, eds. 1998. *Politics in America (the 103rd Congress)*. Washington, DC: CQ Press.

Ellis, W. C. and W. C. Wilson. 2013. "Minority Chairs and Congressional Attention to Minority Issues: The Effect of Descriptive Representation in Positions of Institutional Power." *Social Science Quarterly*, 94: 1207–1221.

Erikson, R. S. 1978. "Constituency Opinion and Congressional Behavior: A Reexamination of the Miller-Stokes Representation Data." *American Journal of Political Science*, 22: 511–535.

Erikson, R. S. and G. C. Wright. 1980. "Policy Representation of Constituency Interests." *Political Behavior*, 2: 91–106.

Federal Reserve Board. 2020. *Report on the Economic Well-Being of U.S. Households in 2019, Featuring Supplemental Data from April 2020.*

www.federalreserve.gov/publications/files/2019-report-economic-well-being-us-households-202005.pdf

Fenno, R. F. 1978. *Home Style: House Members in the Districts.* Boston: Little, Brown.

Fenno, Richard F. 1991. *Learning to Legislate: The Senate Education of Arlen Specter.* Washington, DC: CQ Press.

Fiorina, Morris P. 1974. *Representatives, Roll Calls, and Constituencies.* Lexington: Lexington Books.

Firth, David. 1993. "Bias Reduction of Maximum Likelihood Estimates." *Biometrika*, 80(1): 27–38.

Frantzich, Stephen. 1979. "Who Makes Our Laws? The Legislative Effectiveness of Members of the U.S. Congress." *Legislative Studies Quarterly*, 4(3): 409–428.

Freddie Mac. 2018. *The LGBT Community: Buying and Renting Homes.* www.freddiemac.com/fmac-resources/research/pdf/Freddie_Mac_LGBT_Survey_Results_FINAL.pdf

Gaddie, Ronald K. and John C. Kuzenski. 1996. "Institutional and Personal Legislative Specialization in the United States Senate." *Southeastern Political Review*, 24(1): 3–19.

Gamble, K. L. 2007. "Black Political Representation: An Examination of Legislative Activity within U.S. House Committees." *Legislative Studies Quarterly*, 32: 421–446.

Gay, C. and K. Tate. 1998. "Doubly Bound: The Impact of Gender and Race on the Politics of Black Women." *Political Psychology*, 19: 169–184.

Gilens, Martin. 2012. *Affluence and Influence: Economic Inequality and Political Power in America.* Princeton: Princeton University Press.

GLAAD. 2019. *Accelerating Acceptance 2018: Executive Summary.* https://www.glaad.org/files/aa/Accelerating%20Acceptance%202018.pdf

Glassman, Matthew E. and Amber H. Wilhelm. 2017. "Congressional Careers: Service Tenure and Patterns of Member Service, 1789–2017." CRS Report for Congress, January 3, 2017.

Grant, Lawrence V. 1973. "Specialization as a Strategy in Legislative Decision-Making." *American Journal of Political Science*, 17(1): 123–147.

Green, Donald P., Bradley Palmquist, and Eric Schickler. 2002. *Partisan Hearts and Minds: Political Parties and the Social Identities of Voters.* New Haven: Yale University Press.

Griffin, John D. and Brian Newman. 2005. "Are Voters Better Represented?" *Journal of Politics*, 67(4): 1206–1227.

Griffin, John D. and Brian Newman. 2008. *Minority Report: Evaluating Political Equality in America.* Chicago: University of Chicago Press.

Griffin, John D., Brian Newman, and Christina Wolbrecht. 2012. "A Gender Gap in Policy Representation in the U.S. Congress?" *Legislative Studies Quarterly*, 37(1): 35–66.

Grossman, Matt and David A. Hopkins. 2016. *Asymmetric Politics: Ideological Republicans and Group Interest Democrats.* New York: Oxford University Press.

Haider-Markel, Donald P. 2010. *Out and Running: Gay and Lesbian Candidates, Elections, and Policy Representation.* Washington, DC: Georgetown University Press.

Hamilton, Alexander, James Madison, John Jay, and Lawrence Goldman. 2008. *The Federalist Papers.* Oxford: Oxford University Press.

Hanretty, C., B. Lauderdale, and N. Vivyan. 2018. "Comparing Strategies for Estimating Constituency Opinion from National Survey Samples." *Political Science Research and Methods*, 6(3): 571–591.

Hansen, Eric R. and Sarah A. Treul. 2015. "The Symbolic and Substantive Representation of LGB Americans in the US House." *The Journal of Politics*, 77(4): 955–967.

Hawkesworth, M. 2003. "Congressional Enactments of Race-Gender: Toward a Theory of Raced-Gendered Institutions." *American Political Science Review*, 97: 529–550.

Hawkings, David and Brian Nutting, eds. 2004. *Politics in America (the 103rd Congress).* Washington, DC: CQ Press.

Haynie, Kerry L. 2002. "The Color of their Skin or the Content of their Behavior? Race and Perceptions of African American Legislators." *Legislative Studies Quarterly*, 27(2): 295–314.

Hero, Rodney E. and Caroline J. Tolbert. 1995. "Latinos and Substantive Representation in the U.S. House of Representatives: Direct, Indirect, or Nonexistent?" *American Journal of Political Science*, 39(3): 640–652.

Hutchings, Vincent L. 2003. *Public Opinion and Democratic Accountability: How Citizens Learn About Politics.* Princeton: Princeton University Press.

Hutchings, Vincent L., Harwood K. McClerking, and Guy-Uriel Charles. 2004. "Congressional Representation of Black Interests: Recognizing the Importance of Stability." *The Journal of Politics*, 66(2): 450–468.

Jacobson, Gary C. 2013. *The Politics of Congressional Elections*, 8th ed. Boston: Pearson.

Kessler, Daniel and Keith Krehbiel. 1996. "Dynamics of Cosponsorship." *American Journal of Political Science*, 90(3): 555–566.

Kingdon, John W. 2005. *Agendas, Alternatives, and Public Policies*, 2nd ed. New York: Longman.

Koger, Gregory. 2003. "Position Taking and Cosponsorship in the U.S. House." *Legislative Studies Quarterly*, 28(2): 225–246.

Kramarow, Ellen A. and Patricia N. Pastor. 2012. *The Health of Male Veterans and Nonveterans Aged 25–64: United States, 2007–2010.* NCHS Data Brief (101). Centers for Disease Control and Prevention. www.cdc.gov/nchs/data/databriefs/db101.pdf

Kuklinski, James H. and Richard C. Elling. 1977. "Representational Role, Constituency Opinion, and Legislative Roll-Call Behavior." *American Journal of Political Science*, 21(1): 135–147.

Lawless, Jennifer L. 2004. "Politics of Presence? Congresswomen and Symbolic Representation." *Political Research Quarterly*, 57(1): 81–99.

Lax, Jeffrey R. and Justin H. Phillips. 2009. "How Should We Estimate Public Opinion in the States?" *American Journal of Political Science*, 53(1): 107–121.

Lee, Frances E. and Bruce I. Oppenheimer. 1999. *Sizing Up the Senate: The Unequal Consequences of Equal Representation.* Chicago: University of Chicago Press.

Leighley, Jan E. 2001. *Strength in Numbers? The Political Mobilization of Racial and Ethnic Minorities.* Princeton: Princeton University Press.

Lewis-Beck, Michael S., William G. Jacoby, Helmut Norpoth, and Herbert F. Weisberg. 2008. *The American Voter Revisited.* Ann Arbor: University of Michigan Press.

MacDorman, Marian F. and T. J. Mathews. 2011. *Understanding Racial and Ethnic Disparities in U.S. Infant Mortality Rates.* NCHS Data Brief (74). Centers for Disease Control and Prevention. www.cdc.gov/nchs/data/databriefs/db74.pdf

Mansbridge, Jane. 1999. "Should Blacks Represent Blacks and Women Represent Women? A Contingent 'Yes'." *Journal of Politics,* 61: 628–657.

Matthews, Donald R. 1959. "The Folkways of the United States Senate: Conformity to Group Norms and Legislative Effectiveness." *The American Political Science Review,* 53(4): 1064–1089.

Mayhew, David R. 1974. *Congress: The Electoral Connection.* New Haven: Yale University Press.

Mazzi, Patricia. 2017. "Ileana Ros-Lehtinen to Retire from Congress." *MiamiHerald.com.* www.miamiherald.com/news/local/community/miami-dade/article147718764.html. Accessed March 6, 2018.

McCrone, Donald J. and James H. Kuklinski. 1979. "The Delegate Theory of Representation." *American Journal of Political Science,* 23(2): 278–300.

Miler, Kristina C. 2010. *Constituency Representation in Congress: The View from Capitol Hill.* New York: Cambridge University Press.

Miler, Kristina C. 2018. *Poor Representation: Congress and the Politics of Poverty in the United States.* New York: Cambridge University Press.

Miller, W. E. and D. E. Stokes. 1963. "Constituency Influence in Congress." *American Political Science Review,* 57: 45–56.

Minta, Michael D. 2009. "Legislative Oversight and the Substantive Representation of Black and Latino Interests in Congress." *Legislative Studies Quarterly,* 34(2): 193–218.

Movement Advancement Project, Center for American Progress, GLAAD, Human Rights Campaign. 2019. *Understanding Issues Facing LGBT People in the U.S,* 2nd ed. www.lgbtmap.org/file/Understanding-LGBT-Issues-2019.pdf

Osborn, T. and J. M. Mendez. 2010. "Speaking as Women: Women and Floor Speeches in the Senate." *Journal of Women, Politics and Policy,* 31: 1–21.

Park, David K., Andrew Gelman, and Joseph Bafumi. 2004. "Bayesian Multilevel Estimation with Poststratification: State-Level Estimates from National Polls." *Political Analysis,* 12(4): 375–385.

Popkin, Samuel L. 1991. *The Reasoning Voter: Communication and Persuasion in Presidential Campaigns.* Chicago: University of Chicago Press.

Rapp, David, ed. 2006. *Politics in America (the 103rd Congress).* Washington, DC: CQ-RollCall, Inc. http://library.cqpress.com/pia/document.php?id=OEpia109_0.1

Reingold, Beth. 2000. *Representing Women: Sex, Gender, and Legislative Behavior in Arizona and California*. Chapel Hill: University of North Carolina Press.

Riley, Michael, ed. 2008. *Politics in America (the 103rd Congress)*. Washington, DC: CQ-RollCall, Inc. http://library.cqpress.com/pia/document.php?id=OEpia110_0.1

Schiller, Wendy J. 1995. "Senators as Political Entrepreneurs: Using Bill Sponsorship to Shape Legislative Agendas." *American Journal of Political Science*, 39(1): 186–203.

Schiller, Wendy J. 2000a. "Building Reputations and Shaping Careers: The Strategies of Individual Agendas in the U.S. Senate." In *Congress on Display, Congress at Work*, edited by William T. Bianco, pp. 47–68. Ann Arbor: University of Michigan Press.

Schiller, Wendy J. 2000b. *Partners and Rivals: Representation in U.S. Senate Delegations*. Princeton: Princeton University Press.

Sellers, Patrick. 2009. *Cycles of Spin: Strategic Communication in the U.S. Congress*. New York: Cambridge University Press.

Sinclair, Barbara. 1989. *The Transformation of the U.S. Senate*. Baltimore: Johns Hopkins University Press.

Smooth, W. 2010. "Standing for Women? Which Women? The Substantive Representation of Women's Interests, and the Research Imperative of Intersectionality." *Politics and Gender*, 7(3): 436–441.

Stewart, Charles III and Jonathan Woon. 2019. Congressional Committee Assignments, 103rd to 114th Congresses, 1993–2017: House, January, 2019.

Stimson, J. A. 1999. *Public Opinion in America: Moods, Cycles, and Swings*, 2nd ed. Boulder: Westview Press.

Stimson, J. A. 2003. *Tides of Consent: How Public Opinion Shapes American Politics*. New York: Cambridge University Press.

Stimson, J. A., M. B. MacKuen, and R. S. Erikson. 1995. "Dynamic Representation." *American Political Science Review*, 89: 543–565.

Sulkin, Tracy. 2011. *The Legislative Legacy of Congressional Campaigns*. New York: Cambridge University Press.

Swers, Michele L. 2002. *The Difference Women Make: The Policy Impact of Women in Congress*. Chicago: University of Chicago Press.

Swers, Michele L. 2007. "Building a Reputation on National Security: The Impact of Stereotypes Related to Gender and Military Experience." *Legislative Studies Quarterly*, 32(4): 559–595.

Swers, Michele L. 2013. *Women in the Club: Gender and Policy Making in the Senate*. Chicago: University of Chicago Press.

Szaflarski, Magdalena and Shawn Bauldry. 2019. "The Effects of Perceived Discrimination on Immigrant and Refugee Physical and Mental Health." *Advances in Medical Sociology*, 19: 173–204.

Tate, Katherine. 2014. *Concordance: Black Lawmaking in the U.S. Congress from Carter to Obama*. Ann Arbor: University of Michigan Press.

Thomas, Reginald. 1989. "Claude Pepper, Fiery Fighter for Elderly Rights, Dies at 88." *NYTimes.com*. https://archive.nytimes.com/www.nytimes.com/learning/general/onthisday/bday/0908.html. Accessed March 6, 2018.

Thomas, Sue. 1994. *How Women Legislate*. New York: Oxford University Press.

Uslaner, Eric M. and Mitchell Brown. 2005. "Inequality, Trust, and Civic Engagement." *American Politics Research*, 33(6): 868–894.

Villarroel, Maria A., Tainya C. Clarke, and Tina Norris. 2020. Health of American Indian and Alaska Native Adults, by Urbanization Level: United States, 2014–2018. NCHS Data Brief (372). Centers for Disease Control and Prevention. www.cdc.gov/nchs/data/databriefs/db372-h.pdf

Volden, Craig and Alan E. Wiseman. 2012. "Legislator Effectiveness and Representation." In *Congress Reconsidered*, 10th ed., edited by Lawrence C. Dodd and Bruce I. Oppenheimer, pp. 237–264. Washington, DC: CQ Press.

Volden, Craig and Alan E. Wiseman. 2018. "Legislative Effectiveness in the United States Senate." *Journal of Politics*, 80(2): 731–735.

Warshaw, Christopher and Jonathan Rodden. 2012. "How Should We Measure District-Level Public Opinion on Individual Issues?" *Journal of Politics*, 74(1): 203–219.

Wawro, Gregory. 2001. *Legislative Entrepreneurship in the U.S. House of Representatives*. Ann Arbor: University of Michigan Press.

Wayne, Alex. 2004. "American Indian Housing in Spotlight." *CQ Weekly* (June 26): 1537. http://library.cqpress.com/cqmagazine/weeklyreport108-000001225571.

Weissberg, Robert. 1979. "Assessing Legislator-Constituency Policy Agreement." *Legislative Studies Quarterly*, 4(4): 605–622.

Weissman, Judith, Laura A. Pratt, Eric A. Miller, and Jennifer D. Parker. 2015. Serious Psychological Distress among Adults: United States, 2009–2013. NCHS Data Brief (203). Centers for Disease Control and Prevention. www.cdc.gov/nchs/data/databriefs/db203.pdf

Williams, M. 1998. *Voice, Trust, and Memory: Marginalized Groups and the Failings of Liberal Representation*. Princeton: Princeton University Press.

Williams, Richard. 2006. "Generalized Ordered Logit/ Partial Proportional Odds Models for Ordinal Dependent Variables." *The Stata Journal*, 6(1): 58–82.

Williams, Richard. 2016. "Understanding and Interpreting Generalized Ordered Logit Models." *The Journal of Mathematical Sociology*, 40(1): 7–20.

Wilson, J. M. and P. Gronke. 2000. "Concordance and Projection in Citizen Perceptions of Congressional Roll-Call Voting." *Legislative Studies Quarterly*, 25: 445–467.

Wright, G., R. S. Erikson, and J. P. McIver. 1987. "Public Opinion and Policy Liberalism in the American States." *American Journal of Political Science*, 26: 81–103.

Index

For EU product safety concerns, contact us at Calle de José Abascal, 56–1°,
28003 Madrid, Spain or eugpsr@cambridge.org.

www.ingramcontent.com/pod-product-compliance
Ingram Content Group UK Ltd.
Pitfield, Milton Keynes, MK11 3LW, UK
UKHW010250140625
459647UK00013BA/1763